CRIMES OF THE HEART

Brian Marriner is a prolific writer and one of Britain's leading true crime authors. He regularly contributes to crime magazines both in this country and in the US, including *True Detective*, *True Crime Monthly* and *Master Detective*. He has written several editions of *Murder Casebook*, has been a collaborator on many books, and has made appearances on both TV and radio. He is currently the author of four published works, including the novel *A Splinter of Ice*. An expert in criminology and forensic science with an encyclopaedic knowledge, his book *Forensic Clues to Murder* was described by Colin Wilson as 'the definitive text on forensic medicine, which is destined to become a modern classic.' Brian Marriner lives in Yorkshire.

By the same author

A Splinter of Ice
Forensic Clues to Murder
Cannibalism, The Last Taboo!

CRIMES OF THE HEART

Brian Marriner

ARROW

Published by Arrow Books in 1994

1 3 5 9 10 8 6 4 2

First published by Arrow Books Limited
Random House, 20 Vauxhall Bridge Road
London SW1V 2SA

Random House Australia (Pty) Limited
20 Alfred Street, Milsons Point, Sydney,
New South Wales 2061, Australia

Random House New Zealand Limited
18 Poland Road, Glenfield
Auckland 10, New Zealand

Random House South Africa (Pty) Limited
PO Box 337, Bergvlei, South Africa

Random House UK Limited Reg. No. 954009

ISBN 0 09 930317 5

Set by Intype, London
Printed in Great Britain by Cox & Wyman Ltd, Reading, Berks

To my father, and in memory of my mother

CONTENTS

INTRODUCTION

It was in 1924 that Fryn Tennyson Jesse, in her classic book *Murder and Its Motives* first gave us her classification of the six motives for murder. They were: for gain; for revenge; for elimination; for jealousy; for lust of killing; and from conviction. It remains a pretty comprehensive list to this day, and although odd cases crop up now and again which seem to defy classification or even explanation, or which perhaps straddle two or more of the six motives given, the original list serves us well and is a useful guide to the student of murder.

Or, it should be said, to the student of human nature, since murder is an extreme expression of impulses found within us all. Crimes inspired by love, whether romantic love or sexual obsession, have been with us ever since humankind came into existence, and if this collection of true crimes of passion serves to prove anything, it is that basic human nature never changes.

I have tried to avoid, wherever possible, the old stale cases which surface in every book of this kind. Instead, I have adopted a somewhat unusual format. Chapters deal alternately with contrasting old and new cases, to prove the point that despite every technological advance and increased sophistication, we remain primitive creatures under the skin, driven by urges we cannot always control.

When we give in to those urges, the result can either be a sordid debacle, or an awe-inspiring tragedy of the highest order. Aristotle wrote that the purpose of tragedy is to 'cleanse the soul by means of pity and terror.' Pity we shall feel, because crimes of passion are not of equal stature. The Everest heights are represented by cases like Rattenbury and Stoner, which almost break the heart. The ocean depths are represented by cases which inspire only terror and contempt.

But all are cases which represent human beings *in extremis*.

1

THE BODY ON THE MOOR:
CHARLOTTE DYMOND
1844

The girl lay on her back, her pretty green gown open to the stomach, immodestly revealing her plump thighs. She lay a foot away from a small moorland stream, one arm outstretched, a leg bent comfortably, face turned toward the sky. She might have been gazing up at the passing clouds, lost in a pastoral reverie, but for one obvious fact – her throat had been cut wide open.

The wound was some eight and a half inches in length, beginning at the back of the neck, continuing around the left side and across the front – leaving a gaping wound which penetrated the windpipe – and finishing just past the right ear. The cut was two and a half inches deep and had obviously been inflicted with great force. Strangely, there was no blood at the scene, or any sign of a struggle, except for a necklace which lay just above the victim's head, its coral beads scattered. The weapon was missing.

The mystery of the nine-day disappearance of Charlotte Dymond, an eighteen-year-old servant girl, had been solved. The other mystery – the identity of her killer – seemed to have been solved even before her body was found. Matthew Weeks, a young fellow servant in the same household as the dead girl, had already been judged and found guilty by his neighbours. All that remained was the formality of a trial and a ritual hanging...

The value of the Charlotte Dymond case is that it serves as a kind of time-capsule, affording us a valuable glimpse into the past. We can see how justice was administered in 1844, and even learn something of the lives of ordinary people then, although we shall never fully penetrate the secrets of those lives. For it happened in Cornwall, that mysterious county of storm-lashed coves and desolate moors which ends in a rocky finger pointing out into the Atlantic towards America – that fabled land to which so many poor people of the region emigrated in the 'Hungry Forties'.

By 1844 Queen Victoria had ruled for seven years over the richest and most powerful empire in the world, protected by the most powerful navy afloat. But while wealth was paraded in the great palaces and mansions, vice and poverty flourished among the people. It was a time of desperate poverty for the nation – some two million people were on the pauper rolls – and the fishermen, miners and farmers of Cornwall felt the pinch as much as any.

The Cornish have always been a race apart, of Celtic origin, distrusting strangers. Accused of being 'clannish', most of them are related in some way to one another, and it is almost impossible for a stranger to learn the secrets of these close-knit village folk. There are some things which they refuse to speak about – even among themselves – as if they are taboo subjects. One of these is the murder of Charlotte Dymond; because either the wrong man was hanged, or else it was no murder at all . . .

Fortunately, the case has been well-documented in contemporary records – even the original document of the brief to prosecuting counsel in 1844 survives – and the trial was extensively reported by both local and national press. But today the only reminder of what took place in 1844 is a monument of granite high on Rough Tor, Cornwall's second highest hill, towering above Bodmin Moor. The inscription on the monument reads: *Erected By Public Subscription In Memory Of Charlotte Dymond Who Was Murdered by Matthew Weeks, Sunday, April 14, 1844.* The monument stands near where Charlotte's body was found, pointing skywards like an accusing finger. Over the years there have been many reports of sightings of a girl walking the moor, dressed in a shawl and bonnet – the ghost of a girl who rests uneasily in her grave.

It began on a farm called Penhale, owned by a sixty-one-year-old widow, Philippa Peter. Together with her unmarried son John, and two servants, she managed the 147-acre holding. The farm was isolated, a large stone house a couple of miles away from Davidstow on the northern edge of Bodmin Moor. Matthew Weeks, the principal farm-hand, had worked at Penhale Farm for seven years. Aged twenty-three, with pock-marked, sullen features, he was lame in his right leg, and when he smiled he revealed a gap-toothed mouth. His only good feature was a mop of curly light-brown hair. He had been keeping company with Charlotte Dymond, a fellow-servant and something of a coquette. Certainly she had a reputation as a flirt.

On Lady Day, 25 March, which was the day when servants were hired and fired, Charlotte was paid off by Mrs Peter after eighteen months' service. She received four shillings in change, which included two silver four-penny pieces. But since she had nowhere else to go, she remained at the farm for the time being. Taken on to replace her was twenty-one-year-old John Stevens, who seemed to spend his time spying on Matthew Weeks. This was not difficult, since both shared a bedroom. Stevens was quick to note that Weeks bought a knife and owned a cut-throat razor. He also noted the jealousy existing between Weeks and a man called Thomas Prout, who boasted he would take Charlotte away from Weeks. In fact, Stevens witnessed a bitter row between Weeks and Prout over Charlotte.

On the afternoon of Sunday, 14 April 1844, Charlotte and Matthew dressed in their best finery – Charlotte in a green gown with red shawl, brown silk bonnet and a black handbag – and set off for a walk. Matthew Weeks returned home alone at nine-thirty that evening, and when asked where Charlotte was, replied: 'I don't know.' He then went to bed. The following morning he got up to pursue his normal activities around the farm, and Mrs Peter went to make up his bed. She was surprised to find his stockings – which she had put out clean the day before – covered in mud up to the knees. His best trousers, too, were muddy. Growing suspicious, Mrs Peter questioned Weeks about his movements the day before. He said he had walked with Charlotte as far as Higher Down Gate, some three-quarters of a mile from the farmhouse, and there they had parted; she to walk in the direction of Bodmin Moor, he to walk to a village in the opposite direction.

With each week that passed with no sign of Charlotte, gossip mounted. A local farmer, Isaac Cory, had seen Matthew Weeks walking with Charlotte on the Sunday a good deal further on than Higher Down Gate. The couple had been wearing pattens, metal overshoes which kept one's shoes or boots clear of the mud. They also left a distinctive oval pattern in the turf, which Isaac Cory had spotted.

On the Tuesday, 16 April, an increasingly worried Mrs Peter decided to tackle Weeks about the missing girl, threatening to bring him before a magistrate if he did not tell the truth. It was then that he mumbled an explanation. Charlotte, he said, had found a new position at a place called Blisdale, and had gone there on the Sunday. Since she couldn't travel so far in one day, she intended breaking her journey by sleeping out on the moor. It was a flimsy tale: why would Charlotte have walked out with only what she stood up in, leaving all her other clothing behind?

By Saturday, 20 April, local concern and rumour were at a height, with men in public houses openly baiting Weeks, stopping just short of accusing him of murder. During this period John Stevens saw two silver fourpenny pieces in Weeks's possession. Mrs Peter had not paid

Weeks with such coins. Again Mrs Peter tackled Weeks about the missing girl, telling him that if he had indeed done away with the girl he ought to be 'hung in chains'.

On Sunday, 21 April, Matthew Weeks went out, and Mrs Peter took the opportunity to search his room. In the jacket he had worn on the day Charlotte disappeared, she found a handkerchief belonging to Charlotte. And Week's razor was missing . . . Matthew Weeks did not return to the farm. He had fled the district, perhaps fearing that his alibi for Charlotte – that she had gone to a family called Laxton at Blisdale – was to be broken. John Stevens had been sent to check, and the Laxtons told him that they had never seen Charlotte, nor offered her a position. By his flight Weeks seemed to have acknowledged his guilt.

Two days after his flight, local opinion was satisfied of his guilt and neighbours were determined to search the moors for his victim's body. The search party followed patten prints in the moorland turf, measuring the length of them by notching a stick. The prints ran out on rocky ground and the search party divided into two groups. In the rocky ground around Rough Tor, two local men – Simon Baker and William Northam – stumbled across the body of Charlotte. Missing from the body were the bonnet, shoes and pattens, handkerchief, shawl, handbag and gloves. Some fifty yards away searchers found patten marks in the marshy ground, as if a couple had stood face to face. One set matched the measurement notched on the stick.

Local surgeon Thomas Good was sent for; he examined the body where it lay, noticing that the undergarments were wet, and bloodstains on them a pale pink, as if washed by stream water. It was possible, he thought, that the stream level had been higher recently, reaching halfway up the body. That would account for the lack of blood – it had drained directly into the stream – and might also explain the missing weapon: it could have been washed away far downstream. The body was placed on a cart and taken back to Penhale Farm, to rest in a barn while awaiting further examination.

The following day, both autopsy and inquest took place in the barn. First the autopsy, performed by Surgeon Good. With a Davidstow constable, Thomas Rickard, acting as witness, the surgeon stripped the body of clothing. It had been formally identified as being that of Charlotte Dymond, both by the constable and by John Stevens. The surgeon's report stated:

> I found a wound in the neck eight inches and a half in length including a small portion of the larynx. The small portion of the larynx was attached to the windpipe; the oesophagus was partly divided and the instrument had not only gone through the soft part but had partially separated two of the vertebrae by entering a little way into the cartilage between them. Much force must have been used in giving the wound ... The wound was the cause of death. I do not think the instrument used was a very sharp one ... I do not think she could have inflicted the wound herself. I examined the rest of the body, which was healthy. The bladder was empty, but this might have happened after death. The uterus was healthy and there was no sign of pregnancy or violation ... The hymen was ruptured but the rupture did not appear to be recent.

Next came the inquest. The coroner was Joseph Hamley, himself a surgeon, and his son Edmund, a solicitor, acted as deputy. Witnesses and jury members had been arriving at the farm all day. Nineteen witnesses gave evidence, including Cory, who had seen Weeks on the moor with Charlotte, and a local preacher, William Gard, who had actually seen a couple on Rough Tor at the relevant time. The man had been lame ... Richard Pethwick, a local farmer, had been riding on the moor on the Sunday. He had spoken to the couple, asking them if they were lost. 'The man was lame ... ' Then the physical evidence was produced. The broken coral necklace, a shirt belonging

16

to Weeks with bloodstains on it, and Charlotte's handkerchief which had been found in his pocket.

Without adjourning, the twelve-man jury brought in
their verdict: ' . . . that Matthew Weeks, late of the parish
aforesaid, not having the fear of God before his eyes but
moved and seduced by the instigation of the Devil . . . did
murder Charlotte Dymond.' Within twenty-four hours of
the verdict the coroner had issued a death certificate for
Charlotte, giving the cause of death as: 'Wilfully murdered by Matthew Weeks.' He also issued a warrant for
the arrest of Weeks.

Constable John Bennett set off in pursuit of the fugitive. He soon discovered that Weeks had visited the
Stevens family – some ten miles from Penhale Farm – on
the day he fled. He arrived about three and left at nine
in the evening, having spent six hours chatting to two
girls, Elizabeth Stevens and her friend Eliza Butler. Not
knowing of Charlotte's disappearance, but knowing of
her engagement to Weeks, they asked after her. Weeks
answered their questions readily, displaying no unease.
He seemed very calm and relaxed. At one point he even
took from his pocket Charlotte's black handbag to show
them.

The trial led Constable Bennett to Plymouth – Weeks
had a sister living there – and he was in fact arrested at
his sister's house. He was told that he was being charged
with having murdered Charlotte Dymond, and his clothing was searched. In a side pocket was a pair of gloves
which had belonged to the dead girl. Asked what he was
doing in Plymouth, Weeks said that he had hoped to take
passage on a ship to Jersey. Questioned about his
relations with Charlotte, he said he 'had not kept company with Charlotte since Lady Day, but some other
chaps had'.

By 25 April Weeks had been returned to Davidstow to
face the magistrates. The hearing took place in an inn,
with Weeks handcuffed to a steel bar which ran from
floor to ceiling. All the original inquest witnesses were

17

called to repeat their evidence, and the various forensic items were produced once again. This hearing attracted great local attention, and by the second day of the hearing the local newspaper, the *West Briton*, headlined the case: 'CORONER'S INQUEST – CHARGE OF WILFUL MURDER.' On the third day of the hearing, the *Western Flying Post* announced in bold type: 'HORRID MURDER – CORNWALL.' The report went on: 'Little doubt is entertained of the guilt of Weeks, but what could have induced him to commit such an atrocious deed is rather uncertain. Reports say that it was jealousy – that the deceased was coquettish and favoured the advances of other young men.'

Weeks had no real defence: the evidence seemed damning. Even his plea of 'not guilty' and his statement to a solicitor seemed contrived. In that statement he said he had gone for a walk with Charlotte that fateful Sunday, but denied having murdered her. His statement read: 'I went along with her a little way . . . and then she said she did not want me to go any further. I wished her well and bid her good afternoon, and she left me, and I left her.' The statement had been dictated – he could neither read nor write – and the wording was obviously that of his solicitor.

No doubt it was not justice as we perceive it today. Weeks had no opportunity to defend himself – accused persons were not able to speak on their own behalf – and he had been branded a murderer by the coroner's death certificate and found guilty before trial by the press. But all his actions had been consistent with guilt, and it was not surprising that the magistrates found that he had a case to answer and had him lodged in Bodmin Gaol to await the next Assize Court.

While Weeks lay in jail, the moor was searched for Charlotte's missing clothing. Isaac Cory and his wife found them hidden in a two-feet-deep pit a half-mile from where the body had been found. Constable Rickard witnessed the find. Hidden under moss in the pit were the missing items belonging to Charlotte: her shoes, shawl, bonnet, and the steel pattens she had been wearing. Constable Rickard also found something else of great significance. Searching the stream bank close to where the body had been found, he noticed a loose clump of turf. When he lifted the turf he found a hole beneath, containing a great quantity of blood.

By Tuesday, 30 April, the case was national news, with the *Morning Chronicle* headline of: 'DREADFUL MURDER IN CORNWALL'. Even *The Times* carried the story. Charlotte's funeral had taken place on 25 April, the body being carried from Penhale Farm to be buried in Davidstow churchyard. In July, the local temperance movement held a massive rally on Rough Tor; as many as ten thousand people attended. There were side-shows, wrestling matches and stalls selling soft drinks. A black flag was flown over the spot where Charlotte's body had been found, and placards invited penny subscriptions to erect a granite monument in her memory. As much as one hundred pounds would have been collected – certainly enough to erect the monument which stands to this day on that bleak moor.

The Bodmin Assize trial of Matthew Weeks began on Friday, 2 August 1844. Frederick William Slade was the defence barrister, and Alexander Cockburn, QC, led for the Crown. Mr Justice Patteson presided. But first a special grand jury had to consider whether, on the evidence, a 'true bill' had been proved against the defendant. It was in effect a pre-trial hearing. (The last grand jury heard evidence against the Dartmoor mutineers in 1933, after which grand juries were abolished.) Had the grand jury returned a verdict of *ignoramus*, there would have been no trial; but the twenty-three man jury returned a verdict of 'true', and from that moment Weeks faced a trial proper for his life. The judge took his seat in the packed courtroom, and then the prisoner was put in the dock.

The *Royal Cornwall Gazette* described him as 'being

about 5ft 4ins high, and lame . . . on the whole Weeks could not be called ill-looking, although he has rather an insignificant appearance. He looks not more than eighteen although he is four years older. He has a good head of hair of a brownish colour and curly; his eyes are what are commonly called down-looking, the eyebrows overhang, and he is slightly marked with smallpox.'

The indictment was read to Weeks and in a low voice he replied: 'Not guilty.' The twelve-man jury was sworn in, and the trial began.

Cockburn made his opening address. He went through the story piece by piece: Charlotte's disappearance, Weeks's muddy trousers, his flight from justice. The prosecution said it would prove wilful murder. One by one the witnesses were put up. Those who had found the body described the scene: no blood either on the ground or the body, and no signs of a struggle. Surgeon Thomas Good was put through a thorough cross-examination.

In his evidence he had stated that the wound was deeper on the left side than on the right, with the obvious inference that the assailant must have attacked Charlotte from the front, presuming that he was right-handed. He went on to say: 'The wound was inflicted with great force, probably with a knife, though not very sharp because the edges of the wound were somewhat ragged.' However, under cross-examination from the defence, Good admitted that since the body lay sloping downwards, with the head facing the stream, such a cut would have drained all the blood from the veins directly into the water. He added: 'It was the sort of wound a person might inflict upon himself.'

The prosecution re-examined. Was it likely that Charlotte had cut her own throat? 'I think it's possible, but not likely . . . I am not prepared to say, with reference to the extent, how much of such a wound a person could inflict upon himself.' He agreed that she could have been killed a little away from the stream and then carried to where she was found. But this raised the vexed question of *why had no blood been found on Weeks's clothing*? If he had cut her throat from in front, or carried her, then he must have received some blood on him, yet none was found . . .

The witnesses who had seen Charlotte with Weeks on Rough Tor, less than a hundred yards from where her body was found, proved damning, sealing Weeks's fate. Cory had seen the couple; Pethwick had spoken to them and was now prepared to state: 'I swear that the prisoner was the man beyond belief.' Much was made of the impressions of the pattens found on the moor, the prosecution trying to identify them as belonging positively to Weeks.

That same Friday, at about seven in the evening, Slade rose to put the defence case. He spoke for only an hour, in contrast to the prosecution's nine and a half hours, but then, there was so little he could say . . . He complained that the press had created a bias against his client which must affect the jury's decision. He declared that the Crown had failed to establish any motive; nor had they proved that Weeks had ever been in possession of a knife, nor shown him to have any bloodstains on his clothing – which *must* have covered the real murderer – if indeed it *was* murder. It was entirely possible that after Matthew Weeks had left her, Charlotte had met another man on the moor – perhaps by prior arrangement – who had then killed her. As for Weeks's 'flight from justice', it was a reasonable action to walk out on the farm in view of the local suspicion and hostility. In short, the Crown's case was purely circumstantial.

When he sat down, it was the turn of the judge to sum up the evidence to the jury. It was impossible to believe that Charlotte could have inflicted the wound upon herself, he said; and while the Crown had failed to show any motive for the murder, Weeks had been identified as being the last person seen in her company. 'It is a case of circumstances entirely. Nobody saw him commit the act, if he did do it. Circumstantial evidence is always to be very carefully and cautiously examined, for there is nothing so apt to deceive one for, when any preconceived notion is taken up, how easy it is to dovetail a number of circumstances together and fancy that a very clear case is made out when, in truth, it is not so.

'Nevertheless, it has often been said that circumstantial evidence, if well-weighed and examined and if it does bring the matter home to the mind, is often more satisfactory than direct testimony because, in direct testimony, a motive may be suspected whereas, in circumstances, there is often no doubt at all. When they are put together and examined and compared, they tell a story which cannot lead to direct falsehood.'

The judge finished his summing-up just before ten, and the jury retired for thirty-five minutes before returning with a verdict of guilty. The black cap was placed on the judge's head as he addressed himself to the prisoner.

'Matthew Weeks, the jury, after a very full and patient investigation of this case, have come to the conclusion that you are guilty of the offence with which you are charged, having murdered the poor girl Charlotte Dymond . . . The circumstances of this case do not disclose to the jury or to me the motive which induced you to commit the offence . . . The time you will pass in this world is now very short, your age is very young, still, that does not justify me in holding out the slightest hope that the extreme sentence of the law will not be carried out in your case, that there will be any mercy shown to you.

'There is no hope for you in this world, and my earnest entreaty is for you to endeavour to obtain that mercy from the Almighty which man cannot grant you . . . You shall be taken hence to the place from whence you came and be hung by the neck until you are dead. Your body shall be buried within the precincts of the prison; may the Lord have mercy on your soul.'

Even before he had finished speaking, Weeks had fainted. He arrived at Bodmin Gaol still in a state of collapse at about midnight. He remained in this condition until his death. The *West Briton* reported: 'He has been so affected by, and deeply sensible of his awful situation, that he is constantly fainting, and it is thought he can scarcely be kept alive until the appointed time.' The *Illustrated London News* for 10 August claimed that: 'Weeks has subsequently admitted his guilt, but says it was not a premeditated act.' Weeks had written three letters the day before his death – or rather dictated them – worded in such a way as to tacitly admit his guilt. In a letter to his employer, Mrs Peter, for example, he included a passage which read: 'And I thank the judge and jury too, for they have given me no more than what was due.' The letter ended with the traditional: 'I am a sinner quite undone.'

However, there was a much more explicit confession. It appears to have been part of the duty of the prison chaplains to secure confessions from convicted men, to clear the consciences of those in authority who had convicted them. The day before he died, Weeks dictated a confession to Governor Everest, and the chaplain, Kendall. The confession said, in part: ' . . . We strolled together on the moor . . . Towards dusk we had words about other young men . . . She then said: "I shall do as I like." This expression aroused my anger . . . I took out my knife and went towards her to commit the bloody deed . . . I approached behind her and made a cut at her throat . . . She immediately fell backwards, the blood gushing out in a large stream . . . I never thought of murdering Charlotte Dymond till a few minutes before I cut her throat.'

The following day, Monday, 12 August 1844, a crowd of twenty thousand people gathered outside the prison to watch the execution. As the clock struck twelve midday, Weeks was led out of the prison gate, his arms pinioned. The governor and the chaplain accompanied him, the chaplain reading a prayer as the procession made its way to the scaffold. According to contemporary press reports,

Weeks could barely walk. 'The little strength that yet remained was fast waning.'

The executioner waited on the drop; he was George Mitchell of Somerset, aged seventy. He quickly pulled the cap down over Weeks's face and then adjusted the noose around his neck. While the chaplain still prayed, the bolts were withdrawn and Weeks fell into eternity with a dreadful crash. His body hung lifeless, fingers still clutching a handkerchief he carried. Some in the crowd fainted at the sight. After hanging for one hour and a minute, the body was taken down and removed into the prison for burial. According to one reporter, for the *West Briton*, the grave already prepared for Weeks's body was a bare four feet deep and was flooded with water. The coffin must have floated . . .

Ballads have been written and sung about Charlotte Dymond for almost a century and a half, and various writers have dealt with the case. One, Pat Munn, has even produced a meticulous work of research attempting to prove that Matthew Weeks was innocent. I do not find such arguments convincing. On the evidence before them, I believe that the jury reached the only possible verdict. The suggestion that Charlotte may have committed suicide does not – unlike Matthew Weeks's coffin – hold water. The alternative theory – that an innocent man was sacrificed because he was an outsider and therefore more suitable to be hanged than a reputable local man – is equally untenable.

What the Charlotte Dymond case does prove is that although customs change, human nature remains the same over the centuries. Jealousy – that warped expression of love – has been responsible for murders throughout the history of man, and will continue to provide a recurring motive.

2
BURNING PASSION
1987

There is an old adage to the effect that there is no fool like an old fool, which serves both to illuminate and illustrate this case of the older man who fell in love with a much younger woman, and when she betrayed him, killed her. But the *method* with which he chose to kill belied a savage and insane jealousy. The knife would have been kinder – as it was for Charlotte Dymond – bludgeoning quicker, throttling easier. Yet he chose to burn her alive; such is the depth of hatred which lies on the other side of the coin of love.

Love betrayed turning to hatred is a common theme in murder, yet because of the extreme cruelty of the killing, this murder is of the kind which has fortunately become rare today, a throwback to the savagery of earlier centuries. Shakespeare would have understood this murder perfectly, and might well have made of it a powerful drama. Lacking the dramatist, we must content ourselves with a straightforward account of a very tangled affair.

Ten years earlier, in 1977, Michael 'Derek' Hearne was a wealthy factory owner, aged fifty, living in some luxury at Rawtenstall, Lancashire. His teenage daughter became friendly with a pretty girl who had just moved into the area, sixteen-year-old Shelley Page. Shelley's father had just died, and she was in need of solace and somewhere to live. She moved in with Hearne as his housekeeper, but soon he was besotted with her and she quickly became his lover. But although her Sugar Daddy bought her everything she wanted, she had a string of affairs with other men, many of them married.

Hearne had the advantage of age and maturity. Although every affair caused him intense anguish, he would wait patiently for it to end, knowing that such full-blown passions would quickly burn themselves out.

But the cost was not measured only in emotional scars but also in financial terms. He began neglecting his furniture factory, falling prey to swindlers, and his capital was rapidly becoming depleted as he showered Shelley with flashy clothes, jewellery, expensive holidays and a luxury car.

After he became the victim of a fraud which cost him £59,000, Shelley persuaded him to sell his business and buy her a pig farm in Cumbria. They moved to Cumbria in 1982. When the pig farm failed, principally because Hearne was a collar-and-tie man who was happier behind a desk – the couple moved to Thiefside Cottage in Calthwaite, where neighbours assumed that Shelley was Hearne's daughter.

Within five years Hearne was virtually penniless – and then Shelley left him. In 1986 she moved in with Graham Martin, the twenty-seven-year-old manager of a local tyre depot, whom Shelley had met through a shared interest in grass-track racing, and within a short time they became engaged.

Hearne knew that his lover was gone for good, that she would never return to him. The hideaway cottage he had bought for them both to share, near Penrith in the beautiful Cumbria landscape, now seemed a cold and desolate place, the very light having gone from it, its beating heart stilled.

Hearne was now approaching sixty, and Shelley was still only twenty-five. Hearne stayed alone at the cottage, nursing his grief, trying to overcome the agony of being jilted. But then Shelley made the mistake of going to visit him on the evening of 1 October 1987 . . .

We must try to picture Hearne's despair at this time.

With his money and lover gone, he had been reduced to selling beefburgers from a caravan on the A6 in an effort to scratch a meagre living. He blamed Shelley and her new lover for his plight. He spent the lonely nights plotting how to exact his grisly revenge.

On the evening of Thursday, 1 October 1987, Shelley arrived at Thiefside Cottage with Graham Martin. They were returning Hearne's car, which Mr Martin had seen it through its MOT. There was some forced, polite conversation, but the sight of his former lover, obviously pregnant, with her husband-to-be sent Hearne insane with fury.

On the pretext of going to make some tea, Hearne went into his bedroom and grabbed a shotgun he had bought just days before. Coming back into the sitting room, he shot Shelley in the stomach. Graham Martin struggled to get the weapon off the older man, ejected the cartridges and threw it away, after a confused struggle. But then Hearne threw a lighted petrol-soaked rag at him, setting his clothing ablaze. Mr Martin rushed outside to roll in the grass to put the flames out. When he staggered back to the cottage he saw Shelley lying on the floor 'on fire from head to toe'. Hearne had set fire to her and the cottage, making a funeral pyre to mark his shattered romance.

Carlisle fireman Cliff Harding happened to be driving past and noticed the smoke. He braked to a halt and saw the cottage blazing. He was on his way home from work and was still in uniform. He rushed to the scene of the blaze and saw Hearne struggling with Graham Martin on the ground. He stopped the scuffle and then made a desperate attempt to drag Shelley's body out of the inferno. He said later: 'I stopped the car on instinct. There were people standing outside the blazing cottage but they weren't doing anything. They were just watching two men fighting on the ground.

'I went up and stopped the fighting. I didn't grapple or anything, but when they saw me they must have thought I was a policeman because I was still wearing my uniform. One of them was cut on the face and Graham Martin was burned on both arms and ears. I got hold of Hearne and put him into a car. I told him not to move and told a man not to let him out of the car.

'I just went straight in, I didn't think about it at the time because I didn't know what was going on.' He noticed a shotgun on the path as he attempted to force his way into the blazing cottage. 'I couldn't get her out,' he said. 'I got halfway along the corridor but couldn't get any further because the fire was round the ceiling and flames were rolling across the hallway. She was lying half-way into the hall and I could see her bottom half, but it was quite a severe blaze.'

Hearne was taken to a police station and detained, while Mr Martin was rushed to the Cumberland Infirmary in Carlisle, suffering from burns. A special late-night sitting of Penrith's magistrates' court remanded Hearne in custody.

At his trial at Preston Crown Court on 27 April 1988, Michael Charles William Hearne pleaded not guilty to the murder of Michelle Joyce Page. Mr Benet Hytner, QC, prosecuting, told the court about the background to the horrific murder. He explained how in 1978 Michelle – known as Shelley – went to live with Hearne at his home in Rawtenstall, and related the events which followed.

Mr Hytner said that Shelley was burned to death, and without suffering burns she might have survived. The fire badly damaged the cottage and spread to an adjoining property.

Home Office pathologist Dr Edmund Tapp testified that an examination of Shelley's badly burned body revealed that she had inhaled smoke before she died. He said the most likely cause of her death was the burns which covered the whole of her body. He added that the one-and-a-half-inch-diameter shotgun wound in her abdomen would probably have proved fatal, but if she could have been operated on by skilled surgeons within an hour, her life could have been saved. Another forensic scientist, Philip Jones, said he had found petrol traces on the remains of Shelley's clothing in the fire-damaged cottage.

Then Graham Martin went into the witness box. Fighting back tears, he told of how his pregnant wife-to-be was shot by her former lover and left to die in the blazing cottage. Mr Martin told the court that Shelley had twice complained to him that Hearne had threatened to kill her. On the first occasion she telephoned Mr Martin in the middle of the night to say Hearne had broken into her bedroom and was going to kill her unless she stopped seeing Mr Martin. In February 1987 she told Mr Martin that Hearne had come at her with a carving-knife.

The court heard that on 1 October the previous year, Mr Martin and Shelley went to Hearne's cottage to return his car which Mr Martin had been working on. They were talking in the lounge and Hearne left the room saying he was going to make a cup of tea.

Mr Martin said he was cleaning his hands with a penknife by the fire when, out of the corner of his eye, he saw a flash, heard a bang, and saw Shelley fall to the floor. He turned around and saw Hearne standing in the doorway with a shotgun. He grabbed the gun and pushed Hearne through the doorway and through a glass-panelled door. After a struggle in which he hit Hearne several times he managed to open the gun and eject the cartridges, which he threw away.

Inside the house he saw Shelley lying on the floor bleeding badly from a wound in her abdomen. 'She was appealing for help. She said she was dying,' Mr Martin said. On the way out he saw Hearne coming towards him. There was another struggle and he ran to a neighbour's house to call for help.

Returning to the cottage, he saw smoke coming from the front door and could see that Shelley was on fire. 'She was burning from head to toe.' He then went into the kitchen for water, but when he returned Hearne threw

29

a petrol-soaked rag at him, setting his clothes on fire. After rolling in the grass to put out the flames, Mr Martin tried to get back inside the cottage but was driven back by the intense heat. Then he and Hearne began fighting again, until separated by a passing fireman.

On the second day of the trial Hearne went into the witness box to give evidence on his own behalf. He told the jury that he had never intended to shoot his former lover, who had left him after nine years and planned to marry another man. He claimed he had bought the shotgun as a birthday present for his daughter, and on the evening of 1 October planned to frighten Shelley by trying to shoot himself in front of her. The previous day, he said, he had tried to commit suicide but the gun did not fire.

He related that Shelley and her fiancé, Graham Martin, arrived at Thiefside Cottage to return his car. He told Mr Martin he did not wish to cause problems between them. He was under the impression that Shelley was miserable because Mr Martin was becoming possessive, due to him, Hearne said. Mr Martin replied that he was fed up of Shelley having to run round after him.

Hearne left the room. He accepted that he must have got a loaded double-barreled shotgun which was under the mattress in his bedroom, but he could not remember clearly what happened next.

'I never intended to shoot her,' he claimed. 'I loved Shelley and Shelley loved me. I don't remember coming to the open door of the sitting room and I don't remember the gun firing. I didn't consciously squeeze the trigger. The first thing I knew, it was Shelley saying she had been shot and to get an ambulance.' After the shooting, he said, he vaguely remembered Mr Martin coming at him, swearing and with fists flying, and he was pushed through the glass-panelled front door.

'I vaguely remember getting the petrol-can from the boot of the car, which was parked right outside the front door. I was going to destroy myself with the petrol, but

30

I didn't get the chance. I was going to pour petrol on the settee and sit on it. Shelley was in the far end of the room. She wasn't shouting or screaming. I remember saying to Shelley: "I love you, I'm going."

'I sprinkled petrol on the settee and there was a whoosh. There was an open coal-fire a short distance from the settee. As far as I know I was blown through the window. The next thing I remember I was in the middle of the garden.'

He said that even though Shelley had become engaged to Mr Martin, he had hopes of her returning to him. He said Shelley had confided to him that the first time Mr Martin could not afford to buy her what she wanted, she would be away.

He told of his background; how he had once been a wealthy factory-owner whose upholstery business collapsed because he became the victim of a fraud. He had always bought Shelley what she wanted, he said. He claimed that he and Shelley had last made love in May of the previous year – five months after she became engaged to Mr Martin. But he thought Mr Martin was the father of her unborn child, he said.

Under cross-examination, he agreed with Mr Hytner that nobody other than himself could have shot her. Mr Hytner asked: 'In these circumstances, you must have intended to kill or seriously wound Shelley?' Hearne replied: 'That I'm aware of – no.' He was asked why he had struggled with Mr Martin to hang on to the gun after the shooting. Hearne said: 'I never heard the gun go off. I don't know why I held on to the gun.' Mr Hytner asked: 'Why didn't you call an ambulance?' Hearne replied: 'I don't know.'

Mr Hytner dismissed his claim that he had intended to kill himself by setting himself on fire with petrol. He told Hearne: 'When you realized you would not get her back, you decided that no one else was going to have her. You first shot her and burned her to death.' Hearne replied: 'No, sir.'

Psychiatrist Dr Marion Swann, called by the prosecution, said that Hearne had more personality defects than most people. But she could not say without further investigation if he had a personality disorder. She did not think he suffered from an abnormality of the mind, and saw no evidence that his responsibility for his actions was impaired by any disorder.

But for the defence, psychiatrist Dr Colin Protheroe testified that Hearne *was* suffering from a personality disorder. Dr Protheroe said that Hearne was an extremely possessive and irritable man who, when provoked, experienced high emotions and a tendency to lose control. Dr Protheroe said he had interviewed Hearne three times since his arrest, and found difficulty in getting direct answers from him.

'Sometimes he would become extremely angry with me if I repeated something I understood he had said and he disagreed with ... On a number of occasions we discussed the associations Shelley had had with a number of men, and his reactions were one of anger. Immediately he would break down and cry and almost beg me not to say something undesirable about her. I think I suggested something about his early relationship with Shelley and he shouted at me and ordered me out of the room.

'I see Mr Hearne as having certain personality traits which amount to a personality disorder. He had a predisposition to behave in an excessive manner when under stress.' Dr Protheroe said that Hearne could have lost control on the night Shelley died. He added that Hearne was a self-opinionated, egocentric man who would have found his riches-to-rags fall from wealthy factory-owner to dole-queue traumatic. Hearne boasted of the Mercedes car he had and the many girls he could take out on the town.

At the end of the four-day trial the jury found Hearne guilty by a majority verdict. Mr Justice McPherson jailed him for life.

After the case it was revealed that within days of the

murder, thieves looted the burned-out cottage and neighbours were plagued by sightseers and ghoulish souvenirhunters. Thiefside Cottage was so named because the spot on which it stood was where highwaymen used to ambush coaches in bygone days.

Mr Martin remained bitter about the loss of his wife-to-be and unborn child, saying: 'He has destroyed everything I had. When he killed Shelley he took my life as well . . . I want him to feel pain like Shelley did. I want to do what he did to her – set him on fire.'

The real victims of murder are those who are left behind. Murder is an event which shatters any number of lives. His daughter remembers Hearne as a mild man who never showed any signs of violence. She said: 'On the night it happened, I think he was hoping Graham would shoot him.'

Shelley's sister said that Hearne was possessive and jealous. 'He controlled her so she couldn't have her own life', she said. She added: 'He always had plenty of money, but after he bought the pig-farm he was constantly skint. It's true Shelley wanted the farm – but who else would have taken the advice of an eighteen-year-old?'

It might seem the stuff of opera: Hearne's simmering jealousy exploding twelve months after his lover ditched him for another man. But there is nothing romantic about a girl burning alive from head to toe – and the child she was carrying inside her. Perhaps the old adage should be amended to read: 'There is no fool *so dangerous* as an old fool.'

3
MARIA MARTEN: THE SECRETS OF THE RED BARN
1827

A slice of criminal history was put on the market when Corder's House, a timber-framed building in the Suffolk village of Polstead, was offered for sale by the present owner for £335,000 in October 1989. He had bought it in 1977 for £48,000 – a symptom of inflation.

The house was once the home of one of the greatest villains of melodrama, William Corder, who was hanged for the killing of a twenty-five-year-old farm girl, Maria Marten, in the Red Barn then adjacent to the house. The barn was demolished years ago after generations of grisly souvenir-hunters had made the building unsafe by hacking away chunks of timber. The case is now known as 'The Red Barn Murder' – since that was where Corder buried the body of his victim – but at the time it was known simply as 'The Polstead Murder'.

The crime took place over a century and a half ago and served to inspire many plays, ballads, books, and even a children's puppet theatre. It is hard to see, from a modern viewpoint, why the case aroused so much interest at the time. It was often referred to as 'The Mystery of the Red Barn Murder' but in truth there was no mystery. It was a plain and simple case of a man wanting to dispose of a mistress who had outlived her charm. He killed her and buried her in the barn – where the body was sure to be discovered in time – and displayed no special cleverness or talent for murder.

Over the years a number of myths have evolved around

the case, like ivy hiding the nature of the tree. It is time the facts were made plain.

Maria Marten has long been portrayed as a paragon of virtue, a beautiful girl with the qualities of a lady, a shining, bright-faced symbol of innocence cruelly betrayed. Nothing could be further from the truth. Maria Marten was a product of her time, of poor nourishment and poor social conditions. She had a wen at the side of her neck and was missing two teeth. As for her virtue, she was something of a slut in rustic surroundings, having borne three illegitimate children to three different men.

Maria Marten found herself trapped in a rural environment of some nine hundred inhabitants, each of whom knew everyone else's business, and although only nine miles from Colchester and fifteen from Ipswich, it might as well have been the dark side of the moon.

Born at Polstead on 24 July 1801 in a cottage, Maria was taken into the home of the local clergyman to act as a nursery maid, and stayed there until she was twelve. Any gloss of sophistication she may have had she obtained there, having caught a glimpse at the parsonage of a strange new world of books and clean linen.

Then she was forced to return to the cottage to look after her father and several other children, including her sister Ann, aged four, and became in short a household drudge. Maria was well-built and attractive; moreover, she longed for love. At the age of eighteen she was more than ready to be seduced by Thomas Corder, son of a wealthy local farmer, who made her pregnant. The baby died in infancy and was buried in the local churchyard.

Maria then began a relationship – in fact it had begun while she was still pregnant by Thomas Corder – with a Peter Matthews, a gentleman of some standing, to whom she bore a child, Thomas Henry. Mr Matthews at least paid maintenance for his love-child, some five pounds a quarter.

Then a few years later she was seduced by the other Corder brother, William, and bore him a child. The baby

35

died within weeks in mysterious circumstances and was buried secretly in a field by Corder. The fact that Maria had had relations with two sons from the same family was a source of lively scandal in the neighbourhood.

William Corder was born in 1803. His parents, John and Mary Corder, farmed some three hundred acres in Polstead and had eight children. When John Corder died in December 1825, he left a widow and six surviving children – four sons and two daughters – and had every reason to hope that one of them would take over the running of the farm. But by 1828 only one male child was left to carry on the family name: William Corder. Thomas died in February 1827 when he fell through ice covering a local pond and drowned. Within eighteen months another two sons, James and John, had also passed away.

William, son of a yeoman farmer, had aspirations to being a gentleman and had no taste for honest employment. From an early age he displayed signs of a dissolute nature, lying, stealing and talking his way out of the scrapes he got into with a plausible tongue. He was soon nicknamed 'Foxy' because of these habits. Of slight build and only five foot four in height, he had a sickly complexion and poor eyesight. Agricultural labour was not for him: he would have the life of a gentleman by fair means or foul.

He once sold stolen pigs, and began associating with a local villain by the name of Beauty Smith, who had previously been transported for pig-stealing. He and Corder had been pig-rustling, but Smith was arrested for horse-stealing in another county and was transported for life, leaving Corder in the clear and unscathed by any punishment. However, Smith did once predict that Corder would meet his end by hanging . . .

Corder began courting Maria sometime in March 1826 and soon got her pregnant. She kept this secret as long as she could, but when she was forced to tell her parents, Corder became a frequent visitor to the cottage, having assured them of his intention to marry Maria when the time was right. Maria's baby died within four weeks of birth and Corder took the body away in a box, burying it secretly by night. He warned Maria that the parish constable had a warrant to take her in for bastardy, which was a lie designed to frighten Maria and keep her in check. But the possibility remains that Corder might have murdered the child.

The couple often quarrelled fiercely, particularly when the five-pound note sent every quarter for the upkeep of the child failed to arrive and Maria accused Corder of stealing it. A solicitor and postmistress were willing to swear to the fact that Corder had intercepted the letter, but Corder persuaded Maria to drop the charges by threats and promises. The threat was his claim to have been shown by the parish constable a writ about to be served on Maria for burdening the parish with pauper children. Maria knew nothing of the law and was suitably frightened. The promise was that Corder would marry her. Once Mrs Corder overheard a quarrel between the pair in which Maria declared vehemently: 'Very well; if I go to jail, you do too.' Corder's reply was: 'Every shilling I have shall be yours.'

The proposed wedding turned into something of a farce. On Monday, 14 May 1827, Corder arrived at the cottage to take Maria to Ipswich for the wedding. Maria arrived home in the early hours still unwed. Two more attempts were made on the Wednesday and Thursday, but each time something went wrong and Maria arrived back home without a ring on her finger.

However, on Friday 18 May, Corder arrived at the cottage in great haste, saying: 'I am come, Maria. Make haste, for I am going!' He said she had been disappointed too often and he intended to marry her that very day. Maria was still afraid of the village constable and that writ. 'How can I go at this time of day, in broad daylight, without anyone seeing me?' she protested. Corder explained his plan to her. Maria would dress as a man and, carrying her clothes in a bag, would go to the Red Barn and wait. Corder would walk with her to make sure the coast was clear. That evening, when dusk had fallen, he would arrive at the barn with a horse and gig to take her away.

Maria agreed to this plan. With her stepmother's help she packed her dresses in a bag, keeping on her white stays and flannel petticoat, and a green silk scarf around her neck. Then she put on trousers, a striped waistcoat, and a man's hat to hide her long hair. The stepmother watched Maria and Corder walk away in the direction of the Red Barn in the fading evening light. She was never to see Maria again.

When Corder arrived back in Polstead alone two days later, Mrs Marten asked him what had happened to Maria. Corder explained that there had been another hitch in their wedding plans. A special licence had failed to arrive from London and it might be several weeks before the marriage could take place. But he had settled Maria comfortably with a friend of his in Ipswich, a Miss Rowland, and made sure she was well supplied with money. He said he would marry Maria at Michaelmas; first he had to see to the gathering of his mother's harvest.

Whenever Mrs Marten asked awkward questions about Maria, Corder would tell her that Maria was well, and would read her letters purporting to come from Maria. But when Corder attended his brother's funeral, the Marten family noticed that he was carrying an umbrella belonging to Maria. When taxed about this, Corder said he had visited Maria recently and had borrowed the umbrella from her. With such lies and deceptions Corder kept the fact of Maria's disappearance obscured for some months on end.

Corder settled some legal matters relating to the farm, and when he left Polstead he had with him some four hundred pounds – a fortune for the time. He said he was going to a watering-place for his health. Corder did go to Seaforth, and later to the Isle of Wight, in the winter of 1827 – but there was one curious point: he took with him the keys to the Red Barn, which had never before been kept locked. Corder had indeed gathered in his mother's harvest, but stored beneath the floor of the barn, under the grain and crops, lay the body of Maria Marten.

Mr and Mrs Marten received a letter from Corder from London, giving them the good news 'Maria is now my wife' and saying that she was in lodgings on the Isle of Wight while he was in London on business. He claimed that Maria had written to her parents after the wedding and was upset to have got no reply. In response to further letters he wrote to say that he was 'astounded' that they had not received any letters from Maria. 'It is very odd, I think, that letters should be lost in this strange way . . . I would certainly indict the Post Office, but I cannot do that without making our appearance at a Court Marshall, which would be very unpleasant for us both.' Once again Corder was using the threat of legal action to keep people quiet and stop them from asking questions. But he could not keep them quiet for ever, especially Mr Matthews, who was demanding to hear from Maria – and soon.

Corder wrote back: 'You wish us to come to Polstead, which we would be very happy to do, but you are not aware of the danger. You may depend upon it that if ever we fell into Mr Matthews's hands, the consequences would prove fatal.'

For month after month Corder succeeded in allaying the suspicions of the Marten family, but finally Mr Marten wrote saying that if Maria did not send money to pay for the support of her child, the boy would have to go on the parish for assistance. Corder immediately sent a guinea. The last thing he wanted was for the authorities to begin seeking the whereabouts of Maria.

Meanwhile, Corder was in London enjoying himself. Always a libertine – he used to boast of his sexual conquests – he was meeting women in pastry shops in Fleet Street and elsewhere. He was lodging at the Bull Inn in

Leadenhall Street, and now began advertising in newspapers for a wife. One advertisement in the *Morning Herald* of 13 November read: 'A Private Gentleman, aged 24, entirely independent, seeks female for marriage state . . . The lady must have the power of some property, which may remain in her own possession.'

Corder received some forty-five letters as a result, and after advertising in the *Sunday Times* on 25 November, received a further fifty-three replies. One was from a Miss Mary Moore, who shortly afterwards became Mrs Corder. They were married in the Church of St Andrew in Holborn, afterwards moving to Grove House, Ealing Lane, Brentford, where Mrs Corder opened a school for young ladies. Mrs Corder was devoted to her new husband, but was anxious about his sleeping habits. He frequently groaned in his sleep and gnashed his teeth . . .

The months had gone by and Maria's parents had heard nothing from her and consequently grew worried. Her stepmother was particularly suspicious. When she asked Corder to get Maria to write, he made vague excuses about her hand being crippled with rheumatism, or that she was too busy.

Much has been made of Mrs Marten's miraculous 'dreams of murder'. After ten months she finally persuaded her husband to search the Red Barn, telling him that she had twice dreamed that Maria was buried there. It is likely that these 'dreams' were a subterfuge, an excuse for forcing her reluctant husband to act. She certainly never mentioned them at the trial.

The husband finally went with a neighbour, William Pryke, and began prodding the floor of the barn with a mole-catcher's tool. He withdrew it at a particularly soft spot of earth smelling of something rotting. Digging quickly revealed the body of Maria Marten, lying doubled up. Around her neck was the green silk scarf she had gone away with.

The coroner was informed and he summoned a jury to hear the case. After viewing the decomposing body, the inquest jury then proceeded to the Cock Inn for the formal inquiry. The coroner persuaded the jury to adjourn the inquest while a constable was sent to London to apprehend William Corder.

Constable Ayres from Boxford was chosen for the task, and having been given his instructions and money for his expenses, he set off for the capital. It seems incredible that he could have hoped to trace Corder among the teeming millions in the metropolis, but trace him he did. He went first to the Police Office in Lambeth Street, and served his complaint. The magistrate seconded a London police officer, Mr Lea, to assist Constable Ayres in his task.

They went first to Corder's last known lodgings, as revealed by his letters, at 6 Gray's Inn Terrace, where the new Mrs Corder's family lived, and were told that Mrs Corder was running a school 'somewhere in Ealing'. It was a vague description, but Lea and Ayres set off immediately for Brentford. Leaving Constable Ayres at the Red Lion Inn, Lea inquired at local pubs about any new schools having opened in the area. None had – and there were dozens of schools in the vicinity. However, Lea did learn that a load of goods had been delivered to one particular school some four months previously.

Lea next traced a young girl who went to that school. She told him that the headmistress had a husband whom she called Mr Corder . . . The following morning Lea waited outside the school in Ealing Lane, and when the front door was opened to allow a gentleman to deliver his daughter, Lea pushed through the open door and saw Corder shaking hands with one of the parents. Tactfully, Lea drew Corder to one side, and in the privacy of the drawing room told him that he was arresting him on a very serious charge relating to the murder of Maria Marten. Corder protested that he knew no one of that name and asked if he might finish his breakfast. The helpful Mr Lea said: 'Yes, and if any questions are asked or suspicions aroused as to my being here, you may say

41

I am come to arrest you for debt, and I shall not contradict you.'

When they were about to leave, Mrs Corder demanded to know the reason for Mr Lea's visit and why her husband should go with him. Her brother, Mr Moore, came downstairs and asked Mr Lea what authority he had; after all, Corder was a gentleman and Mr Lea obviously of the lower classes. Mr Lea replied that he was arresting Corder for murder. 'Murder!' Mr Moore exclaimed. 'You must be mistaken in this person, for I am sure he would never commit murder. He has not the courage to kill a mouse . . . He has married my sister lately and from what she says he is the most kind, tender-hearted and indulgent husband.'

When Corder's trunks were subsequently searched, several erotic books bound in leather were discovered, including *Fanny Hill*, and dozens of printed advertisements for a wife.

Lea took Corder to the Red Lion and placed him in the custody of Constable Ayres, who recognized him at once. Together they produced Corder at Lambeth Street Police Office on 23 April, where a magistrate ordered that Corder should be taken with all possible speed to Polstead. The trio travelled by coach, and fellow-passengers were astonished at Corder's cheerfulness: he frequently laughed and told obscene jokes.

When the coach arrived at Colchester, Corder was taken to the George Inn. A large crowd had gathered to watch the arrival of the already infamous man, and they crammed into the inn to catch sight of him. Ayres took Corder into a private room, while Lea went to the local gaol to ask the governor to lodge Corder overnight in one of his cells. The governor refused: the officer had no warrant committing Corder to his prison.

Ayres went to bed that night handcuffed to Corder, with Corder's free arm handcuffed to the bedpost, and the pair spent a miserable night. Before Corder retired that night, he wrote his mother a letter which read:

Dear Mother, I scarcely dare to presume to address you, having a full knowledge of all the shame, disgrace, and may I truly add, for ever a stain upon my family . . . your very unfortunate son, *William Corder.*

Several important local magistrates and dignitaries visited Corder the next morning, including the local clergyman. Later that day Mr Moore, his wife's brother, arrived on the scene, having travelled from London to comfort Corder. After he had heard some of the evidence, he asked Corder: 'How could you send letters that you were happily living with Maria Marten when, at the same time, you were living with my sister whom you had married?' Corder made no answer to this question.

Lea and Ayres then took Corder in a post-chaise to Polstead, where he was lodged at the Cock Inn, arriving in the early hours of the morning to avoid the waiting crowds. When Corder woke that day it was to discover that the inn was packed to overflowing with some fifteen newspaper reporters from all over the country, and the inquest jury in place. The other rooms in the inn were filled with noisy customers who had made a holiday of the occasion.

Corder and the jury listened to the evidence. George Marten testified: 'I am brother to the deceased. I was ten years old when my sister went away. On the afternoon of that day I saw Corder go from the Red Barn across two fields with a pickaxe on his shoulder . . . I was only twenty rods from him and I saw his face very plainly.'

Phoebe Stowe said: 'I live in the nearest cottage to the Red Barn. One day in last year William Corder came to my house and asked me if I could lend him a spade of my husband's.'

James Lea told of arresting Corder. Mrs Marten identified a green silk scarf as having belonged to Maria, and then burst into tears. Mr Robert Offord, a cutler, testified: 'About this time last year William Corder came to my shop with a small sword with a scimitar blade about

43

twelve inches long . . . he wished it to be ground and made as sharp as a carving-knife . . . ' Mr John Lawton, surgeon, said: 'I was present when the body was viewed . . . The internal bone of the orbit of the right eye was fractured as if a pointed instrument had been thrust into it . . . Such a stab might have penetrated the brain.' In his opinion, a pistol-ball had entered the neck from behind at an oblique angle, causing the injury to the eye socket.

Corder, wearing a black Spanish cloak, looked ill and exhausted and was allowed to remain seated as the coroner read out the evidence against him. The jury then retired, taking an hour to reach a verdict of wilful murder against Corder, and he was remanded to Bury Gaol to await trial at the next Assize. The pub customers celebrated the verdict with heavy drinking and debauchery, finding something comic in the fact of murder.

As soon as the inquest was over, Maria Marten was carried in her coffin to the village churchyard and was laid to rest within sight of the Red Barn. For his part, Corder took the news of the inquest verdict calmly and ate the meal provided for him with a hearty appetite. Many of the jurymen, who had been his friends, called at his chamber to bid him farewell and express their sorrow.

While being driven to Bury Gaol in a post-chaise, Corder told Mr Lea, escorting him: 'I had two frightful dreams on the Friday night before you took me; I dreamt that I saw all my deceased brothers and sisters pass before me, all dressed in white . . . ' On arrival at the prison, Corder told the governor that he very much wanted a Bible and a prayer-book. Before parting from Lea, Corder gave him a silk embroidered purse as a token of remembrance.

The annual Polstead fair – the Cherry Fair – was held on 16 and 17 July, and the star attraction was a theatrical representation of *The Late Murder of Maria Marten*. There were also puppet-shows depicting the murder, and ballad-singers with songs about Corder being 'the hor-

rible murderer'. So Corder's guilt was assumed and pro-
claimed. Guilty as he undoubtedly was, he can hardly be
said to have had a fair trial, although it was to take over
a century for the power of inquest juries to be limited
and for pre-trial reporting to be banned.

The trial began in August 1828. Corder's wife had
visited him regularly in prison and had even taken lodgings in Bury to be near him. Just before the trial the
body of Maria Marten was exhumed; this was because a
witness had complained to the coroner that he was not
satisfied with the stated cause of death: the pistol-ball in
the head. There had also been a stab-wound in the victim's side, proved by cuts in the stays and chemise of the
deceased.

This was true, but since Maria's father had poked the
floor of the Red Barn with a spike for mole-catching, it
is likely that he caused this injury. However, Corder was
to be charged with shooting, stabbing and strangling
Maria Marten.

The Assize Court at Bury was crowded on Thursday,
7 August, when Corder was placed in the dock before
Lord Chief Baron Alexander, having been taken to the
court by Mr Orridge, governor of Bury Gaol. There had
been quite a battle between the public for seats, and some
of the barristers lost their wigs in the mêleé.

Mr Aspell, clerk of the Assize, read out the nine counts
in the indictment against Corder, who listened intently,
now and again peering through an eyeglass at the jury.
The substance of the charges against Corder was that he:
'shot Maria Marten with a pistol, value two shillings,
upon the left side of the face giving her one mortal wound
of the depth of four inches and the width of half an
inch, of which she died instantly; also made an assault
upon her with a sword of the value of one shilling in the
left side of the body between the 5th and 6th ribs to
the depth of six inches and the breadth of one inch, of
which she instantly died; also strangled her with a six-
penny handkerchief, when she instantly died.' The ninth

count on the indictment alleged that he buried Maria Marten in the Red Barn, covering her with 'five bushels of clay of no value'. It is difficult to understand why the precise value of every piece of evidence had to be emphasized, unless all evidence was forfeit to the Crown.

The judge, jury and spectators gazed at a detailed model of the Red Barn, while the prosecuting counsel, Mr Andrews, displayed the plans of the building with the grave-site marked. Corder, with a pale complexion, sandy beard and large sorrowful eyes, wearing blue trousers and white silk stockings and pumps topped with a velvet doublet, stood in the dock with a faint smile on his lips.

Mr Andrews said that the prisoner was the son of respectable parents, and Maria Marten was the daughter 'of parents from a humbler station in life'. The couple had been intimate, with the result that an infant was born illegitimately, who died aged three weeks. Corder had twice made arrangements to marry Maria Marten, only to have something go wrong with his plans each time. But on Friday, 18 May, Corder had called at the Martens' cottage at noon and insisted that she come with him to Ipswich to be married that day. He persuaded her to dress as a man so that neighbours should not recognize her, and her female attire was placed in a bag and taken to the Red Barn. Maria left by the back door dressed as a man, a green silk scarf around her neck. Corder left by the front door. Both made their way towards the Red Barn – and that was the last anyone saw of Maria Marten.

In the weeks that followed, Corder told different people various stories about her whereabouts. To some he said she had sailed to France on a steam-packet; to others he said he had left her in the care of a Miss Rowlands at Yarmouth. When one woman asked him if they intended to have more children, Corder replied sharply: 'No, Maria Marten will have no more children.'

Subsequently Corder wrote to Maria's father and stepmother, claiming to have married her in that city, but the Martens expressed suspicion because Maria had not written personally with the news. Corder claimed that she had, but that her letter had gone astray. Telling of Corder's arrest, the prosecutor said that Corder 'thrice denied' knowing anyone named Maria Marten, but when his dwelling was searched a black velvet bag belonging to Maria was found, containing a brace of pistols.

Mr Marten had searched the Red Barn in April, following his wife's urgings, and had found his daughter's body buried there. She had been shot in the head, stabbed in the side, and strangled with that green silk scarf.

One by one the witnesses testified. Ann Marten said: 'I know William Corder, the prisoner at the bar, and have for nearly seventeen years. He was living at Polstead and was acquainted with Maria; they were intimately connected . . . Maria was delivered of a child at Sudbury. The prisoner said he was the father of the child.' She told of overhearing quarrels between Maria and Corder about the baby's burial place and the missing five-pound note. Corder threatened Maria with the parish, saying they had a warrant out to punish her for producing three illegitimate paupers.

She recounted that Corder had taken Maria away to get married. When she subsequently asked Corder what he had done with Maria, he replied: 'I have left her at Ipswich, where I have got a comfortable place for her.'

Thomas Marten told of finding his daughter's body buried in the Red Barn when he searched it on 19 April, using a mole-catcher's spike to prod the earth. At one spot it came up smelling foul . . . Witnesses told of having seen Corder with a pickaxe. Maria's friend Rachel Burke said Corder had told her that Maria had gone to France in a steam-packet.

Mr Broderick, defence counsel, protested to the judge that a preacher addressing a congregation of several thousands of people at the Red Barn had alluded to Corder as the murderer. Mr Chaplin, the official who caused the prosecution to be brought, was questioned by Mr Broderick, who asked him: 'Did you hear the parson preach in or near the barn?'

Mr Chaplin replied: 'No, certainly not, but I heard of the occurrence.'

'And you took no steps to prevent it?'

'No, I did not.'

'Are there exhibitions going about the neighbourhood representing Corder as the murderer?'

'I have heard so.'

'And you have not interfered to prevent them. Is there not a camera obscura near this very hall at this moment exhibiting him as the murderer?'

'There is a camera obscura, I believe, about the street . . . I was not aware that I have any power to stop them.'

Mr John Balham testified: 'I am constable at Polstead. I know Corder very well. I also knew Maria Marten. I never had a warrant to apprehend her . . . although there was a report about the place that she would be taken up. I have known the young man at the bar all his life . . . I can give him the character of a kind-hearted, good-tempered young man.'

Mr John Lawton, the surgeon from Boxford, gave evidence which was of interest in that it was an early attempt by a scientific man to develop some kind of forensic medicine. He said he had placed the tip of the sword in the wound in Maria's body: it fitted. Likewise the ball from Corder's pistol fitted the hole in the victim's skull. He went on: 'I have the head here and I produce it.'

There was a gasp of horror as the skull was produced and handed around the court. Corder stared at its ghastly grin unmoved. The trial was then adjourned until the following day, the hour having grown late. Corder was kept in a separate room, but ladies and gentlemen of the town raised ladders against the building so they could peek at him through holes in the roof.

Corder entered court the following morning after a

hearty breakfast. The second day was given over mainly to the defence case. Corder was called to read his defence speech to the jury, which he had written down carefully in a book. He began by reminding the jury that defence counsel were not permitted to address the jury on behalf of the prisoner, and so he had to speak for himself. He complained about the newspaper coverage of the case: 'I have been described by the press as the most depraved of inhuman monsters', and begged the jury to ignore any reports they might have read and to listen without prejudice.

He went on: 'It has been well observed that "truth is sometimes stranger than fiction", and never was the observation more strongly exemplified than in my life and circumstances . . . The last few years of my life have been one continual series of misfortunes. I was deprived of all my brothers, three in number, and my father died only a few months before." '

He claimed that Maria had taken from his house two pistols without his knowledge, pistols which he had showed her how to use in the past. He and Maria went to the barn to talk. She bitterly chided him for not showing her the same regard as did her 'gentleman' lover, Mr Matthews. Corder then told Maria that he had decided not to marry her after all, and feeling deeply hurt, he walked away.

But he had scarcely taken a step out of the barn when he heard a loud report. Maria had shot herself. Corder told the court: 'The danger of my situation now flashed upon my mind. There lay the unfortunate girl, wounded to death, and by an instrument belonging to me, and I the only human being present . . . ' In short, he said he had panicked and buried the body, fearing that he would be accused of the crime of murder. Afterwards, he had been forced to lie about Maria's whereabouts in order to cover up his original sin of concealing the body.

It was a clever and plausible tale, but sounded contrived. Corder spoke for thirty-two minutes, begging the jury to believe him and asking them: 'Gentlemen, can any sufficient motive be suggested for such a horrible crime? . . . My life is in your hands.'

Then followed witnesses for the defence, some who testified to having seen Maria Marten shooting with Corder's pistols, others who gave Corder a glowing character reference. At noon the judge began his summing-up to the jury. At 1.50 p.m. the jury retired, returning after thirty-five minutes of deliberation. The verdict was guilty of wilful murder.

The judge placed the black cap on his head and told Corder: 'You stand convicted of an aggravated breach of the great prohibition of the Supreme Being, the Almighty Creator of Mankind: "Thou shalt do no murder."

'The law of this country, in concurrence with the law of all civilized nations, enforces this prohibition of God by exacting from the criminal who violates it the forfeiting of his own life. "He that sheddeth man's blood, by man shall his blood be shed." '

The judge urged Corder to seek solace in religion and to prepare himself for the next world by repenting fully before his execution. He then passed the sentence of death: 'That you be taken back to the prison from whence you came, and that you be taken from thence on Monday next to a place of execution and there be hanged by the neck until you are dead, and that afterwards your body shall be dissected and anatomized.'

Corder had listened to the death sentence with relative calm, but when he heard he was to be dissected he shuddered and almost collapsed, having to be supported by Mr Orridge, the governor of Bury Gaol. Taken back to that prison, Corder was made to don prison garb and was placed in the condemned cell, guarded by two officers so that he should not commit suicide and thus cheat the hangman. Mrs Corder visited him in prison and brought him religious tracts to read, while the governor and chaplain tried in vain to wheedle a confession of guilt out of him.

The scaffold had been erected in a paddock next to the gaol, and on the Sunday prior to the execution the convicts of Bury Gaol, including William Corder, attended chapel for the service. Members of the press were present to observe Corder's reactions, but he held a white handkerchief to his face, obscuring any view of him, for most of the service. However, he was seen to strike himself on the temple when the preacher made reference to his crime, and he appeared to be deeply agitated.

On that Sunday evening, after exhortations from the governor, Corder finally wrote his confession. Dated 1828, from the condemned cell, Bury Gaol, Corder wrote:

> I acknowledge being guilty of the death of poor Maria Marten, by shooting her with a pistol. The particulars are as follows: when we left her father's house we began quarreling about the burial of the child, she apprehending that the place where it was deposited would be found out. The quarrel continued for about three-quarters of an hour, upon this and other subjects. A scuffle ensued and during the scuffle I took the pistol from the side pocket of my velveteen jacket and fired. She fell and died in an instant . . . I was overwhelmed with agitation and dismay – the body fell near the front doors on the floor of the barn. A vast quantity of blood issued from the wound and ran on the floor and through the crevices.

After stating how he buried her body about two hours after her death, Corder went on: 'I declare to Almighty God I had no sharp instrument about me, and that no other wound but the one made by the pistol was inflicted by me. I have been guilty of great idleness and at times led a dissolute life, but I hope through the mercy of God to be forgiven.'

As early as five o'clock on Monday morning hundreds of people began to gather before the scaffold, with gentlemen and their ladies arriving in gigs and chaises and booking every room in every inn in the town. It was the social event of the year. By the time of the execution the crowd numbered some eight to nine thousand people, many having come from as far afield as Cambridge and Newmarket.

Corder spent the early hours of the morning in the prison chapel, and by 11.30 a.m., now dressed in his own clothes, he was led out by the under-sheriff to where the hangman was waiting. It was Foxten, the executioner from Newgate Prison, who had been specially retained for this performance.

There were many women in the crowd, and when a man remonstrated with one of them for being present to witness so brutal a deed, she retorted that she had the right to witness the end of a man who had so inhumanly butchered one of her sex. It was a rare and early example of women's lib.

After he had been hooded and had the rope placed about his neck, Corder said loudly: 'I am guilty – my sentence is just – I deserve my fate – and may God have mercy upon me.'

The crowd remonstrated with the hangman, telling him he had left too much slack in the rope. He grudgingly made adjustments, annoyed to have public interference in his duties. He then cut the rope which supported the platform, and Corder fell. The hangman immediately grasped him about the waist and swung on him to hasten his end. After hanging for an hour, the body was cut down.

The executioner afterwards expressed his chagrin at having been interrupted in the performance of his duties by the crowd and criticized about the length of his rope. Foxten said: 'I never like to be meddled with because I always study the subjects which come under my hands and, according as they are tall or short, heavy or light, I accommodate them with the fall. No man in England has so much experience as me or knows how to do his duty better.' It was a rare note of pride from the hangman.

The public were allowed to view the almost naked

body of Corder as it lay in the Shire Hall, prior to its removal to the county hospital for dissection. Afterwards phrenologists published reports on Corder's head and brain, claiming to have discovered traits of secretiveness and destructiveness.

Looking back on the case now, it is indeed difficult to see what Corder's motive for the deed was – unless he had murdered his new-born infant, and Maria knew, and held it over his head, threatening him with disclosure unless he married her.

The premeditation on Corder's part is readily apparent. He insisted that Maria dress as a man and go to the barn. He followed her there, having the pistol in his pocket. As to whether Corder killed his own love-child by Maria, we must let the evidence speak for itself. Why should Maria have 'apprehended' that the place where the body was buried might be found? What had she – or Corder – to hide if the baby had died a natural death? And why the mystery over the burial place? All we know is that it was a 'field' and the baby was buried at night.

Soon after Corder's execution a melodrama, *The Mysterious Murder in the Red Barn* by Mr West Digges, was performed with great success at the Royal Pavilion, Mile End Road, London, and it has featured in repertory theatres ever since. Another play about Corder was called *Advertisement For Wives*. James Curtis, who attended the trial of Corder and wrote a book on the case, *Maria Marten*, had his copy bound with a large portion of Corder's skin, donated by the doctors who anatomized him. It remains one of the most grisly relics in the library of murder, being recently rediscovered in a university library.

4

BIRMINGHAM'S 'PLASTIC BAG' KILLING
1985

By March 1985, Albert Bowie faced an age-old *dilemma*: he was in love with another woman and his wife stood in the way. Like William Corder, he saw elimination as the only way out. He too hid the body of his victim, but lacking a barn, used a more prosaic garden shed.

The 'eternal triangle' has always been a potent motive for murder. It was, after all, precisely for this reason that Dr Crippen murdered his wife; but today, with the ease with which divorce can be obtained, murder seems both an unnecessary and drastic solution to a simple problem. However, as with so many of today's almost frivolous and stupid murders, Bowie had another reason for disposing of his wife: he wanted to move his young mistress into the family home and needed every penny he could get his hands on – including his wife's money.

A self-employed haulage contractor aged forty-four, Bowie, of Aston, Birmingham, strangled his wife Philomena after what he claimed was a row about a faulty steam-iron, then stuffed her body into a black polythene bag, which he locked in a garden shed. Then, just hours after the deed, he persuaded his seventeen-year-old lover, Linda Graham, to move in with him, telling her that his wife had left him for good and gone to Spain.

When relatives of his wife became anxious about her whereabouts, he told them that she was in Ireland visiting friends. But after almost two weeks with no news – and the strange teenager in the house – the relatives contacted the police, who questioned Bowie. He told them the same story, but they searched the house anyway, finding nothing. They were unable to get into the garden shed because Bowie claimed he had lost the key, but when they returned later to resume the search, they found Bowie in the hallway of his home, together with a bulky plastic bag containing his wife's body, which he was in the process of hiding somewhere else. Presumably, since the police had already searched the house, Bowie thought it the best place to hide the body, on the basis that they were hardly likely to look there again.

The full grisly details emerged at Birmingham Crown Court during a murder trial which began on 28 October 1985. Miss Diane Cotton, QC, prosecuting, told the jury that Bowie was 'besotted' with Linda Graham, buying her a ring and spending large sums on her. In October 1984 Bowie's fifty-six-year-old wife Philomena was made redundant from Hockley bus garage and given a lump-sum redundancy payment, which she put into their joint account.

Miss Cotton continued: 'In April or thereabouts, 1984, the defendant had met this young girl. He seems to have met her quite a lot, and became infatuated with her. From July he was seeing her every night, and from that time had a sexual relationship with her. In February this year he bought her a ring and told her his wife was going to apply for a divorce and leave him.'

Describing the killing of Philomena Bowie, which took place sometime between 11 March and 23 March, Miss Cotton said that Bowie strangled her with an electric flex and then bundled her body into a plastic bag – a dustbin liner – which was deposited in the garden shed. There it remained for two weeks. In the meantime, constant questioning by her relatives preyed on Bowie's mind and on 21 March he told his parents about the killing, and told Linda Graham the following day. She immediately moved out, and her report to the police led them to search the house that same day.

Miss Cotton said that when police questioned Bowie, he told them that he had not had sex with his wife for a long time, and on the day she died they had argued over a broken steam-iron. His wife was sitting on the settee, and Bowie admitted approaching her from behind and putting the electric flex around her neck. 'I just kept pulling until the cord was tight,' he said.

Miss Cotton went on: 'You will hear that he admits that he caused the death of his wife. The issue in this case is whether he is guilty of murder or only manslaughter.' Commenting on the claim that the killing followed a row over a faulty iron, Miss Cotton said: 'The prosecution suggests that what he was really doing was planning to get rid of his wife so he could have Linda Graham to live with him.' But Bowie discovered, just like many a murderer before him, the grim irony of homicide: he lost the very thing he killed for.

Miss Cotton said that Bowie's seven-year marriage had run into difficulties the previous year because the couple had sexual problems. The main problem was the infatuation of a middle-aged man for a teenager 'whom he was impatient to have come live with him'. When his dream came true – for the ten days when his lover lived with him – he kept the grim secret in the garden shed from her.

Red-haired Linda Graham went into the witness box to tell the court that Bowie had said his wife had gone to live in Spain. She moved in with him but, she told the jury, 'there were some clothes of his wife's in the house and we put them in a bag. I said: "Suppose she comes back?" But he said: "She won't be coming back." ' Describing her sexual relations with the man old enough to be her father, she said: 'We wanted to have sex. We used to go to bed together, but he could never manage it. We never went to the pictures, dancing, or to the pub for a drink. We didn't even go on walks together. He only ever took me out in his van on his delivery rounds.'

Breaking down in tears, the teenager told of how, after

ten days of living together, Bowie confessed to her that he had killed his wife. 'He said that they had had an argument and he had strangled her. I could not believe it. I asked him where he had put the body and he said it was in the shed. I left after that.'

On the second day of the trial, Bowie went into the witness box to tell the jury that he strangled his wife because of her taunts about his sexual inability. 'She said something about me not being any good to her or any other woman, and I should only be going to places like gay pubs.' Telling of how they had slept apart for several years, Bowie told of the moment of killing.

'I was standing in the doorway, the new length of flex in my hand to repair the iron. She made some taunting remarks about my sexual inability. The taunting remarks were coming over, and the next thing I knew the cord was around her neck.' He complained that his wife had been a bingo addict who got up late and watched television all day long. The thrust of the defence line was clear: manslaughter due to provocation.

Bowie said that after the killing he left his wife's body sitting on the settee for seven hours, before wrapping it in clothes and putting it in the garden shed. He sat in the armchair for two hours staring at the body, then went to West Bromwich to do a job. He also claimed that he was forced to do housework for his wife, in between working a twenty-two-hour day.

Defence counsel, Martin Wilson, QC, asked him: 'Can you remember strangling your wife?'

Bowie replied: 'No.'

Mr Wilson said: 'Did you form a decision to kill your wife before that day?'

Bowie replied: 'No, sir.'

But, as emerged later, Bowie remained remarkably cool on the day of the murder, even making a business call at Austin-Rover in the evening. (This typical 'cool' behaviour after a murder is not uncommon and is termed by psychiatrists 'disassociation'.)

The prosecution insisted: 'This was a planned, intended murder, and not a situation in which the defendant was provoked at all.' Bowie had told his girlfriend that his wife was due to move out on the day of the murder. 'The reality was that she had no intention of moving out at all, and had even arranged for a niece to stay with her that night.' Bowie, Miss Cotton went on, had taken nearly three thousand pounds from a joint account to spend on the girl.

Miss Cotton, in her closing speech, said Bowie was guilty of deliberate murder, needing to get rid of his wife so that his girlfriend could move in with him. 'He was infatuated with her and wanted to live with her, but he didn't want to leave his home, and there were difficulties over the van, which had been paid for by his wife's sister.' She said that in the days following the killing Bowie had had plenty of time to make up the story about the argument over the iron and the sex taunts which he related to police in his confession.

But Mr Wilson told the jury that Bowie killed his wife 'in the heat of the moment'. He went on: 'Whatever you may think of the girl – that she's immoral or stupid – she has been through the most dreadful of experiences. She has lain beside a man who had killed his wife, with the wife's body at the bottom of the garden.' He claimed that Bowie had made no arrangement to dispose of his wife's body *prior* to the murder – proof that the murder had not been premeditated.

At the end of the three-day trial the jury of eight men and four women took just four hours to unanimously convict Bowie of murder. Applause from the public gallery greeted the sentence of life imprisonment imposed on Bowie. A friend of the murdered woman said: 'Justice has been done. She worshipped that man. She even told me that her husband had befriended a girl of seventeen. She was worried about it, but said he felt sorry for the girl and wanted to help her.'

Bowie, the middle-aged man enmeshed in a web of

passion who so desperately wanted to change his life, has succeeded in that at least. He has swapped his life in Aston with Philomena for a life sentence in one of Her Majesty's prisons. He won't like that one little bit.

5
MADELEINE SMITH: THE MONA LISA OF MURDER
1857

On Thursday, 9 July 1857, a jury in the High Court of Justiciary in Edinburgh found the charge against Madeleine Smith, aged twenty-one, of murdering her lover, Pierre Emile L'Angelier, by the administration of arsenic 'not proven', and she walked free from the court. The controversy that verdict aroused continues to this day, with the question did she or didn't she? still unanswered.

She occupies the same place in the history of crime as Adelaide Bartlett, found not guilty of her husband's murder, and Lizzie Borden. After being acquitted of murdering her parents, Lizzie was branded a killer by the cruel doggerel:

> Lizzie Borden took an axe
> And gave her mother forty whacks;
> When she saw what she had done
> She gave her father forty-one.

But where Lizzie was plain, Madeleine Smith was a raven-haired beauty with a diamond-bright smile and an inner radiance which made her a star in the dock. Today that smile remains as enigmatic as that of the 'Mona Lisa'. Is she smiling at the follies of men – or at having successfully hoodwinked the jury? The facts tell their own story, but are open to all kinds of interpretations. Ultimately, each and every reader must judge for themselves, in the attempt to resolve the enigma which is Madeleine Smith.

It was in March 1855 that Emile L'Angelier first noticed a strikingly beautiful girl walking along Sauchiehall Street in Glasgow. L'Angelier was a twenty-nine-year-old warehouse clerk employed by the firm of Huggins & Company on a salary of a hundred pounds a year. He was so besotted with the nineteen-year-old girl that he persuaded Robert Baird, a friend who knew her, to introduce him to Miss Smith. She in turn was instantly attracted to the Jersey born L'Angelier. That initial fascination was eventually to turn to a destructive hatred worthy of any Greek tragedy, and could rightly be termed a fatal attraction long before the movie of the same name.

L'Angelier was an interesting character, typical of the type of man too big for the small role allotted to him by fate or society. A humble clerk, he had visions of a romantic destiny. When his father died in 1842, L'Angelier, then aged sixteen, was apprenticed to a Glasgow seed merchant. But after five years he threw up his position to go to France and fight with the National Guard during the revolution of 1848. He returned to Edinburgh penniless, but he brought back with him one driving ambition: to marry a wealthy woman and thus enhance his own life. He worked for several firms before settling with Huggins of Glasgow, at first on ten shillings a week.

L'Angelier certainly displayed audacity in hoping to capture Madeleine Smith. She lived in the same city as he did, but on such a different level that she might as well have lived on another planet.

She was the eldest daughter of a wealthy family and had received an excellent education, leaving school at eighteen to join the best society in Glasgow. Talented, beautiful and vivacious, she was the object of desire for every eligible bachelor in the city.

The meeting of L'Angelier and Madeleine Smith was the coming together of two cultures: the working class and the middle class. No lady of breeding should have fallen for a common clerk, but there was something different about L'Angelier. He had an interesting back-

61

ground and a romantic nature. He was gifted with the superb courtesy and sophistication of his French fore-bears. In short, he possessed all the necessary attributes of an exceptional gigolo.

Madeleine, of course, was no ordinary lady. In an age when it was considered shocking for a woman to admit to strong passion, and when the Brontë sisters had to publish their novels under male pseudonyms, Madeleine was a free spirit with a tremendous strength of character and an almost ruthless independence, determined to give her passions full rein.

It was an age when respectable young women were supposed to do nothing but amuse themselves; their whole upbringing had been to prepare them for marriage to a suitable husband with a secure income. It was a dull and confining existence, and Madeleine was bored. There is evidence that, although resigned to her destiny, Madeleine wanted a secret 'fling' before the suffocating marriage of respectability which awaited her, and she was quite prepared to manipulate any lover. She admitted in a letter to L'Angelier that she was 'fast' and confided to him:

> I used to say there were three things I would like to do. First to run off, second to marry a Frenchman, and third, that I would not marry a man unless he had a moustache, and yours is such a nice one.

Yet there was one man who had far more influence over Madeleine than anyone else, and that was her father, a successful architect and strict Presbyterian. A typical Scot, with fixed vision and iron determination, he ruled his family like a medieval patriarch and was determined that his daughter was destined for a brilliant match with a man of her own class and mettle – and, naturally, a man with money of his own. The very idea of his daughter falling in love with a penniless clerk would have caused him to choke with rage.

A lesser man would have given up any idea of possessing Madeleine, but L'Angelier was made of sterner stuff. He pursued her as a stoat pursues a rabbit, and within a few weeks had established such a hold over her that he was able to chide her for her faults and somewhat arrogantly tell her how to behave.

He persuaded Madeleine to agree to marry him, but although she was quite prepared to have a secret engagement, she refused point-blank to tell her father of any such plans. The very idea of approaching her father with such news terrified her. Caught in an impossible situation, Madeleine lied. She claimed she *had* approached her father, but he had refused to give his assent to the match.

In July 1855 a coldly furious L'Angelier wrote the following letter to Madeleine. It was found in his lodgings after his death, and read:

I do not deserve to be treated as you have done. How you astonished me by writing such a note without condescending to explain the reasons why your father refuses his consent. He must have reasons, and I am not allowed to clear myself of accusations . . . I warned you repeatedly not to be rash in your engagement and vows to me, but you persisted in that false and deceitful flirtation, playing with affections that you knew to be pure and undivided, and knowing at the same time that at a word from your father, you would break off your engagement. You have deceived your father as you have deceived me. You never told him how solemnly you bound yourself to me, or if you had, for the honour of his daughter he could not have asked you to break off an engagement such as ours. May this be a lesson to you never to trifle with any again . . . Think of what your father would say if I sent him your letters for perusal. Do you think he would sanction you breaking your vows? No, Madeleine, I leave your conscience to speak for itself.

This is an extraordinary and very important letter, since it contains so many internal clues. Firstly, since it was a draft of a letter, it proves that L'Angelier kept copies of his correspondence. Secondly, after just four months he had managed to exert such an influence over Madeleine that she promised to marry him. Thirdly, there is the arrogant tone with which L'Angelier addresses a beautiful heiress who could have her pick of men. Why did Madeleine put up with it? It can only be because the physical attraction between them was so strong that she was willing to be bullied, and may even have taken a masochistic delight in it. (However, it is very easy to forget that Madeleine had only recently left school and was still a child in her desire for romance, easily swayed by a man some ten years older than herself and far more wordly in his bearing and lovemaking.)

The fourth and most important clue in the letter is the barely disguised attempt at blackmail towards the end: 'Think what your father would say if I sent him your letters . . . ' That threat was to have dire consequences for L'Angelier.

Despite this apparent breach in the relationship, the meetings and letters continued. Miss Perry, an elderly spinster friend of L'Angelier's, and one of Madeleine's servants, acted as a go-between. Even after her father discovered that she was having a liaison with a social inferior and banned any future meetings, Madeleine continued to meet her lover secretly. The father was unaware of this: he had assumed that his word would be obeyed as law.

The Smith family spent the summer of 1855 at their country house, Rowaleyn, on the Clyde near Helensburgh, and the association between Madeleine and L'Angelier continued. Even before this, in the family home in India Street, Madeleine used to let L'Angelier into the house after the rest of the family were asleep.

A year later, when her father began to suspect that the relationship was continuing, he gave his daughter a further warning and was apparently satisfied that she intended to obey him. Madeleine even wrote to the mutual friend, Miss Perry, saying that she had broken off with L'Angelier because 'I felt it my duty to obey Papa'.

But at the same time she was writing to L'Angelier in Jersey, where he was on holiday with his relatives there: 'It will break my heart if you go away. I live for you alone. I adore you. I never could love another as I do you.' In further letters she begs L'Angelier to keep their correspondence secret.

L'Angelier had plans of his own. A secret relationship was no good to him; not even a marriage in defiance of her father. He wanted nothing less than a marriage recognized by her family and blessed with their money, and he was determined that his ambition was not to be denied.

In a letter written on 3 December 1855, Madeleine signs herself 'thine ever dear loving wife, Mimi L'Angelier'. (Mimi was his pet name for her.) In that letter she even discussed the possibility of marriage and the publication of banns.

From holiday at Rowaleyn, Madeleine wrote on 29 April 1856:

> Dearest, I must see you. It is fearful never to see you, but I am sure I don't know when I will see you. Papa has not been a night in town for some time, but the first night he is off I shall see you. We shall spend an hour of bliss. There shall be no risk, only C.H. shall know.

C.H. was Christina Haggart, a Smith family servant who used to ferry notes between the couple. A further letter makes the appointment 'by the gate at half-past ten'. Another letter reveals what happened at that meeting. She wrote: 'Beloved, if we did wrong last night, it was in the excitement of our love . . . I did not bleed in the least, but I had a good deal of pain in the night.' They had become lovers in the full sense of the term.

The effect on L'Angelier was disturbing. He wrote her

a somewhat priggish, even hypocritical letter in which he said:

> Would to God we had not met that night. I am sad at what we did. I regret it very much. Why, Mimi, did you give way after your promise? Think of the consequences if I were never to marry you . . . I will not again repeat what I did, until we are regularly married . . . Mimi, you must make a bold step to be my wife. Speak to your mother. Tell her that you are my wife before God. My conscience reproaches me for a sin which only marriage can efface.

This is a surprising reversal of the usual Victorian roles: a man threatening to withhold sex from a woman until she marries him.

Madeleine's situation was perilous. Enjoying the illicit relationship, the frank carnality of the experience – (for it was plain lust dressed in fancy words) – she realized that it could never come to anything. Her destiny had been mapped out for her by her father and included a suitable husband.

At this point her father produced an eligible suitor for his daughter's hand. Mr William Minnoch was a wealthy merchant, considerably older than Madeleine, but a good friend of the father and a man of excellent character. Mr Smith wanted him as a son-in-law. Accordingly, Mr Minnoch stayed with the Smith family at Rowaleyn in September 1856 and paid court to Madeleine; and when the Smith family returned to Glasgow, it was to a new house at 7 Blythswood Square, just around the corner from Mr Minnoch's. On 28 January 1857 Mr Minnoch proposed to Madeleine and was accepted. They were both aware of the pressure on Madeleine to make a respectable marriage.

Meanwhile the affair with L'Angelier was continuing but showing signs of coming to a natural conclusion and a parting of the ways. Madeleine had been a little girl let loose in the orchard. She had gorged herself on the fruit but was now glutted. L'Angelier, aware of her cooling ardour, hung about her bedroom window, which was on the ground floor at Blythswood Square. Sometimes they talked through the window, sometimes she let him in 'for old time's sake'. But L'Angelier had learned of her impending marriage to Mr Minnoch and returned her latest letter unread.

Madeleine took advantage of this tactical error. She wrote to him saying: 'I felt truly astonished to have my last letter returned to me. But it shall be the last you will have an opportunity of returning to me . . . as there is coolness on both sides, our engagement had better be broken.'

On 2 February 1857, Madeleine wrote to L'Angelier asking him to return all her letters. It was a formal end to the relationship. She explained: 'My love for you has ceased . . . I did love you once, truly, fondly, but for some time back I have lost much of that love.' She added: 'I know you will never injure the character of one you so fondly loved. I know you have honour and are a gentleman. What has passed you will not mention.' Alas, L'Angelier was no gentleman.

Soon after receiving this letter L'Angelier approached a colleague at work, a Mr Kennedy, in a state of extreme agitation and distress. He explained that he had received a letter from Miss Smith breaking off their engagement and asking for the return of her letters. Mr Kennedy advised him to send back the letters and forget all about her. She was obviously unworthy of a man of his character. L'Angelier replied that he would, as a last resort, show her letters to her father. He would ensure that Madeleine never married another man while he was alive.

There followed a series of urgent letters from Madeleine, L'Angelier obviously having made plain his threat to blacken her character and expose her. She wrote: 'I have just had your note. Emile, for the love you once had for me, do nothing until I see you. For God's sake do not bring your once loved Mimi to an open shame.'

A little later she wrote: 'Emile, write to no one, to Papa nor to any other . . . Oh, Emile. Be not harsh to me. I am the most miserable, guilty wretch on the face of the earth. Emile, do not drive me to death.'

Feverishly, Madeleine made arrangements to meet him secretly, and the letters continued. 'Emile, for God's sake do not send my letters to Papa . . . I will die.' And later: 'Emile, do nothing until you see me . . . ten o'clock tomorrow night.' Later still: 'On my bended knees I write to you . . . and ask for mercy . . . do not inform on me – do not make me a public shame . . . I shall be undone. I shall be ruined . . . Despise me, hate me, but do not make me the public scandal . . . ' Finally, a secret meeting was arranged.

Around this time Madeleine sent a servant boy with a note to a chemist's shop to buy prussic acid. The chemist refused to supply it – it was an offence under the new Poisons Act. On 11 and 12 February Madeleine contacted L'Angelier, promising to renew their relationship. On Thursday, 12 February, L'Angelier dined with Miss Perry, mentioning that he was seeing Madeleine on the following Thursday.

On Thursday, 19 February, L'Angelier was let into the house in Blythswood Square by Madeleine via her bedroom window. She gave him a cup of cocoa. When he returned to his lodgings he was violently ill.

On Saturday, 21 February, Madeleine bought an ounce of arsenic from a chemist named Murdock, explaining that it was to kill rats at the family home. Since the Smith family were regular customers of his, he supplied her with the poison with no hesitation – but she had to sign the poison register.

The following day, Sunday, according to L'Angelier's own diary which was found in his rooms after his death, he again met Madeleine secretly, in the dining room, and drank a cup of cocoa she had prepared for him. That night he lay in agony in his lodgings with severe stomach pains.

On Wednesday, 25 February, Madeleine went back to Murdock's chemist shop to complain that the arsenic he had supplied was not white. Mr Murdock explained that under the new law arsenic had to be mixed with a proportion of colouring matter – either soot or indigo.

A week later, on Wednesday, 4 March, Madeleine wrote to L'Angelier expressing her sympathy at his illness and suggesting he should go to the Isle of Wight to recuperate. He replied with a note asking acidly why she wanted him to go so far away.

On Friday, 6 March – all these dates were later ascertained by the police – Madeleine visited another Glasgow chemist, Mr Currie, and bought a further supply of arsenic. On that same day she left for a brief stay at the Bridge of Allan. On 17 March she returned to Glasgow and the following day visited Mr Currie again for another ounce of arsenic.

On Thursday, 19 March, L'Angelier, on sick-leave from his firm, left for a holiday at the Bridge of Allan, just missing a note from Madeleine making an appointment for that same night. On 21 March the letter begging him to come and see her was forwarded to him by a fellow-lodger via the French Consulate in Glasgow.

On Sunday, 22 March, L'Angelier returned to his lodgings and asked his landlady, Mrs Jenkins, for some supper. He seemed to be in excellent health. Afterwards he went out, taking a pass-key for the front door and explaining that he might be late back.

At 2.30 a.m. the next morning, Mrs Jenkins was awoken by a violent ringing of the front door bell. She hurried downstairs and opened the door to find L'Angelier lying on her front step, moaning in agony and almost unconscious from abdominal pains. He said he was so sick he had feared he would not get home, and told her he had suffered previous attacks. Mrs Jenkins got him into bed with a hot-water bottle.

However, by four o'clock his condition had deteriorated so rapidly that Mrs Jenkins sent for the nearest doctor, a Dr Steven. Dr Steven could not come – he was ill himself – but he sent a prescription, asking to be called again if there was no improvement.

At seven o'clock L'Angelier lay in a coma. A frightened Mrs Jenkins sent for Dr Steven, who arrived and immediately gave the patient morphia. The doctor asked if L'Angelier was a heavy drinker; he was puzzled that so young a man should have such a serious stomach complaint. Mrs Jenkins said that L'Angelier was a temperate man, and she was puzzled because this was the second time he had been out late at night and returned home ill.

The doctor sat with the patient for an hour, then left. L'Angelier, drifting in and out of consciousness, asked Mrs Jenkins to send for Miss Perry, the spinster lady who had been his friend and confidante, but before Miss Perry could arrive he was dead.

When L'Angelier's firm heard of his sudden death they were very concerned. He had been a popular employee. Since there was no provision under Scottish law for an inquest into the death, the firm decided to make their own inquiries into the circumstances, and sent a warehouseman, William Stevenson, a close friend of L'Angelier's, to find out what he could.

From a fellow-lodger, Stevenson discovered that Dr Steven had only seen L'Angelier on the morning of his death. L'Angelier's usual doctor was a Dr Thomson. He reported this back to his firm, and since Dr Steven refused to issue a death certificate, the firm commissioned both him and Dr Thomson to carry out a postmortem. They carefully opened up L'Angelier, securing the contents of his stomach in a sealed jar before examining the stomach itself. The signs of some irritant poison were clear – certainly clear enough for Stevenson to approach the procurator-fiscal of Glasgow and ask him to investigate the case as one of murder.

Accordingly, the body of L'Angelier was removed for analysis by Dr Penny, Professor of Chemistry at Glasgow University. He found one-fifth of an ounce of arsenic in the stomach contents alone – a massive dose. The professor reported: 'First, that the matters subjected to analysis and examination contained arsenic; and, secondly, that the quantity of arsenic found was more than sufficient to destroy life.'

The industrious Stevenson had searched L'Angelier's room and found the incriminating letters from Madeleine; still more of her letters were found in his desk at his work-place. As a result, on Tuesday, 31 March, Madeleine Smith was arrested and charged with the wilful murder of Emile L'Angelier.

Before the opening of the trial, on 30 June 1857, the police spent much time tracing her purchases of arsenic and transcribing the letters as exhibits in the case – letters which they claimed she was so anxious to keep private that she had killed. As an example of the police thoroughness, there were no less than 214 exhibits in the case, with eighty-nine witnesses being cited, of whom fifty-seven actually testified. Thirty-one witnesses were called for the defence.

The trial began in Edinburgh before Lord Justice-Clerk Hope, and Lords Handyside and Ivory. (Such three-judge trials were common in Scotland.) The prosecution was led by the Lord Advocate and the Solicitor-General, Mr Maitland, and the Advocate-Deputy, Mr Mackenzie. The defence was represented by the Dean of Faculty, Mr Inglis, together with Mr George Young and Mr Alexander Moncrieff. The wealth of Madeleine's family ensured that she would get the best possible defence team.

There were three separate counts in the indictment, including administering arsenic on 19 or 20 February causing illness, and on a third occasion on 22 March causing death.

An accused person was not then allowed to go into the witness box to give evidence on their own behalf. That right came only in 1898. They could only produce a written 'declaration' or statement. In her declaration

Madeleine frankly admitted her relationship with L'Angelier. She stated:

> 'My name is Madeleine Smith. I am a native of Glasgow;
> twenty-one years of age. I reside with my father, James Smith,
> architect, at No. 7 Blythswood Square, Glasgow. For about
> the last two years I have been acquainted with Emile
> L'Angelier . . . who lodged at No. 11 Franklin Place . . . I have
> met with him on a variety of occasions . . . I had not seen M.
> L'Angelier for about three weeks before his death, and the
> last occasion I saw him was on a night about half-past ten
> o'clock. On that occasion he tapped at my bedroom window,
> which is on the ground floor and fronts Main Street. I talked
> to him from the window . . . I did not go out to him, nor did
> he come in to me . . . The last note I wrote to him was on
> the Friday before his death, viz, Friday the 20th of March
> current . . . In consequence of that note I expected him to
> visit me on Saturday night, the 21st current, at my bedroom
> window, in the same way as formerly mentioned, but he did
> not come and sent no notice. There was no tapping on my
> bedroom window said Saturday night, or on the following
> night, being Sunday. I went to bed on Sunday night about
> ten o'clock and remained in bed until the usual time of getting
> up next morning, being eight or nine o'clock. M. L'Angelier
> was very unwell for some time . . . and complained of sick-
> ness, but I have no idea what was the cause of it. I remember
> giving him some cocoa from my bedroom window one night
> some time ago . . . I have bought arsenic on various
> occasions . . . I used it as a cosmetic and applied it to my
> face, neck and arms diluted with water . . . I had seen the use
> of it recommended in the newspapers. I never administered
> or caused to be administered to M. L'Angelier arsenic or
> anything injurious. And this I declare to be the truth.'

The essence of Madeleine's statement was that she admitted nothing. The prosecution would have to prove everything. They were well prepared to do so and had every
reason to expect to convince the jury that Madeleine
Smith had poisoned her lover to keep her guilty liaison
secret.

The prosecution case was naturally built on circumstantial evidence; after all, nobody had actually seen Madeleine poison her lover. But the inference was to be drawn from her actions and letters. She had admitted buying arsenic. She admitted having given L'Angelier cocoa. She had begged L'Angelier not to publish her letters to him; he had threatened to do so. She had the means, method and opportunity – and the motive too.

Scottish trials do not begin with a speech from the prosecutor telling the jury what he intends to prove. Instead, after the jury has been sworn and the charge put to the prisoner, the prosecution begins calling its witnesses.

Mrs Jenkins, landlady of the deceased, said: 'I knew the late M. L'Angelier. He lodged in our house ... His usual habits were very regular. He was sometimes out at night, not very often, but he has been late. His general health was good until about January.'

She gave details of the two previous sicknesses prior to the fatal one, adding: 'I knew he expected to be married about the end of September 1856.' Coming to the final illness she said: 'He suffered great pain. I said to him: "Were you not taking anything which disagreed with you?" He said: "I never approved of medicine ... " He got very bad at four o'clock. I said I would go for Dr Thomson in Dundas Street. He thanked me, but said it would be too much trouble too early.' Later she fetched Dr Steven, and when she told L'Angelier that the doctor thought he would get over it, L'Angelier replied: 'I am far worse than the doctor thinks.' Several times he said to the landlady: 'If I could get some sleep I would be better.'

This is interesting testimony on two points. The first is that L'Angelier had plenty of opportunity to say, in the hours before his death, that he had been poisoned. He said nothing. On the other hand, if he had taken the arsenic to commit suicide – as the defence was to suggest

73

– then he would have known that no amount of sleep would make him better.

The landlady continued with the revolting details. 'He vomited a great quantity of stuff. The chamber-pot was quite full.' But she added: 'L'Angelier had an illness one night about the end of August or beginning of September. He said his bowels had been very bad and he had not been in bed all night.'

L'Angelier's friend William Stevenson told of collecting L'Angelier's belongings from his lodgings and finding a letter in his vest pocket. It read: 'Why, my beloved, do you not come to me? Oh, beloved – are you ill? Come to me, sweet one. I waited and waited for you but you came not. I shall wait again tomorrow night.' The land-lady had testified that when Stevenson read this note he had exclaimed: 'This explains everything!' Certainly it was that note which had first aroused his suspicions.

In cross-examination Stevenson admitted that he had not marked all the letters he had found, and that: 'I understand that L'Angelier corresponded with a number of ladies in the South and in France . . . He was a vain person – vain of his personal appearance – much so.'

Dr Hugh Thomson said: 'It did not occur to me at the time that these symptoms arose from the actions of any irritant poison.' But later he had said to Stevenson: 'It was such a case as if it had occurred in England a cor-oner's inquest would be held.' The next morning Mr Stevenson called again and said that Messrs Huggins & Co. requested me to make an inspection.'

Together, he and Dr Steven carried out that 'inspec-tion', or autopsy. He described cutting open the abdomen and removing the stomach after both ends had been tied off. The contents of the stomach were decanted into a bottle, then the stomach was slit open and its lining examined. Ulcers in the mucous membrane made them suspect poison. Dr Steven then testified, saying he had declined to give a death certificate unless he made an examination.

Dr Frederick Penny was the Crown's expert witness, a great authority on poisons. He had carried out several tests on the stomach contents, including the Marsh test and Reinsch's process, and determined that in the eight-and-a-half fluid ounces of the stomach contents there were almost eighty-three grains of arsenic – or nearly one-fifth of an ounce. He had himself purchased arsenic from the chemist's shops of Mr Murdock and Mr Currie in order to carry out tests to determine how much colouring matter they contained. The great mystery for the professor was that while he had easily detected arsenic in the stomach, he could find no traces of any indigo. However, he did establish that by 'peculiar and dexterous manipulation the colouring could be separated from the arsenic – but it would take skill'.

He testified that cocoa would be an excellent medium in which to administer arsenic. The Lord Justice-Clerk thanked him for his testimony, saying: 'Certainly, Dr Penny, more satisfactory, lucid or distinct evidence I have never heard.'

Dr Robert Christian also testified as an expert, pointing out that it was likely that as much arsenic had been vomited out as had remained in the stomach. He agreed that suicides generally took massive doses to ensure death, but insisted: 'I think chocolate or cocoa would be a vehicle in which a considerable dose might be given.'

Mr Thau, who lodged with L'Angelier, said that he had often seen him taking laudanum. 'I saw him take it several times. I once told him that he took too much.' The chancellor to the French Consul in Glasgow testified: 'I do not think it likely that he committed suicide.' But he later added: 'I once heard him speak of arsenic; it must have been in the winter of 1853-4. It was on a Sunday, but I don't recollect how the conversation arose. It lasted about half an hour. Its purport was how much arsenic a person could take without being injured by it.'

A schoolfriend of Madeleine's, Mary Buchanan, said that she had been at school with Madeleine at Clapton, near London, for a year or so, and had heard in a lesson, or in reading in the evening, that Sturian peasants took arsenic to improve their breathing and complexion. She had actually been with Madeleine when she bought some arsenic – 'quite openly'. Chemists testified to Madeleine buying arsenic from them 'openly, and signing her name in the book'.

Thomas Kennedy, the cashier at Huggins & Co., had known L'Angelier intimately and told of how Emile had wept when Madeleine broke off their engagement. 'He said: "She will be the death of me, Tom." ' L'Angelier had threatened to expose Madeleine's letters and said at one point: 'I wish I was six feet under the ground.'

A police officer testified that searches had been made of every shop in the city, but no purchases of arsenic by L'Angelier could be traced. But nor could earlier purchases by Madeleine. She bought her first arsenic on 21 February – but L'Angelier's first illness was on 19 February – a point the defence was to exploit.

Miss Perry, the friend and confidante of L'Angelier, spoke of how the relationship between him and Madeleine grew, and then cooled. 'On 9 March he was talking of his extreme attachment to Miss Smith; he spoke of it as a fascination. He said: "It is a perfect fascination, my attraction for that girl; if she were to poison me I would forgive her." '

On the fifth day of the trial, Saturday 4 July, a legal argument arose over L'Angelier's diary, which the prosecution wanted to introduce into evidence. The Dean of Faculty argued that it should be excluded, saying it was proof of nothing and was probably concocted by a jealous and disappointed suitor. Many of the entries were undated. The judges agreed to exclude it under the 'hearsay' rule. Instead, the love-letters of Madeleine Smith were read, with all their frank glorying in the act of sex.

Defence witnesses included Robert Baker, a grocer from Jersey, who had known L'Angelier well and said: 'He often told me he was tired of his existence and wished himself out of the world.' Of his friends, Mr Laird told of how L'Angelier had once taken up a knife, threatening to plunge it into his own breast. Mr Smith said that L'Angelier had talked of 'self-destruction'. Mr Anderson said that L'Angelier frequently boasted of his success with women. David Hill said that L'Angelier had told him that he took arsenic regularly. Mr Mackay, a merchant from Dublin, had got to know L'Angelier quite well and said: 'I saw quite enough of him to enable me to form an opinion of his character. I considered him a vain, lying fellow.' Janet Christie, who knew L'Angelier from his work, testified to hearing L'Angelier say that French ladies used arsenic for their complexions.

Much was made during the trial of an article in *Chamber's Journal* which advocated the use of arsenic for the complexion, and a succession of ordinary doctors went into the witness box to tell of patients who were arsenic-eaters. They told of patients who had comitted suicide by arsenic, having obtained it from dye-mills where it lay about in large quantities in open casks.

On the seventh day – Tuesday, 7 July – the Lord Advocate made his closing speech to the jury, telling them: 'I now have to discharge perhaps the most painful public duty that ever fell to my lot . . . It is now my duty to draw these details together and present to you . . . in a connected shape, the links of that chain of evidence which we have been engaged for the past week in constructing . . . you will arrive at the conclusion that every link is so tightly fastened – that every loophole is so completely stopped – that there does not remain the possibility of escape for the unhappy prisoner from the net which she has woven for herself . . . '

He said he would avoid, as much as possible, the 'incredible evidence of disgrace and sin and degradation'. He referred constantly to Madeleine as 'this unfortunate lady', 'this miserable girl', or 'poor creature'. But it did not prevent him from trying to put the rope around her neck.

Thread by thread he drew together the case against her, describing L'Angelier as a 'respectable character' threatening to reveal the contents of Madeleine's letters. 'It was then she saw the position she was in – she knew what letters she had written to L'Angelier – she writes in despair for him to give the letters back: he refuses . . . There is one interview – she attempts to buy prussic acid; there is a second interview – she has bought arsenic; there is a third interview – she has bought arsenic again . . . The story is strange, in its horrors almost incredible.'

The entire framework of his speech was designed to show the sequence of events which led to murder, 'To bring clearly before you how these facts *in their order,* bear upon the crime alleged.'

On the eighth day the defence rose to make its final speech to the jury. The Dean of Faculty began by stating bluntly: 'Gentlemen of the jury, the charge against the prisoner is one of murder, and the punishment for murder is death; and that simple statement is sufficient to suggest to us the awful solemnity of the occasion which brings you and me face to face.'

He remarked that the prosecutor had shown compassion for the prisoner in his speech and went on: 'But gentlemen, I am going to ask you for something very different from commiseration. I am going to ask you for that which I will not condescend to beg, but which I loudly and importunately demand . . . I ask for justice.'

Point by point he refuted the prosecution case, which had argued that the three attacks of sickness were part of a *design* to murder L'Angelier. The defence paid much attention to key dates. That first sickness, which was the first charge in the indictment, had taken place on 19 February – yet Madeleine did not buy arsenic until the twenty-first. The Crown had searched all the chemists' shops in Glasgow – yet there was no 'tittle or vestige' of evidence that Madeleine had purchased arsenic until the 21st. The proof that she had not possessed the poison before this date lay in the fact that: 'When the prisoner went to buy arsenic afterwards, on February twenty-first and March sixth and eighteenth, she went about it in so open a way that it was quite impossible for her to escape observation.'

Having demolished the first count in the indictment, Mr Inglis then moved on to the second count. There was simply no *proof* that Madeleine had met L'Angelier on 22 February, the date of the second illness. In fact, his landlady had testified that he did not go out at all that Sunday night. Mr Inglis commented savagely: 'To conjecture in the face of the evidence that L'Angelier was out of the house that night is one of the most violent suppositions ever made in the presence of a jury.' If Madeleine had not administered the arsenic on the first occasion, and he had proved she had not (the judge in his summing-up later instructed the jury that the first count had failed and they should acquit), then ruling out suicide, '*L'Angelier must have had the arsenic from someone else's hands.*' He asked the jury to bear these facts in mind: 'It enables me to take a position from which I shall demolish every remaining atom in this case.'

As for the alleged third meeting, on 22 March, the only proof of that was a letter from Madeleine which was undated. There was nothing to indicate when it was written or on which night the meeting was intended to take place. The plain fact was that no single person could prove where L'Angelier had been on that Saturday night, during the five and a half hours before leaving his lodgings and returning mortally ill. The prosecution had asserted that he met Madeleine – *but where was the proof?*

He turned his attention to L'Angelier, this 'unknown adventurer . . . who intruded himself into the society of this young lady . . . he had a very silly expectation of admiration from the opposite sex . . . he was calculated to be very successful in paying attention to ladies, and was looking to push his fortune by that means.'

He asserted that L'Angelier had set out to seduce and

corrupt Madeleine. As a result: 'She had not lost her virtue merely, but, as the Lord Advocate said, her sense of decency. Gentlemen – whose fault was that – whose doing was that?' While admitting that Madeleine had 'fallen into the depths of degradation' under L'Angelier's influence, he went on: 'He will be a bold man who will seek to set limits to the depths of human depravity; but this at least all past experience teaches us: that perfection, even in depravity, is not rapidly attained, and that it is not by such short and easy steps as the prosecutor has been able to trace in the career of Madeleine Smith, that a gentle, loving girl passes at once into the savage grandeur of a Medea, or the appalling wickedness of a Borgia. There is and must be a certain progress in guilt.' After having spoken for several hours, defence counsel sat down exhausted.

Now came the judge's summing-up. He deplored Madeleine's moral character and the disgusting letters she had written, in which 'she provoked and invited sexual intercourse . . . these letters show an extraordinary frame of mind and as unhallowed a passion as perhaps ever appeared in a Court of Justice.

'This is a letter from a girl, written at five in the morning, just after she had submitted to his embraces; can you conceive or picture any worse state of mind than this letter exhibits? In other letters she uses the word "love" underscored, showing clearly what she meant by it; and in one letter she alludes to a most disgusting and revolting scene between them which one would have thought only a common prostitute could have been a party to. Certainly such a sentence was probably never before penned by a female to a man.'

At the end of the nine-day trial the jury returned with their verdicts of not guilty on the first count and not proven on the second and third counts. A cheer went up in the court, a great release of pent-up emotion. Madeleine smiled.

There are some wags who maintain that the peculiarly

Scottish verdict of 'not proven' means 'Go away and don't do it again.' Its legal effect is to free the prisoner without clearing them of blame. In a letter written afterwards to the matron of the prison where she had been held, Madeleine declared that she was not happy with the verdict.

Madeleine had impressed everyone during the trial with her cool composure and remarkable vitality. During the trial she was showered with letters from men seeking to marry her, although on her release from custody she found that her former friends shunned her. Her parents had not sat in court during the trial, but had taken to their beds from shame. When she left the court as a free woman, Madeleine, who had changed her clothes and put on a bonnet and a dark veil, was taken in a carriage by her brother to the railway station. They took a train to Rowaleyn, arriving at ten o'clock that night. Of her welcome home we know nothing. The Smith family moved out of Glasgow and sought oblivion, Madeleine's two sisters never marrying.

Madeleine herself moved to London, mixing in the company of artists – people as bohemian as herself. In 1861 she married George Wardle. He was closely associated with the Pre-Raphaelite Brotherhood movement, of which William Morris was a leading light. Morris had founded a factory to produce artistic wallpaper and furnishings for the home. It was a vaguely socialist venture, designed to bring culture to the masses, and a great commercial success. Madeleine's husband became general manager. The couple lived in Bloomsbury and joined the Socialist League.

Although the PRB movement was primarily artistic, it was also radically political, demanding the emancipation of women, the vote for all, and more daringly, promoting the idea of free love. Madeleine became the leading hostess of the movement, and had numerous famous guests to dine at her table. It is said that she once served a meal to George Bernard Shaw, and that at another soirée

George Du Maurier (unaware of her real identity) remarked: 'Madeleine Smith's beauty should not have saved her from the scaffold.' She led a happily married life for twenty years, presenting her husband with a son and daughter.

When her husband died, Madeleine was forced to leave her Bloomsbury home and for the next ten years lived in retirement at Leek in Staffordshire, on the small income left by her husband and an allowance from her wealthy brother-in-law. But when her allowance ceased, on the death of her brother-in-law in 1909, she decided to emigrate to America, at the age of seventy-four, to join her son. She survived her second husband – a man named Hora – and lived in poverty in Brooklyn, dying in April 1928, aged ninety-three. She was buried in Mount Hope Cemetery, New York. Noted for her smile, she took her secret to the grave, never revealing in word or writing the answer to that teasing question: did she or didn't she do it?

The answer lies somewhere in her personality, that strong self-willed search for sensation. F. Tennyson Jesse wrote of 'the *violence* of her personality', by which she meant her impetuous and intense *demand for more life*, her refusal to accept life as it is lived conventionally, a demand for self-expression at all costs. Jesse goes on: 'Nowadays she could have become a business woman, or gone on the stage, or lived in a bachelor flat and had love affairs.' There are those who swore she would make a great actress.

But it was a damn close-run thing. When the jury were polled, it transpired that two had voted for guilty. Perhaps the remaining thirteen members of the jury had voted 'not proven' because they too could not solve the riddle of Madeleine Smith with an easy conscience.

One thing is certain: had Madeleine Smith been able to go into the witness box and give evidence, then she would have been destroyed in cross-examination. She would not have had the answers to many vital questions, such as: why, if she was engaged to Mr Minnoch, she was writing such affectionate notes to L'Angelier. She knew he was threatening to destroy her, so just how would she have resolved her problem if L'Angelier had not conveniently died? And why did she choose to try arsenic as a cosmetic – years after she had seen it recommended – just at the precise moment that L'Angelier was threatening her?

Madeleine Smith was perhaps fortunate that she could not go into the witness box, and so the question mark remains beside the name of the Mona Lisa of murder.

6
THE 'REGGIE PERRIN' DEATHS
1986

Can you imagine what it's like to become the innocent victim of someone else's private dream? That is what happened to a Stockport housewife and her daughter. The dreams of the husband left them both dead, buried in shallow graves in a Welsh forest, while the husband-killer lived out the rest of his fantasy.

In his classic *The Seven Pillars of Wisdom*, T. E. Lawrence – the famed 'Lawrence of Arabia' – wrote: 'All men dream; but not equally. Those who dream by night in the dusty recesses of their minds wake in the day to find that it was vanity; but the dreamers of the day are dangerous men, for they may act their dreams with open eyes, to make them possible.'

Robert Healey was a dreamer. His life was in a mess. He was sexually infatuated with his twelve-year-old step-daughter and nagged by his wife. Like many people, he regretted his mistakes and the life he had made for himself. He longed to begin all over, start out afresh. But he felt trapped. Like Madeleine Smith, he felt a burning demand for more life.

Instead of taking the rational step of seeking a divorce, he decided to remove what he felt to be the impediments in his life. Murder seemed to be the only solution.

Such cases are quite common in the annals of homicide, and illustrate how most killers suffer from a warped kind of thinking. They lack the ability to work out logical solutions to their problems, to think themselves out of a mess, and so resort to short cuts. Only a violent response seems left to them. What they lack, of course, is plain common sense.

For Robert Healey, the moment to make his dream reality came on the night of 29 July 1986. Something in his brain snapped, and first he killed his wife, and then his stepdaughter. In an ordinary domestic murder of this kind the killer either attempts suicide immediately after the act, or feeling very remorseful, surrenders himself to the police. But this was not the style of Robert Healey, because he was a dreamer.

He was also heavily influenced by the successful television comedy series *The Fall and Rise of Reginald Perrin*. In fact, he had every episode of the series on videotape at his home. The plot of the series revolves around Perrin – played by Leonard Rossitter – faking his own death by drowning. Healey adopted this idea with relish. He threw himself into the role with all the enthusiasm of a 'method' actor.

For the police it began simply enough, with the finding of a man's clothing on a lonely beach at Prestatyn, North Wales. It was a hot summer's day, with the mist just clearing from the sea, when a man out walking came across the pile of clothing. He looked out to sea, thinking of an early morning swimmer, but no one was to be seen, and his next thought was of a death by drowning. He phoned the police, who were soon on the scene. A search of the clothing established that it belonged to a Robert Healey, thirty-eight, a driving instructor from Stockport, in the Greater Manchester area. Also found was what purported to be a suicide note to the man's mother, which read in part: 'I don't know what to do anymore. I may as well die now.'

It seemed a routine suicide, and Welsh police contacted Manchester police, asking them to visit the man's address at Longread Avenue, Hazel Grove, Stockport, and inform relatives of the man's apparent death.

When Manchester police called at the house they found it empty. Neighbours reported that they had not seen either Mr Healey or his wife, Greeba, or her daughter, Marie, for some time. Inside the house was yet another suicide note to his wife, Greeba, aged forty. This read: 'You tell me I can't even make love right. My life is over. I hope the fish and crabs eat my body . . . I'm going to drown myself. I do not want to live anymore.' Police also found a note written by Greeba to her husband some time previously, which read: 'Bob, I love you. Goodbye . . . '

It looked as if the wife had left her husband, and he had then decided to kill himself. But Healey's sister had information for the police which made them reluctant to accept the situation at face value. What had begun as a routine suicide case was now being investigated by Detective Chief Superintendent Clive Atkinson as a possible double murder. Blood had been found in the house . . . Where were the missing wife and stepdaughter? Why hadn't Healey's body been washed ashore? What had happened to Mrs Healey's car? These were the questions which nagged at the senior detective. Every instinct born of his long experience warned him that something was badly wrong with the scene as it had initially presented itself.

Forensic scientists were called in to examine the house. Attempts had been made to wash a bedroom wall, but close inspection revealed the presence of particles of human blood. The bed in the stepdaughter's room had been made up with fresh sheets and blankets, but examination of the mattress revealed traces of sperm. Sexual activity had taken place in the bed of a twelve-year-old child . . .

That alone was enough to set alarm bells ringing in Superintendent Atkinson's head. He initiated in-depth inquiries.

Healey had sold his driving instructor's car to a family relative for cash just before the family vanished, and he had emptied his bank account of some four hundred pounds. Were these actions consistent with a man determined to end his life? There was more. Healey had first obtained a birth certificate in the name of his brother-in-law, then used it to apply for a passport in that name. This was the method adopted by the British former Postmaster General John Stonehouse when he faked his death by drowning off a Florida beach in the seventies, reputedly inspired by details given in the best-selling novel *The Day of the Jackal*. It is said that life imitates art, and certainly this case has some disturbing echoes of fiction.

When Superintendent Atkinson saw the video cassettes of *Reginald Perrin*, he was certain that Healey had copied the plot. Relatives of the missing man confirmed that he was a keen fan of the series. It was all too coincidental. On 5 August, less than a week after the finding of the clothing on the beach, Superintendent Atkinson told a press conference: 'There is a strong possibility that this man's wife and stepdaughter are dead. The case is now virtually a homicide investigation.' It was at this point that the national press dubbed the case the 'Reggie Perrin Mystery'. It was not to remain a mystery for long.

There had been a nationwide hunt for Mrs Healey's car, a blue Vauxhall Chevette. Within days this was found abandoned in a Birmingham car park, its seats heavily stained with blood. The car was towed away for analysis, and scientists were able to match the blood to the bloodstains found at the Healey home.

It was almost three weeks later that a seventy-seven-year-old man out walking in woodland at a remote area in Caerwys, North Wales, spotted a pinkish object sticking up from the carpet of rotting vegetation and leaves. He poked it with his walking stick and recoiled in horror when he realized that the object was a human hand. At that spot, just eight miles from the beach where the clothing had been found, police recovered two bodies from shallow graves just twelve inches deep. They were badly decomposed, naked, and had no jewellery on them.

At the mortuary, anguished relatives identified the remains as being those of Greeba Healey and her daughter Marie. A pathologist then carried out a postmortem, which revealed that Mrs Healey had been subjected to a frenzied attack, and had died from skull fractures caused by a heavy blunt instrument. Marie had died from 'massive asphyxiation', the pressure applied to her having distorted her features. Both females had had sexual intercourse shortly before death. The hunt was now on for the 'Reggie Perrin Killer'.

There was press speculation that Healey was in France, or perhaps Spain, but he had spent those three weeks wandering around London, lost among the teeming crowds of the capital. He had rented a flat under a phoney name, and spent his time visiting churches and keeping a journal about his murders. This was a highly emotional 'Diary of Death' kept in a cheap red exercise book, in which he recounted the killings, his motives and the aftermath. One chapter, headed 'Life With G.', described the misery of his life with Greeba; others told of his fascination with Marie, and the night of the murders was recounted in stark, chilling detail. In fact, the diary was a carefully constructed 'excuse' for the killings. When he read in the newspapers about the discovery of the bodies, he knew the game was up. He went to Scotland Yard and gave himself up, handing the diary to police officers with the words: 'It's all in here.'

It wasn't, of course. Not the whole truth. Just Healey's subjective account, which omitted several important facts. The truth would emerge during his trial, which was awaited with great interest.

It was one of those odd cases which captures the public imagination, and it is not hard to see why. Someone once said that the trouble with life is that we cannot rehearse it first. It goes out 'live', with all its blunders, mistakes, pains and miseries. The ideal answer to a severe problem would be for the individual to have the chance to start afresh. In real life this rarely happens. Sometimes important witnesses who testify at trials are given new identities and jobs, but for most of us, we have only the one crack at life.

Healey's trial for double murder began at Liverpool Crown Court with the bearded Healey – he had grown a beard while on the run to disguise himself – pleading not guilty to the charges. On Monday, 23 March 1987, Mr Brian Leveson, QC, began by telling the jury that Healey had deliberately killed his wife and stepdaughter, afterwards faking his own death. It had been a sick charade, said the prosecutor, and Healey had plagiarized the plot of a television series.

The Healeys appeared to be just like any other couple, on the surface, he said, but appearances were deceptive. In fact, the marriage was unhappy, and when Healey sold his driving instructor's car, he was already planning the double murder. Healey's sister was the one person who knew that the Healeys' marriage was on the rocks, and shortly after the family mysteriously vanished, the sister went to her brother's home and found it deserted. She discovered bloodstains on the carpet in the master bedroom. She also discovered the suicide notes. She believed at that point that her brother had killed himself. 'It was a despicable deception,' Mr Leveson commented.

Earlier that same day, Healey cancelled the milk and newspaper deliveries. He withdrew all the money from his bank account. He made the application for the passport in his brother-in-law's name. He maintained the pretence that everything was all right by taking a pupil for her driving test. He even borrowed a coin from a fellow-instructor and pretended to phone home, returning the coin saying, 'I knew she wouldn't be in.'

Mr Leveson said acidly: 'He knew very well that she would not be in, because by then she was long since dead.' Turning to the evidence of the murders, Mr Leveson told of the bloodstains which had been found in the house, the semen traces which matched Healey's blood type found in the bed of young Marie. He suggested that Healey had raped his stepdaughter before brutally killing her. And he had had sex with his wife shortly before murdering her. Was all this sexual activity consistent with the defence story of a confused and unhappy man acting in panic? The bespectacled Healey sobbed in the dock at this point, shaking his head in denial and wringing his hands.

After the killings, Mr Leveson went on, Healey spent five hours cleaning up the house, washing down the walls to remove blood spatters, and changing the bedding on Marie's bed to mislead the police. He put the bodies in his wife's car and drove to North Wales, where he buried them side by side in a wood. He then left his clothing on the beach to fake his suicide, and drove to Birmingham, disposing of the blood-soaked bed clothing along the way by dumping it out of the car. He abandoned the car in Birmingham, taking a train to London, where he rented a flat in Kensal Green under a false name. And while on the run he compiled his diary, which was basically an attempt at self-justification.

(Handing that diary to the police had been a major blunder on Healey's part, because it was now a Crown exhibit, and the prosecution used it to demolish Healey's claims, where the defence might have used it to bolster his story.)

The murders were very carefully planned, Mr Leveson conceded, but not original. He asked the jury: 'Have you seen the Reggie Perrin television series?' He suggested that the Stockport Murders were a direct copy of the comedy show; that Healey had plagiarized the ideas of a script-writer and used them for the purposes of murder.

Mr Leveson showed the jury the red-covered diary. He read out passages in which Healey had recorded his obsession for Marie. 'I worshipped the ground she walked on,' Healey had written. Healey told of how he had first met Marie when she was ten years old. 'She was a girl I would have gone to any lengths to please.' But he complained that as time went by she drifted away from him. 'Gone were the days when she would leave me a note to say she loved me.' Later, Marie told him that she resented him and wanted her real father. Healey wrote sadly: 'There was no conversation from her. I became irrelevant in her life. But she was my special little girl with unique qualities. I would not kill her intentionally.'

Healey bowed his head as Mr Leveson read out passages from the chapter 'My Life With G.', which recorded the deterioration of his marriage. 'I felt like a piece of furniture to be moved around on the whim of my wife.' He wrote of how his wife had once thrown a take-away meal and a can of beer over him during a row.

> My life was reduced to giving driving lessons and paying the bills. I could feel myself screaming. I felt as if my head was about to burst open. I used to bang my head against the wall.

Mr Leveson said: 'The accused jotted down his frustrations with his wife's attitude.' To illustrate this he read out a passage:

> Gradually things went from bad to worse. I became tense, extremely unhappy and frightened. It seemed everything I did was wrong. My life became a living hell. I wanted happiness but found misery.

Turning to the night of the murders – 29 July 1986 – which was headed 'How', Healey wrote that he and his wife went to bed at midnight and made love. Then: 'She ridiculed me and said I was fantasizing about someone else. I only wanted sex and never made love to her at all.' He fell asleep and woke up about three hours later. He felt upset; his wife's words tormented him. He went downstairs for a drink and returned with a rolling pin. He wrote:

> I did not feel right and thought: what am I doing? I hit her over the head with it. I hit her several times. I am not clear

91

about what happened afterwards. I cannot say what possessed me to do it. It was unreal. It was like I was standing back watching someone else. It was like a dream. I was powerless to help. I could not believe I was doing this.

The diary recounted how Marie walked into the bedroom as he was killing her mother, and in a struggle Healey grabbed her by the throat, pinning her up against the wall. With one hand he held the daughter, with the other he continued to rain blows on the mother. The diary went on: 'When I let go of Greeba there was no life in Marie. I did not realize how easily Marie had died. I had not wanted to kill her. I just didn't want her to see what had happened to her mother.'

In a chapter headed 'After', Healey described how he buried the rolling pin and then loaded the bodies into the car. 'Nobody noticed me,' he recorded. Of his life on the run in London he wrote: 'I wandered around London and walked past Downing Street hoping I would be recognized.' He also wrote that he prayed in Westminster Abbey, and hoped someone would sense his mental anguish and approach him. 'As the days went by I found it was more and more a living hell.' He also described how, while praying in St Bride's Church in Fleet Street, two policemen walked in. 'I followed them out, but they weren't interested in me.'

Mr Leveson said that the prosecution did not accept the diary as a true and factual account of what had happened, because medical and scientific evidence conflicted with Healey's account. 'He has had a long time to compose it. He has done his best for himself to place what he did and why he did it in as favourable a light as possible.'

The diary entries were designed to give a portrait of a man possessed; a poor demented creature who hadn't known what he was doing. But Healey had known very well what he was doing, Mr Leveson thundered. According to his own diary account, it had taken him five hours to clean the house, after which came the elaborate plans to cover his tracks with the fake suicide – hardly the actions of a madman.

The central core of the case, the prosecution suggested, was that Healey had been sexually infatuated with his thirteen-year-old stepdaughter. It was the plot of *Lolita*, the man marrying the mother to get at the daughter . . . Healey sobbed heavily in the dock, shaking his head in denial once more.

One by one the witnesses appeared in the witness box to give evidence in the case. Home Office pathologist Dr Donald Wayte said that Greeba Healey had a splintered skull and had been struck over the head at least fifteen times. Marie had been asphyxiated with 'massive compression' to her neck, face and chest. Sperm samples recovered from the bodies matched Healey's blood type, both victims having had sex shortly before dying. Other experts testified about matching the blood in the car to that in the bedroom.

A close friend of the family, who had gone on holiday with the Healeys to Majorca a month before the murders, told the court that she noticed that Healey paid more attention to Marie than he did to his wife. 'More attention than I would expect . . . He seemed to stare at her for a long time and was always taking photographs of her and whispering to her.' She said that once on the beach Healey had whispered something to Marie, and she had replied: 'Why me? It's always me. Why not my mum?' The witness added: 'If Marie wanted to go back early and have a shower, the moment she got up he would be following her straight away.' She said she didn't mention her concern to Greeba Healey. 'She would have thought I was trying to put her off her husband, because she knew I never liked him.'

Healey's sister spoke of going to his house on the day he and his wife disappeared. She said: 'My brother married Greeba in November 1985. From what I saw, he and Greeba were not suited. I tried to discuss it with him but he kept saying, "I have got to try." '

On 29 July she learned that Healey had sold his car. This news alarmed her, and that night she and her husband called on Healey. They got no reply, so let themselves into the house with a spare key which her brother had entrusted to her. 'The clock had stopped at 4.45 p.m. The electricity appeared to have been switched off. I looked around the house. I could smell blood in the bedroom. I lifted up the carpet and saw diluted bloodstains. It looked as if someone had tried to clean it.' The sister was fighting back tears as she left the witness box.

Detective Superintendent Derrol Waring testified that he had asked Healey during an interview: 'I put it to you that you had intercourse with Marie in her bedroom and then killed her for some reason. Did Marie threaten to expose your activities to Greeba?' Healey had replied: 'Nothing of the sort.'

Healey's mother gave evidence, telling the jury that she had never liked Greeba. She had made her son's life hell. She had seen her son a few days before the killings, and 'he was in a shocking condition. He only ever spent five minutes with us, his parents, because she didn't like him seeing us. He told me: "I feel so awful. Things are bad and I can't take much more." '

Healey himself went into the witness box, weeping and trembling. Speaking about the night he killed his wife and stepdaughter, he said softly: 'It was like a film. It was like watching myself on television. It was not me there . . . I didn't plan it. I did not know what was going to happen.' He said that after making love to his wife that night – and suffering her taunts about his performance – he fell asleep, waking three hours later with an upset stomach.

'I felt upset. I felt like screaming. I felt frustrated. I felt sick and upset by her words to me. I went downstairs to the kitchen for a drink of Andrews. In the kitchen I stared at things, objects. I took up a heavy lager bottle at first.

94

There was a rolling pin. I picked it up. I didn't know what I was doing ... I was telling myself: "For God's sake stop it! Stop it!" I went upstairs to our bedroom. I walked around the bed. I hit her on the head with the rolling pin. She jumped up. She didn't say anything. She didn't scream, she just moaned. I didn't hear anything after that. I hit her again – I don't know how many times. We were just struggling. Eventually she was down on the floor. I don't remember exactly what happened.'

Trembling violently, he went on, the hushed courtroom listening intently. 'Then Marie walked into the bedroom. I told her to get out. I lashed out and my hand caught her face. She went out and came straight back in again. I made a grab for her. I didn't want her to see her mother on the floor. I don't know how long it was before I realized they were both dead. I wanted to kill myself because of what had happened.'

He said he had written the diary to put the story of his life with Greeba and Marie in perspective, adding: 'I gave myself up to the police because I could not stand the guilt of what I had done.' Healey said there had been week-long rows in his marriage. He had tried to patch up the relationship by sending his wife 'endless bouquets' of flowers. He told the jury: 'Greeba had a funny way about her which I could not understand. But I did not want to lose her because I loved her.'

Defence counsel Mr John Hughill, QC, asked him why he had twice returned to Greeba after leaving her, following rows.

Healey said: 'I went back because I wanted to be with her, despite how it was at times.'

Defence counsel pressed him: 'Did you ever have sexual intercourse with your stepdaughter, Marie Walker?'

Healey replied firmly: 'No, sir.'

In cross-examination Mr Leveson said to Healey: 'I put it to you that on the night of the murders there was none of the sobbing and wringing of hands you have shown to the jury.'

Healey insisted: 'There was!' He agreed that his actions after the murders – the fake suicide notes and the disposal of the bodies – had been those of a rational man. When Mr Leveson suggested that he had copied the Reggie Perrin show, Healey denied this, although agreeing that he was a keen fan of the show and had video cassettes of the programme.

In his closing speech for the prosecution, Mr Leveson told the jury: 'There is no evidence in this case that the defendant is not responsible for his actions. I tell you bluntly that Healey killed his wife without any provocation whatsoever, and that he killed Marie after having intercourse with her. The proper verdicts in this case are guilty of deliberate and wilful murder on both counts in the indictment.'

For the defence, Mr Hughill made an impassioned plea for his client, describing the misery of his marriage. He went on: 'You have seen a tortured soul before you. He is sane and ordinary, but I don't expect you to like him. You cannot envisage the pressure that man has been through. He seems to have been dominated by his relationships with members of the opposite sex. All the evidence indicates that these offences were the work of someone whose mind had snapped under the strain.'

He ended: 'There is no doubt that he did kill these two women, there is no doubt that he will be rightly punished for what he has done. But it would be terrible if he were to be punished for what he has not done. If you have any doubt about his state of mind at the time of the killings, then you must convict him of manslaughter.'

Summing up at the end of the six-day trial, Mr Justice McNeill said: 'There was the forensic evidence of sexual activity in Marie's bedroom, and the prosecution claim that the relationship between the accused and Marie is the key to this case. On the other hand, you have heard Healey's denial of any sexual involvement . . . you have listened to his own account, both written down and in the witness box. How much influence did the television series about Reggie Perrin have on his mind? These are matters for you, members of the jury . . . '

After retiring for three hours, the jury returned with unanimous verdicts of guilty on both counts of murder. Healey stood weeping in the dock, his head bowed as the judge told him: 'You know there is only one sentence for these crimes. You will go to prison for life.' After the case, Superintendent Waring revealed that Healey already had convictions for sex offences.

To students of murder, Healey's bald and graphic account of the killings – 'I went upstairs. I hit her on the head – It was not me there. It was like watching someone else . . . ' and his emphasis on his altered state of consciousness is familiar territory, and is typical of the out-of-the-body feelings of the killer, almost like a description of alien possession. Psychiatrists call it 'disassociation'. The individual cannot face up to what he has done and goes through a process of denial. He lies to himself.

But whether mad or bad, Healey was a very dangerous man, the 'dreamer of the day'. Two innocent people paid with their lives for his dream.

7
THE PUZZLE OF CONSTANCE KENT
1860

According to the strict criteria of motives established by F. Tennyson Jesse, the case of Constance Kent does not belong to that sub-category of murder known as the *crime passionnel* because it contains no sexual element. But the definition is too limiting. If ever there was a crime of the heart, it was that committed by Constance Kent – if indeed she was guilty.

Despite her conviction, despite her own confessions of guilt, there are plenty of reasons for concluding that she was innocent of the crime for which she was sentenced to death, and that the real culprit escaped justice.

In 1860 Constance Kent, then aged sixteen, was living with her father and stepmother in a large house, Road Hill House, in the village of Road, on the Wiltshire-Somerset border. The ninth of ten children born to Mary Ann and Samuel Kent, Constance was a disturbed child – and not without reason. She had seen her mother die and her father marry their former governess, with whom he had almost certainly been sleeping while his wife was still alive. He had fathered two more children and had made her pregnant with a third, and Constance and the other inconvenient reminders of the first marriage were relegated to the servants' quarters.

A knowledge of the social background to the times is crucial to any understanding of the case. Women of the middle class were brought up to observe a 'code of manners' which was harsh and stifling. Regarded as intellectually inferior to men but morally superior, they were educated for marriage, bred to become breeders in turn. Those women who remained spinsters could not hope to find paid employment; they became unpaid drudges in their parents' household. Even if married, they were not expected to enjoy sexual intercourse. An influential physician of the time, William Acton, wrote in all seriousness that women who made an effort to enjoy sexual intercourse risked cancer of the womb. Life for the middle-class girl in those days was incredibly dull and stifling, and such a suffocating existence might have been designed for outbreaks of wild and irrational violence. It would have been a fury at fate itself . . .

Although Constance, a plain and deeply religious girl, was the central character in the drama, a far more significant figure was her father. The son of a London carpet manufacturer – although reputed to be the illegitimate son of the Duke of Kent, father of Queen Victoria – in 1829 Samuel Savile Kent married Mary Ann Windus, aged twenty-one, some seven years his junior. Mary's father was a well-respected merchant in London, and also a Fellow of the Royal Society of Antiquaries.

By 1833 the couple had three children, of which the only boy died in infancy. Samuel Kent held a partnership in a drysalter's firm in London, but was forced to give up his position because of a respiratory ailment. However, his father-in-law used his influence to get Kent appointed to the position of sub-inspector of factories for the West of England, a post created by the passing of the new Factory Act. The post required Kent to travel a great deal through Devon, Somerset, Wiltshire and Dorset, a duty which was to keep him busy for the next thirty years.

Mrs Kent had to remain at home, occupying a series of large but understaffed rented dwellings and trying to cope with her brood of children. Like most Victorian husbands, Mr Kent kept her permanently pregnant. And, like most Victorians, Mr Kent insisted on an outward show of affluence which he could ill afford. The family had to have the best in clothes and horses, even though Mr Kent's salary could not stretch to it. The cost of velvet curtains was bread and butter for dinner. Mr Kent earned eight hundred pounds a year, and he had a private income of two or three hundred more, but it was inadequate for his needs. Even the servants gossiped about the meanness of the household budget.

From 1835, until Constance's birth in February 1844, Mrs Kent had five more babies, of whom only one survived, a son named Edward. Worn out by her continual confinements, a nursemaid who termed herself a 'governess' was hired to care for the new infant, Constance. The governess, twenty-one-year-old Mary Pratt, was the daughter of the local greengrocer. She was destined to become the second Mrs Kent.

The following year, 1845, Mrs Kent gave birth to her tenth and last child, William. At this point Mr Kent decided to move into a separate bedroom in another part of the house, leaving his wife alone in the seclusion of her room. Perhaps it was Mr Kent's form of birth-control, or perhaps he had tired of a woman he had literally worn out by over-breeding. Certainly Mrs Kent was now very frail.

With the mother effectively out of the way, Mary Pratt grasped the reins of the household, taking charge of the two eldest daughters, Mary Ann, aged fifteen, and twelve-year-old Elizabeth. When the three eldest children were eventually sent away to boarding schools, it was quickly rumoured that Mary Pratt was mistress of the Kent household in every sense of that term. Mr Kent was believed to be sleeping with his young governess . . .

In the sixteen years of existence following her birth, Constance was brought up not in a household of maternal love, but in a situation of constant domestic tensions. Servants kept leaving because of the poor pay. The real mother was a shadowy figure in a dark and curtained room. The new mistress was no older than her sisters. And Mr Kent was going through a bad patch. He had hoped for promotion to the Board of Factory Commissioners, but instead found himself hauled up before them to explain the rumours about his wife's seclusion and her replacement by a young mistress. He was sternly reminded that factory inspectors needed to display public probity, and the presence at functions of an accomplished wife was a positive asset. His daughters, too, needed the companionship of girls of their own class.

Kent wrung his hands, explaining that his wife was an invalid who depended on his daughters for care. He hinted that his wife was insane, and she had been secluded for her own protection. When the issue was raised again, much later, Kent produced his family doctor to assert that Mrs Kent had been insane from as early as 1836. This was patently untrue, since during the period she was allegedly insane her husband had bred five children by her, and the evidence was that Mrs Kent did not go into seclusion until after the birth of her last child in 1845.

Whatever the reasons for the falsehoods Kent told the Commissioners – probably to cover up an illicit affair with the governess and to protect his job – Constance and William grew up knowing their mother only as an invalid, and the governess as the person who dictated their lives. There is some evidence that Mrs Kent was aware that the governess had supplanted her in her husband's affections, but there was little she could do. She could not face the scandal of an open break, or return to her family, since she had married Kent against her parents' wishes. She became resigned to the situation.

Constance and her younger brother William were very close, and they were favourites of their mother. Evidence of the mother's love came in 1851, when Constance was seven, and her adored elder brother Edward returned home briefly from his naval training school. The mother gave Edward her family Bible, making him promise to keep it always. She also made arrangements to place one

101

thousand pounds of her inheritance in trust for Constance, perceiving that her daughter was destined for spinsterhood and determined to give her a good start in life. She was well aware that her husband would make no effort to spend time or money on finding Constance a suitor.

This must have enraged the husband, struggling to keep up a lifestyle which he could not afford. Perhaps in revenge for his wife's secret financial arrangement, he removed Edward from his naval training school and placed him in a cheaper boarding school, to the boy's bitter disappointment.

A year after making that secret legacy to Constance, Mrs Kent died in great agony of an ailment diagnosed by the family doctor as 'an obstruction of the bowels'. Strangely, her health had been generally good prior to her untimely end.

In August 1853, after the year of traditional mourning was over, Samuel Kent married Mary Pratt, with Constance, aged nine, as a bridesmaid. The eldest boy resented the governess taking the place of his mother and went to sea. He died abroad, leaving only the three girls and William from the first family.

Mr Kent lost no time in breeding from his new wife, and the children of the first marriage, especially Constance and William, became neglected, their education ignored. A mark of their fall from favour was that they had beds in the servants' quarters. The new Mrs Kent ruled the children with 'a severe hand', according to one servant, boxing their ears or confining them to their rooms as punishment.

It was later alleged that Constance was an unruly child, with an obstinate and impassioned nature, yet at school she was awarded second prize for good work and behaviour.

Such was the background to the events of 30 June 1860. On the fatal night of 29 June, the occupants of Road Hill House slept soundly. In one bedroom were Mr

102

and Mrs Kent, the wife being again pregnant. Their three children: Amelia, five, Francis Savile, three and a half years, and infant daughter Eveline, were elsewhere in the house. Young Savile slept in the second-floor nursery with his baby sister and a nursemaid. The four children from the first marriage were asleep in their rooms on the third floor.

At about five o'clock on the morning of 30 June, nurse-maid Elizabeth Gough awoke, and pulled the bedclothes more securely around the twelve-month-old girl sleeping beside her. She noticed that Savile was missing from his cot, but assumed that the boy's mother had taken him into her own bed. She went back to sleep, wakening at 6.15 a.m. She got up, made the bed and read a chapter from the Bible. It was not until an hour later that she knocked on the door of her mistress's bedroom to enquire if she had Master Savile with her.

When she heard that Savile was missing from his cot, Mrs Kent came running from her bed in a panic. She said she had not seen the boy since he had been put to bed at eight o'clock the previous evening. Soon the news that the child had vanished had gone through the house-hold. Constance came out of her tiny room on the third floor rubbing her eyes and asking what all the fuss was about. Both she and her two sisters said they had not seen the child or heard any disturbance in the night.

The housemaid hurried downstairs and reported back in some agitation that the door was ajar and a window was open. There had been a spate of cut-throat murders in the area, and Mr Kent dressed hurriedly, swearing that his child had been kidnapped by gypsies. He set out by trap to the nearest police station, at Trowbridge.

While he was away, two nearby cottagers, men by the name of Benger and Nutt, who had been alerted to the news of the disappearance, began searching the grounds of the house, no doubt hoping for a reward. Shortly before Mr Kent returned, they found the body of

Francis Savile in a disused closet in shrubbery across from the stable yard.

The body had been wrapped in a blanket taken from his cot, and his throat had been cut with such force that his head was almost severed from his trunk. There was also a deep stab wound over the heart, which had been inflicted after death, since it had not bled. An attempt had been made to stuff the tiny body down the closet.

The absence of blood at the scene suggested that the child had been killed elsewhere and his body carried to the privy to be concealed. The sight of the mutilated corpse filled everyone with horror. It was a wicked crime, the injuries inflicted in a gratuitous and almost casual manner. According to many reports, the crime was only eclipsed in casualness by the clumsy efforts of the local police. I must confess that I find it difficult to criticize them. Faced with an apparently motiveless crime, they did their duty as best they could.

The two men who had found the body, Benger and Nutt, carried the corpse into the house, to a distraught Mrs Kent. Soon afterwards Mr Kent arrived home, followed shortly by Superintendent Foley and a couple of his men. Although noting that the mould on the sill of the open window had not been disturbed and that the window showed no signs of having been forced, Foley accepted initially that the crime had been committed by an outsider. It was impossible to believe that someone from such a respectable household could have been the culprit, and Mr Kent himself had suggested the possibility that gypsies were responsible. Mr Kent did much to divert police suspicion from his house, and in retrospect it is difficult to see why gypsies should have kidnapped a child simply to murder it.

On that Saturday police officers searched the kitchen at Road Hill House and found stuffed in a furnace a chemise covered with blood. It could well have been menstrual blood from Constance or her sisters, but the superintendent decided to station two constables in the kitchen all night to see if anyone in the household got up to try and destroy the incriminating garment. No one did, and Foley dismissed the chemise as a red herring. He failed even to mention it in his report to Scotland Yard – an omission for which he was later to be bitterly criticized.

However, by the Monday local suspicion centred on a member of the Kent family as the murderer, proof that the Kents were unpopular in the area. It was thought suspicious that the nursemaid had waited so long before informing her mistress that the child was missing.

The inquest was held on the Monday, with people already muttering about the improper relationship which had existed between Kent and his governess while his wife was still alive – although the relevance of this to the murder was not stated. Local feeling was running very high against the stepchildren too.

A curious incident in Constance's early life was recalled. In 1856, when she was twelve, she and her brother William ran away from home during the summer holidays, with the avowed intention of boarding a ship at Bristol to sail away to find their brother Edward, who was then in the West Indies. However, they only got as far as Bath before police picked them up as suspected runaways.

The strange feature was that Constance had disguised herself as a boy, cropping her hair short and wearing her brother's clothing. The local press carried a report about the escapade in which police were quoted as saying that Constance had been 'a little hero', never breaking under questioning which had reduced her brother to tears. She had remained calm and stoical. Once again Mr Kent had to explain his daughter's behaviour to the Board of Factory Commissioners, and he complained that she was an 'intractable child, lacking in feminine delicacy and having an impassioned nature'. Both children were severely punished, Constance being locked in the cellar for two days.

Now this incident was brought up again, with hints that Constance was 'unnatural' and sexually peculiar in dressing as a male. Yet, of course, dressing as a male had been an eminently sensible way of escaping detection.

Local people were filled with such a mob-lust that the coroner refused to allow the children to be questioned in the Temperance Hall, where inquests were usually held, and instead had the inquiry adjourned to Road Hill House. There Constance and William were questioned, as were the housemaid who had discovered the open window and the nursemaid who discovered that the child was missing. The two men who found the body also testified.

The inquiry came to a dead end. There appeared to be no motive for the crime, the mother was obviously heartbroken, and Mr Kent had no reason to dispose of one child from so many, and no one else in the household had a motive. Nor did burglary seem a likely prospect. In the end the jury returned a verdict of 'Wilful Murder against a person or persons unknown'.

This did not satisfy either the mob or the press. The coroner, Mr Sylvester, had declined to question Mrs Kent, not wishing to add to her anguish, but *The Times* for Wednesday, 11 July, was highly critical of his compassion and demanded a full-scale investigation into the murder. ' ... The inference is plain that the secret lies within someone who was within the household,' it stated, and argued that the entire household should be held 'collectively responsible for this murderous and dreadful event' and confined in the house until the matter had been cleared up. Mr Kent also came in for some criticism from the paper:

We should like to know why the father went to Trowbridge immediately the child was missed; why he thought it had been stolen and how he accounted to himself for the *modus operandi* of the thief; why he didn't first search the premises, raise the neighbourhood and call in all conceivable help.

Public suspicion had now focused on the father. Pressure was mounting for action, *any* action. On Tuesday, 10 July, Superintendent Foley arrested the nursemaid, Elizabeth Gough, on suspicion. A chest flannel which proved to fit the nurse had been found down the lavatory with the child's body. On Monday, 16 July she was brought before the magistrates. At first Mrs Kent said she had never been in the habit of taking the child from its cot at night, and it was unlikely that the nurse might have thought she had done so, since she was eight months pregnant and the child was quite heavy. Later, she changed her testimony, saying that the nursemaid might reasonably have assumed that she had taken the child after all. The magistrates found no case to answer and discharged Elizabeth Gough. But while in custody she had mentioned to a policeman's wife that one of Miss Constance's nightdresses was missing, and if found might lead to the murderer . . .

The public were furious that an innocent servant had been put through such an ordeal, but it wasn't over yet for Elizabeth Gough.

In mid-July the local police admitted their bafflement and turned to Scotland Yard for help. The famous Chief Inspector Jonathan Whicher was sent to lead the investigation. (Wilkie Collins, in his novel *The Moonstone*, based his fictional Sergeant Cuff on Whicher.) This case was destined to become Whicher's downfall.

He arrived on the scene two weeks after the murder, studied the evidence and talked to witnesses. Superintendent Foley had been assisted by a Dr Parsons in his inquiries, and the doctor mentioned something he thought was odd. The nightdress Constance Kent was wearing at the time was clean, with starch still on the collar, but she had supposedly been sleeping in it for almost a week.

Almost immediately, Whicher fixed his suspicions on Constance, mainly because of the escapade when she had run away from home. To him, this indicated mental instability. He examined the household laundry list and saw that Constance was supposed to have three night-dresses, but could only produce two. When asked to account for the missing garment, she said it had been lost in the laundry. While laundries are notorious for losing garments, this clinched the case for Whicher.

On Friday, 20 July, he took Constance in custody to a magistrates' court behind closed doors in the Temperance Hall, hoping no doubt that the grim experience would frighten her into a confession. But when the warrant was read out to her, she cried out passionately: 'I am innocent! I am innocent!' The magistrates remanded Constance in custody to Devizes Gaol for one week.

While local people nodded their heads wisely and agreed that Whicher had once again solved a difficult case, the local press took a very different line, furiously accusing Whicher of using Constance as a scapegoat and arguing: 'Any other inmate of the house having commit-ted the murder could easily have taken the garment from the wash bundle for the purpose of throwing suspicion by pointing it at Miss Constance.' It added that all who knew her were certain of her innocence.

When Constance appeared again before the magistrates for the formal hearing of the case against her, Whicher had gathered no new evidence, apart from enlisting as witnesses two schoolfriends of Constance's who testified that she was unhappy at home and had expressed 'a dislike through jealousy of the deceased'. It was also noted that the new stepmother often taunted Constance that she was as insane as her mother had been . . .

But other witnesses described how Constance had been seen 'romping' with Savile on the afternoon before his death, and painting a little picture for him. Elizabeth Gough was re-examined, and stated: 'I have never heard Miss Constance say anything unkind towards the little boy that is dead.' Constance sat demurely listening to the evidence, dressed in black, her gloved hands folded in her lap.

The lawyer hired for Constance had no difficulty in getting the magistrates to throw the case out, the evidence being so flimsy. In a passionate speech he argued that although Constance had told schoolfriends that the younger children were preferred to her, 'where is the step-mother who will not prefer her own children to those of a former wife?' He went on: 'Is it likely that the weak hand of this young girl . . . can have inflicted this dreadful blow? Is it likely that hers was the arm which nearly severed the head from the body? It is perfectly incredible.'

He complained that 'this young lady had been dragged from her home like a common felon,' and her reputation had suffered a 'judicial murder' which had ruined her life. 'Her prospects are clearly blighted . . . '

Constance was released from custody, and her sisters clasped her in affection. On Saturday Elizabeth Gough was once again arrested, only to be released shortly afterwards. Constance was quickly placed in a convent in France to escape the publicity and embarrassment. The mob now turned its fury on the hapless Inspector Whicher, accusing him of having acted in an unwarranted manner in ever arresting the innocent young lady.

Whicher's conduct was even commented on in the House of Commons. One member stated that the inspector had acted in a most objectionable manner; after all his boasting of the evidence he could produce, the young lady had been discharged by the magistrates and they believed that there was not the slightest doubt that she was innocent of the charge.

Whicher never recovered from this setback to his career, and when the Criminal Investigation Department was created at Scotland Yard in 1878, it was not Whicher who was chosen to head it, but one of his protégés, Superintendent Adolphus Williamson.

Fickle public opinion, deprived of one victim, now fastened its attack on Mr Kent. The common theory put forward was that Kent had been having sexual relations with the twenty-three-year-old nursemaid; young Savile had awoken and seen what was going on, and Kent had murdered his own child to shut his mouth and preserve his good name, Elizabeth Gough being an accessory to the crime.

A letter to *The Times* put the case as follows:

> Suppose that something was taking place beneath the roof that night, supposing the child awakening from sleep 'saw a man where a man should na' be,' would that not supply a motive for the crime? To my mind, two things which occurred next morning are fraught with suspicion – the ostentatious reading of the Bible for an hour by the nurse, who knew the child was missing, and who ought immediately to have made enquiry in Mrs Kent's room, and the decision which was at once arrived at that the child had been murdered. If the police would follow out these two points, they would perhaps be more successful than in their 'fussy activity' about the night-dress of a schoolgirl.

On Saturday, 11 August suspicion was diverted from Elizabeth Gough when a working-man gave himself up to the police and made a statement confessing his part in the murder. He claimed that Mr Kent had handed the child out to him from the open window and promised him a sum of money to murder the child, but as Mr Kent had not paid, and the curse of God was upon him, he had decided to confess. He was found to be insane, having no connection with the crime, but it served to inflame feelings against Mr Kent still further.

Yet, for all the fuss and various suspects, the murderer must have been a member of the Kent household – a fact which the public did not forget. Ruined, and with their reputation in tatters, the Kent family had to leave Road Hill House and settled in Wrexham in North Wales.

The years passed and the case faded from the public consciousness. Constance grew to womanhood in her convent. Three years later she was permitted to return to England, and in 1863 enrolled in a High Church establishment in Brighton, St Mary's Home, which was affiliated to a hospital. Under the name of 'Emilie Kent', Constance spent the next eighteen months training as a children's nurse.

But something quite dramatic happened at St Mary's. It has been described as a 'religious conversion', but may well have been a psychological passion to become a martyr: a kind of religious mania. She was under the supervision of the Revd A. D. Wagner, Perpetual Curate of St Paul's Church, and he appeared to have a strong influence over her. In the hot-house atmosphere of the religious establishment, with Revd Wagner urging her to save her soul, Constance decided that the only way she could be accepted fully by her new friends was as a poor sinner seeking salvation. She decided she had to publicly confess that she had indeed murdered young Savile five years previously, and in Holy Week, 1865 – shortly after her twenty-first birthday – she informed Revd Wagner of her decision.

The advice he gave her was that she was right to do so in order to gain eternal salvation. Consequently, on 25 April Constance went to Bow Street Magistrates, accompanied by Revd Wagner and the Mother Superior, to see the Chief Magistrate, Sir Thomas Henry, by appointment. Superintedent Durkin and Chief Inspector Williamson of the Detective Force were also present. The meeting was held in Sir Thomas's private room.

Sir Thomas was reluctant to accept Constance's confession, fearing that she had come under Roman Catholic influence. He was at pains to ensure that she had freely given herself up and was aware of the fate that awaited her. 'I hope you understand that whatever you say must be entirely your own free and voluntary statement and that no inducement that may have been held out to you is to have any effect upon your mind?'

Constance: 'No inducement ever has, sir.'

Sir Thomas: 'I am most anxious that you should consider that.'

He questioned Revd Wagner closely, trying to ascertain

if there had been some sinister Catholic conspiracy at work. Finally – even reluctantly – he had to commit Constance to appear before Wiltshire magistrates. The two police officers took her in a cab to the railway station and accompanied her on the journey. She was now formally under arrest.

She was tried at the following Wiltshire Assizes before Mr Justice Willes. Dressed in black, her face veiled, she stood in the dock as the Clerk of Assize read out the charge against her. 'Constance Emilie Kent, you stand charged with having wilfully murdered Francis Savile Kent at Road Hill House on the 30th of June 1860. How say you – are you guilty or not guilty?'

In a low voice she replied: 'Guilty.'

The judge asked her: 'Are you aware that you are charged with having wilfully, intentionally and with malice killed your brother? . . . And you plead guilty to that?' The prisoner hesitated. The silence stretched out until the judge was forced to ask again: 'What is your answer?' Again there was silence from the dock, a silence stretched almost to screaming-point. The judge repeated the full charge over again, and this time Constance said 'Guilty.'

There could be no trial. Constance had pleaded guilty and it only remained for the judge to pass the only possible sentence: that of death. Her counsel, Mr Coleridge, QC, addressed the judge, saying: 'My Lord, acting on the prisoner's behalf I desire to say two things – first . . . the guilt is hers alone . . . and secondly, she was not driven to this act, as has been asserted, by unkind treatment at home, as she met with nothing there but tender and forbearing love . . . '

The judge donned the black cap and sentenced Constance to hang, saying, in part: 'You appear to have allowed your feelings of jealousy and anger to have worked in your breast until at last they assumed over you the influence and power of the Evil One.' At this point the judge

112

burst into tears for several minutes, a scene which caused Constance herself to sob heavily.

The sentence of death was eventually commuted to one of life imprisonment. A doctor had been asked by the Government to examine the prisoner to test for insanity. Dr Bucknill published his report in the press, in due course, expressing the opinion that she was both sane and truthful. He gave details of her confession to him, which read: '... a few days before the murder she obtained possession of a razor from a green case in her father's wardrobe ... She took the child from his bed and carried him downstairs ... She says she thought the blood would never come ... so she thrust the razor into his left side ... She secreted her nightdress, eventually burnt it in her own bedroom, and put the ashes in the kitchen grate ... As regards the motive, although she entertained a great regard for the present Mrs Kent, yet if any remark was at any time made which in her opinion was disparaging to any members of the first family, she treasured it up and determined to revenge it. She had no ill-will against the little boy, except as one of the children of her stepmother ... '

She had written a letter to her solicitor before her trial which was now made public. It read:

Devizes. May 15th.

Sir, It has been stated that my feelings of revenge were excited in consequence of cruel treatment. That is entirely false. I have received the greatest kindness from both the persons accused of subjecting me to it. I have never had any ill-will towards either of them on account of their behaviour to me, which has been very kind. I shall feel obliged if you will make use of this statement in order that the public may be undeceived on this point.

I remain, sir, Yours truly,
Constance Kent

Constance Kent served twenty years of her life sentence, in both Portland Prison – where she occupied her time

113

making religious mosaics – and Millbank. A prison inspector who saw her during this time described her as 'a small, mouse-like creature ... She was a mystery in every way. It was almost impossible to believe that this insignificant, inoffensive little person could have cut her infant brother's throat under circumstances of peculiar atrocity.'

Constance was released in 1885, aged forty-one. It is believed that she emigrated to Australia, where she became matron of a nursing home, dying in 1944 aged one hundred. Her father had died in 1872 of a liver disease.

And there we have it. A straightforward account of a complex case with the means, method and opportunity available to Constance, and the motive established as revenge. The murderer had escaped detection for five years before her conscience betrayed her and she made a belated confession. The good Inspector Whicher is vindicated, and justice was done. Or was it? Let us look again, this time more carefully, at the evidence in the case, noting two inconsistencies which seem to point to Constance's *innocence*.

THE INNOCENCE OF CONSTANCE KENT

The quest to establish the innocence of Constance Kent is by no means new. Even at the time and despite her confession, some journalists believed in her innocence, viewing her as more a victim than a self-confessed killer, and even the public exhibited some sympathy towards her.

The fact that Constance was alleged to have admitted her guilt in the confessional to the Revd A. D. Wagner was viewed with suspicion by the *Brighton Gazette*, which asked in a leader: 'Is the Confessional of the Anglican Church sealed against the law of the land?' The *Pall Mall Gazette* for 26 April said: 'Now instances of false confession have certainly occurred, and it must be said with some plausibility that such an occurrence was particularly likely to take place in the case of an enthusiastic young woman of strong devotional temperament, who might work herself up into the notion that it was good work to denote herself for the sake of her family and who, by the mere fascination of the event, might even have had her imagination so deeply affected that she might bring herself to think she had really done it.'

Other newspapers followed the same line. The *Standard* for 26 April wrote: 'We simply attach no judicial importance to her confession drawn up at St Mary's Home . . .' The *Express* for 13 May complained: 'What life was possible for Miss Kent after Revd Wagner had begun to tell the inmates of the house that one of their number was a murderer?' Even the *News of the World* voiced the suspicion that the confession had been brought about by the sinister influences of Revd Wagner and the Mother Superior.

After Constance's confession had been made public, stunning the nation, her local newspaper, the *Trowbridge and Wilts Advertiser*, insisted on Constance's innocence and expressed its suspicion of the alleged confession. The fact was, and remains, that the only evidence against Constance was her own confession, and she was convicted on that basis. It could not have happened in Scotland, because under Scottish law no person can be convicted on their confession alone: there has to be corroborating evidence. But under English law people can still be convicted on the sole basis of their confession alone.

At the time of writing, twenty-year-old Bruce Lee from Hull, who has a low IQ, holds the record of being Britain's most prolific killer, having confessed in 1980 to the murder by arson of twenty-six people. In January 1981 he was sent to a mental hospital by Leeds Crown Court without limit of time – the equivalent of a life sentence. It was a short hearing because Lee pleaded guilty. On 14 March 1982 he retracted his confession, and a Home Office inquiry cleared him of at least half the murders – they were in fact accidental deaths due to a fire in an old people's home where repairs were being carried out, probably started by a workman's blow-torch. Yet Lee remains incarcerated . . . Emotionally and mentally unstable people *do* make false confessions, as police forces throughout the world are only too well aware. With that in mind, from our vantage point in time we ought properly to view Constance's confession with caution, even suspicion.

Many books have been written about the case of Constance Kent. In his *Cruelly Murdered*, Bernard Taylor asserts that Constance was the real murderer, having stabbed Savile in the side with a knife. The father, who had been sleeping with the nurse, found the body soon afterwards and cut the throat to mislead the police into thinking that the murder was one of a series committed in the area with a cut-throat razor. His intention, therefore, was to protect his daughter Constance.

Yseult Bridges, in his *Saint With Red Hands*, argues that the real murderer was Mr Kent, who was having sex with nursemaid Gough when the three-year-old Savile woke and saw what was going on. He put his hand over his son's mouth to prevent him from waking Mrs Kent, but accidentally suffocated the child, then had to fake a murder to save his own skin, the nursemaid being an accomplice to the deed. Constance then confessed to protect her father – although why she should have felt this to be necessary *five years after the event* makes little sense.

Both views seem untenable. Constance claimed she had stabbed the child in the side with a cut-throat razor – which would have been virtually impossible. And had she really cut the throat she would never have wondered 'whether the blood would ever come'. She would have been drenched in it. Her confession reads like something imagined by a person *who was not there*. But would a father, wishing to fake the murder of his favourite child,

116

almost sever the head from the body? It seems an act motivated only by an insane hatred. But where is the evidence for Constance's hatred or desire for revenge?

Let us review the facts. The children of the first family were made to sleep on the third floor with the servants, yet at the time of the murder there were three empty rooms on the second floor, where Constance's father and stepmother and their three children slept. And Constance was often punished by being locked in a room for days on end and deprived of food – but even this was not especially cruel in a period when it was considered quite proper for parents to birch their children. At the time of her confession Constance was at pains to point out that she had not been motivated by revenge and had been well-treated by her parents.

It has been suggested that Constance may have committed the murder as a desperate act against her fate; unmarried daughters of the period ended up as drudges or governesses in other people's households, like the Brontë sisters. But how could a murder so foul have helped Constance?

If not Constance – then who? Journalists at the time considered that there were at least two other persons in the house who could have committed the deed. Without daring to name him, the *Bath Chronicle* suggested Mr Kent as the prime suspect – a man who while sleeping with the nursemaid had to kill his son to still his tongue. The medical evidence supported the suffocation theory: there was bruising and blackening around the mouth and it is likely that the child was dead before the mutilations with the knife – hence the lack of bleeding. Dead bodies don't bleed. He could even have used the nurse's chest flannel – or brassière – to suffocate the child, that same cloth which was found stuffed down the closet with his son's body.

Additional support for this theory is that young Savile was known to be a tell-tale, always running to his mother with stories. To avert disgrace, a possible divorce and the

117

certain loss of his position as a factory inspector, Mr Kent may well have sacrificed his young son. And Constance too . . .

Let us examine Mr Kent's extraordinary behaviour after the murder. Why rush out of the house to go for the police some three miles away? He could have sent servants for the police, and in any case there were policemen living closer than Trowbridge. Wouldn't it have been more natural to search the house first in case the child had wandered? Why immediately assume murder?

When Kent left the house in a hurry, all that was known was the cot was made up, the coverlet neatly pulled up to the pillow, and the child was missing. But on his way to Trowbridge Mr Kent told a turnpike-keeper: 'I have had a child stolen and carried away in a blanket.' Yet the fact that a blanket was missing from the cot was not discovered by Elizabeth Gough until *after* Kent's departure. It was an extremely incriminating remark, which went unnoticed by Inspector Whicher, who had immediately fastened on Constance as the culprit and ignored any conflicting evidence.

Just as incriminating was Kent's behaviour with the police. He kept them out of his house until noon on 30 June 1860, telling them: 'The murderer will not be found here.' The local police were naturally a little servile towards a gentleman like Mr Kent. He told police officers that the killers could have been nearby cottagers whom he had prevented from fishing in his stream, former nursemaids, or even gypsies. True, he had upset locals by prosecuting local children for theft and by enclosing common land, but there was not a shred of evidence to support any of his suppositions.

When the 'bloody night-shift' was found in the kitchen stove – a garment made of a coarse material likely to have been worn by a servant – Kent was told of the find by the police, who never considered him a suspect and treated him as a collaborator. Kent came up with the suggestion that they should trap the killer by hiding in his kitchen all night, in order to catch the culprit when she came down to remove the incriminating garment. The police duly returned secretly that night and were locked in the kitchen by Kent, who explained that it was customary to bolt the kitchen door and he did not wish to arouse the killer's suspicions by leaving it unsecured. As a result the officers remained trapped in the kitchen all night, with no access to the scullery, where the garment lay in the stove. Kent had supplied them with beer and cheese, and when he unlocked them in the morning the garment in the stove was missing. They had been duped, and only Kent could have achieved this.

As a member of the gentry in the area, Kent influenced all who were likely to question him. His lawyer managed not only to spare Kent and his wife from any questioning, but even from making an appearance at the inquest. The coroner removed some hostile members from the jury and so constructed a packed jury. Mr Kent tried all along to impede the police inquiry. This was realized at the time, but was ascribed to his desire to shield Constance. He could equally have been shielding himself.

In the few days after the murder, Kent went out of his way to loudly accuse the laundress of stealing Constance's missing third nightdress. He was both pointing the finger of suspicion at Constance and suggesting that the 'bloody shift' and the missing nightdress were one and the same. And with her history of 'strange' behaviour – running away from home dressed as a boy – Constance made a natural scapegoat.

Did Mrs Kent suspect the truth? The evidence is that by mid-July she had decided to side with her husband and Elizabeth Gough. She summoned the magistrates to amend her original statement about never having taken Savile from his cot. Now she said she might well have done so, and said she had once told Gough: 'Nurse, do not be frightened if I come in and take the child away.' Perhaps Mrs Kent knew that to protect her husband, she had to protect her rival in love too.

At around this same time, while Gough was detained in another house in custody, a witness overheard Gough saying to Mrs Kent: 'How can I bear it? I must give in – I can't hold out any longer.' Mrs Kent allegedly replied: 'Oh, don't say that! You have done so well so far – do keep it up – you must, for my sake.'

We turn now to the mystery of Constance's confession, made five years after the murder and when she was safe and unsuspected. A confession in which she was at pains to add the words: 'I, Constance Emilie Kent, alone and unaided, on the night of 29 June 1860, murdered at Road Hill House, Wiltshire, one Francis Savile Kent. Before the deed was done no one knew of my intention, and no one assisted me in the crime, nor in the evasion of discovery.' The internal evidence contained in that confession makes it suspect. For it to work, Constance must have been able to enter the nursery without waking the nurse, remove the child without it crying out, remake the cot while holding the child in one arm, and make her way down the stairs and out of the window. Why not out of the door? She then had to cross the yard, past the dogs – they did not bark that night, very like the clue in the Sherlock Holmes story – and she then had to take the child into the disused closet and cut its throat, where she says she thought the blood 'would never come'. There was no quantity of blood found in the closet: the child's throat had been cut elsewhere. But Constance, if innocent, could not have know that . . .

It is evident that Constance was deeply attached to her religious order. Shortly after her twenty-first birthday, when she came into her legacy, she begged Revd Wagner to accept eight hundred pounds for the church. He refused the gift. She then stuffed it into alms boxes around the place, but Wagner retrieved it all and handed it back to her. He did not want her money – he wanted her soul.

On Wednesday of Holy Week Constance decided she wanted to be confirmed in the church. Revd Wagner refused. Obviously he made it plain that she could not be accepted as a full member of the faith without confessing her awful deed. He alone knew her real identity and revealed it to the Mother Superior that same day. Together they heard Constance's confession and no doubt stage-managed it all. On the following Monday Revd Wagner travelled to London to see the Home Secretary, carrying Constance's written confession with him. It was a superb piece of publicity for his church and his view that the confessional should be kept. He had praise heaped on him from all quarters for his good work in bringing so notorious a sinner to penitence.

In the fevered atmosphere of that religious establishment Constance had found real peace and sense of purpose – yet now was deprived of confirmation unless she confessed. The deeply religious Constance thought it her duty to do as she was told – as did most women of the time – and she confessed in order to be confirmed and so join the church in spirit and body. It was that simple. Confirmation was the bribe.

Constance never consulted her father before making that confession. He learned of it by reading about it in his morning paper. He visited her in Devizes Gaol and she fell into his arms. She put her arms around him and sobbed: 'My course is due to you and God.' She had cleared him with the words 'alone and unaided . . . '

Surely the psychological explanation for her confession after five years of silence is now clear: to gain the acceptance of her religious guides and friends, she had to confess – even if innocent – and offer herself as a sacrificial lamb. The price of acceptance was to confess to a crime she had never committed. It was a price she was prepared to pay. Christ, after all, was an innocent who had sacrificed his life for others. Constance had hinted as much to her father: 'My course is due to you and God.'

Her female duty was to obey men; she had been conditioned to it. She obeyed first her tyrant father, and then her spiritual advisor, Revd Wagner. Both used her for

121

their own ends. Behind the scene the truth was probably recognized – hence the judge's tears when he sentenced her to death, and the commutation of the death sentence to one of life imprisonment.

It is to be hoped that during her twenty years in prison, Constance felt always that her false confession had earned her a special place in heaven. It certainly earned her a place in the annals of murder.

8
THE LYONS' CORNER HOUSE
MURDERS
1945

It is difficult to find a modern case to serve as both a parallel and a contrast to Constance Kent's. The nearest I can find is one from 1945 – although there are some features from Graham Young's which bear a resemblance. Young, who died on 1 August 1990 in his cell in Parkhurst Prison, was an obsessive poisoner, the most notorious mass-poisoner in Britain this century. At the age of fourteen he poisoned his father, stepmother and sister. On 5 July 1962 he was tried at the Old Bailey and sent to Broadmoor. After his release in February 1971, he was found a job with a photographic firm, where he promptly began systematically poisoning his workmates with thallium. Tried at St Albans Crown Court on 19 June 1972 for two murders and many attempted murders, Young was found guilty and jailed for life.

However, even though it was a case of murder within the family, Young cannot be equated with Constance Kent or indeed any crime of passion. He was a scientific killer who kept careful notes of the symptoms exhibited by his victims and the doses given. Cold and emotionless, he was like a scientist pulling the wings off flies to observe their agonies. Graham Young did not have a heart – which is ironic, since he died in his prison cell from a heart attack.

Much better for our purposes is the case of Jacques Tratsart. It is more *revealing*. Murder can show us the inner workings of the human heart more precisely than any other form of human activity, even if the act of murder – as is so often the case – takes us into the realm of abnormal psychology.

In the case of Jacques Tratsart, a young man who attempted to murder his entire family and succeeded in killing his father and sister in the most public fashion, the ordinary reader might well have difficulty in identifying the motive. In fact, patricide is one of the oldest forms of murder, and since the beginning of recorded history there have been many instances of sons who hated their fathers badly enough to kill them. It is part of the age-old continuing revolution of youth against age. The son rebels against his father, and in turn has his own son rebel against him. The clue to this case lies in the book which Tratsart began to write in an asylum for the criminally insane. Its opening sentence was: 'This is a world of youth: all men over forty scram!'

It began – or rather ended – in that most ubiquitous of institutions: a Lyons' Corner House. These restaurants were a common feature of every major city and flourished for over half a century, ever since the first one was opened in Piccadilly in 1894. They enjoyed their greatest vogue between the two world wars, the chain growing to no less than 250 establishments, which were only gradually phased out in the sixties. As restaurants-cum-tearooms, they gave the ordinary man in the street the opportunity to visit a restaurant and be waited upon for a few pence. The waitresses, in their smart black and white uniforms, were known as 'nippies', and Lyons' Corner Houses were ideal meeting places for lovers, friends or family outings. One of the most famous was in Oxford Street, near Tottenham Court Road, in London. A playwright might have used it as the setting for a romantic comedy; in fact this particular restaurant became the setting for murder.

Jacques Adrian Tratsart – known as 'Jack' – was an unhappy young man. He was twenty-seven years of age, unmarried, and lived alone. His father, John Tratsart, was a Belgian who had come to England before the First

124

World War and made a home in Norbury, south London. He was a shoemaker by trade. He had six children from his wife, and when she died in 1937 he married his housekeeper. That 'act of betrayal', as the son saw it, sowed the seeds for murder.

When the Second World War broke out, the Tratsart family were evacuated to Northampton – all save Jack, the eldest son, who was a toolmaker and therefore had a 'reserved occupation'. He was short-sighted and had to wear spectacles. When he took them off to rub his eyes, he brooded over his father, and the fact that the rest of the family had taken his side and given tacit approval to his new marriage. Jack was a manic-depressive who had been treated by a specialist for his condition, without any great success. In the dark hours of the night he must have lain awake for hours, thinking about revenge – because he was also a hopeless insomniac.

At the end of the war, the family in Northampton made moves to return to London, to the house in Norbury, and Jack did not like this new turn of events. However, he decided to turn it to his advantage. It was arranged that he would meet his father, now aged fifty-seven, his brother Hugh, and two of his sisters, Claire and Anne, at the Lyons' Corner House in Oxford Street. Also present would be Jack's mother's middle-aged sister, a Miss Coemans. The ostensible purpose of the meeting was to discuss the impending move back to Norbury, but Jack had other plans . . .

In some ways it was a tragic family. Twenty-eight-year-old Claire was epileptic, and Hugh suffered from palsy. To Jack, who had been outraged by the suffering and casualties of the war, the world was a bleak place full of unbearable pain and injustice. He was known to have been particularly outraged by the Italian treatment of the Abyssians. In his view, his brother and sister were crippled by ailments and might as well be dead; as for his father, he despised him. He deserved to die. Jack decided to kill all three members of his family and then commit suicide.

In a sense, Jack's problem was that he was seeking justice in a basically unjust world. 'Life being what it is, one dreams of revenge . . . ' the painter Paul Gauguin wrote in his *Journal*. Jack, too, was dreaming of revenge. He was a walking bomb, waiting to go off. He had bought a pistol from a sailor for five pounds two years previously, so he had the means and the motive. The family meeting was to prove the opportunity.

A fortnight before the end of the war, and ten days before Hitler's suicide in the Berlin bunker, the family met at the Oxford Street Lyons' Corner House for tea. The restaurant was crowded as the family of six sat around a table talking. The family was engaged in an animated discussion, laughing and chatting, and few who noticed them could have thought that the young man in spectacles who was fiddling around with a pistol under the table had anything sinister in mind. It might have been a water-pistol or an airgun. But it was real enough.

The date was 20 April 1945, the time 5 p.m. Six shots suddenly rang out, bringing the babble of conversation in the crowded restaurant to a shocked halt. In the hushed silence, three members of the family were seen to fall, with blood pouring from wounds in their heads and bodies. The young man in spectacles stood over them, a smoking pistol in his hand. As members of the public began to scream and hide themselves under tables, two soldiers nearby seized Jack Tratsart and subdued him. He made no attempt to struggle.

The ambulance service and the police were telephoned, and the staff at the restaurant calmed down the patrons, encouraging them to finish their meals. The murder scene was screened off, and a police constable who had hurried into the restaurant telephoned the police station in Tottenham Court Road to inform them of multiple murder in the heart of the metropolis. London had long been used to sudden death by aerial bombardment, but cold-blooded murder still had the power to shock and cause sensation. The case was headlined in the press.

The first detective on the scene was Detective Inspector Robert Higgins. He arrived just as the bodies were being removed. The older man was dead, a woman was dying, and a younger man had been shot in the jaw and was seriously injured. The alleged gunman sat quietly on a chair, still guarded by the two soldiers. He appeared to be unnaturally calm. Although both soldiers swore they had seen the young man brandishing a pistol, a search of his person revealed no weapon. Nor was there any sign of a gun in the immediate vicinity. Detective Inspector Higgins was baffled.

When he asked the suspect where the gun was, the bespectacled young man told him: 'You are the detective; it is your job to find it.' Hundreds of people had witnessed the shootings, but nobody had seen what had happened to the weapon. Certainly he had been in possession of one, since many witnesses had seen him fire the fatal shots, and a search of his pockets revealed nineteen bullets. He couldn't have swallowed the weapon . . .

Eventually Detective Inspector Higgins spotted a strange outline in a nearby light fitting. In the bowl lay the pistol. Tratsart had tossed it up there immediately after the shootings, but in the confusion no one had seen him do this.

Jacques Adrian Tratsart was taken to Tottenham Court Road police station and was questioned while he sipped a cup of tea. He spoke quite freely and without any sign of emotion or remorse, his statement being taken down in writing. He admitted having planned to shoot his family and having purchased the pistol for this purpose, saying: 'The opportunity only comes once, they say. Best to be prepared.' That opportunity had been the family meeting in the Lyons' Corner House.

In the course of his statement Jack Tratsart said:

I have considered killing my brother, Hugh, and my sister,

Claire, for some time, perhaps four or five years really, ever since I came back from Belgium when I was nineteen. My sister Claire is an epileptic and my brother Hugh has never been able to use his hands – a sort of semi-paralysis. They've never stood a chance, and my father didn't help them in their deficiencies. He is miserably, terribly bigoted, and the worst person to have as a father. You know what an epileptic is? She can't get married and her life isn't worth living whatsoever. My sister Claire is a staunch Roman Catholic and all she thinks about is going to heaven. She's got every possible disadvantage and couldn't keep her job. I have been contemplating killing myself over a number of years. I tried once but failed. That was in Belgium. I was the only one of the family who could help Claire and Hugh. My father only thought of making money. I had decided to commit suicide, so I thought I would do a good job while I was about it.

He had loaded the pistol with six bullets and sat at the table in the Lyons' Corner House facing the three women: thirteen-year-old Anne, Claire and his aunt. Beside him sat his father, and his brother Hugh. The statement went on:

I sat in the right position so that nobody could interfere with me shooting them and myself. We all sat talking normal gossip. I got the gun out and the funniest thing happened. I tried three times to fire it and couldn't. I didn't know you had to pull the top back. I decided to shoot Claire first, then my father, then Hugh, and then myself. I pointed the gun across the table at Claire and pulled the trigger, but nothing happened, and only Hugh saw me and grinned. Ten minutes later I repeated the performance and pulled hard at the trigger, with the gun only about two feet from Claire. But again nothing happened. They did not seem to realize that I was going to kill, and when my aunt asked jokingly what I had there, I said: 'Only a water-pistol.' They joked about it and I put it under the table. Then I carried my plan through. I fired two bullets at Claire but did not see what happened. I then fired two at my father and two at Hugh, coming round in a line. I was then standing up and pointed the gun at

128

my head and pulled the trigger once or twice, but nothing happened.

Tratsart was charged with double murder and attempted murder – his father, John Baptiste Tratsart, had died almost immediately and his sister Claire on the way to hospital. Hugh survived the terrible injuries to his jaw. After committal proceedings at Marlborough Street Court, Jack Tratsart was sent for trial at the Old Bailey, but was never to reach there.

Doctors who examined him in prison found him to be unfit to plead, and he was declared insane and sent to Broadmoor. There he learned how to play tennis and the piano, and began writing his book. He died two years later. Had he been hanged it would only have shortened his life by two years, and he was obviously not responsible for his actions – as much a victim as the people he slew.

But Jack Tratsart had acted as judge, jury and executioner, and that can never be forgiven in any society. He had decided to opt out, taking three members of his family with him. G. K. Chesterton once described suicide as being the greatest of all crimes, because the killer effectively kills all mankind – since they cease to exist for him.

Jack Tratsart was a mentally deranged young man who, finding the world an inequitable place, attempted both to change and leave it. With fatal consequences.

9
THE TANGLED WEB OF HENRY WAINEWRIGHT
1874

'O what a tangled web we weave. When first we practise to deceive' – so run the first lines of the poem, and for many people the first great exercise in deception is adultery. Being involved in an affair means living an almost schizophrenic life, torn between spouse and lover, with a necessity to develop a psychopathic talent for lying. For many, the stress of leading a double life is too much and they crack. Most either leave the spouse or confess all. But some see murder as a short-cut out of an impossible situation. 'From the bed to being dead', one might say. The case of Henry Wainewright is the story of one of the most brutal murders of the late nineteenth century, and it is of interest because it demonstrates the stupidity of the killer and the ever-changing pattern of murder.

The typical nineteenth-century murder was for financial gain, the typical murderer being a poisoner hastening an aged relative to the grave to secure an early inheritance. Or perhaps to enjoy a life insurance swindle – as practised by Thomas Griffiths Wainewright (no relation to Henry) who poisoned his pretty twenty-year-old sister-in-law for eighteen thousand pounds, explaining to friends who queried his motives: 'Well, she had such *thick*, *ugly* ankles . . . ' as if that alone was cause enough to kill her. It was a sentiment of black humour of which Oscar Wilde would have approved – indeed, he made Wainewright the subject of a celebrated essay: 'Pen, Pencil and Poison'.

The twentieth century witnessed a new phenomenon: the sex murder. This in turn gave way to the 'motiveless murder' which now plagues us in the form of such monsters as Dennis Nilsen. One could say that in the first stage, murder was committed to satisfy natural hunger – or the relief of poverty. The second stage satisfied the sex hunger, and the present stage satisfies some obscure existential need to feel alive, if only in the act of killing – the individual's need to 'make a dent', as Fromm described it in his *Anatomy of Human Destructiveness*.

But certain human predicaments remain constant motives for murder, and adultery is a prime one. Once the mistress begins making 'impossible' demands, then impossible solutions suggest themselves – or so Henry Wainewright found. The newspapers of the day blazoned his case, and one journal brought out a 'Police News Edition. Price One Penny' under the bold heading: 'THE WHITECHAPEL TRAGEDY. The Life and Trial of Henry and Thomas Wainewright. With Verdict and etc.'

It contained engravings of the principal characters in the drama – and more importantly, from our point of view, a 'memoir' of Henry Wainewright. He is described as being 'well-educated and remarkably intelligent'. His conduct during his trial exhibited 'a strong will and an iron nerve'. He was a prodigal, a spendthrift who had got through his patrimony in a very short time, and was 'too fond of the pleasures of life'. He is described as 'reckless', and an insatiable womanizer. His hedonistic attitude towards life is summed up thus: 'Perhaps at the bottom of all this the moving and active principle was vanity . . . ' Both 'reckless' *and* 'extremely intelligent'? An odd combination; but then, human beings have always been ambivalent, capricious creatures.

Tracing the life history of Henry Wainewright reveals much about the social conditions of mid-Victorian England. His father had been a successful brush-maker in the East End of London, and when he died in 1864 he left the sum of eleven thousand pounds to be divided

131

among his five children. In some respects this sudden windfall seems to have been the cause of Henry's undoing. Before that, he had lived happily on the income from his brush-maker's shop in the Whitechapel Road, living with the wife he had married in 1862, in a house in Tredegar Square. He was extremely popular in the neighbourhood and revealed a flair for literary recitation. He frequently gave lectures on such topics as 'The Wit of Sydney Smith', or readings from Dickens and Hood, at the local Mechanic's Institute. One of his favourite pieces was 'The Dream of Eugene Aram'. (Aram was hanged for murder in 1759 and eulogized in a poem by Thomas Hood some seventy years later. This same poem – the 'Dream' – was also a favourite recitation piece of that other Victorian villain, Charles Peace.)

In 1871 Henry met Harriet Louisa Lane, a twenty-year-old milliner's apprentice, while enjoying himself at the popular local pleasure resort at Broxbourne Gardens. He was much taken by the well-educated girl – she was born at Weymouth, the youngest of seven children, and her father was manager of the Royal Gunpowder Works at Waltham – and she soon became Wainewright's mistress. He set her up in rooms at 3 Sidney Square, Commercial Road, together with her close friend, Ellen Wilmore. Harriet confided to Ellen that Henry was a 'real gentleman'; he gave her an allowance of five pounds a week – a considerable sum for the time – and bought her clothes and expensive gifts. Harriet styled herself 'Mrs Percy King', with Henry being 'Percy King'. It was probably a device to fool the landlady, but certainly Ellen Wilmore knew Henry's true identity.

On 22 August 1872, Harriet bore a daughter to Henry, and in December 1873 another girl was born to the pair. Harriet had already taken the precaution of placing a paid advertisement in the *Waltham Abbey Weekly* informing all who cared to read that she had married, and was now known as Mrs Percy King. Ellen Wilmore seems to have become a nanny to the children, looking after them on the occasions when Henry called to take Harriet out.

By 1874 the pressures of leading a double life had led to serious difficulties for Henry. Following the death of their father, he and his brother Thomas tried to run a brush-manufacturing business as a partnership, but soon dissolved it by mutual consent. Henry kept the shop at 215 Whitechapel Road, and Thomas became the tenant of the Hen and Chickens, where he established an iron-monger's business. Witnesses were to testify that Henry was always free with his money, treating ballet dancers to Champagne and frequently meeting show-girls. Soon he was obliged to tell Harriet that he had to cut her allowance – which did not please her – and like all mistresses, Harriet complained of the long lonely hours spent on her own waiting for her lover. The plight of the 'other woman' is ever thus. On top of all this, Henry found himself in debt to the tune of three hundred pounds and was facing bankruptcy.

Harriet had exhibited an alarming tendency to drink heavily and indulge in noisy quarrels – often in the street. Henry hit on the idea of introducing his brother Thomas as a possible suitor, under the name of 'Edward Frieke'. (The real Edward Frieke was an auctioneer friend of Henry's.) Gradually, the understanding was established that Harriet was to be transferred to 'Edward'. Harriet was not averse to the idea – obviously failing to spot any family resemblance between the two men.

In early September 1874, Harriet got very drunk out-side the house in which Henry had rented rooms for her, and caused a scene in the street. As a result she was given notice of eviction by the landlady. However, only a day or two after the scene in the street, Harriet was a changed woman. The business of the transfer had been openly broached by both men and she was delighted, her future seemingly secure. She told Ellen Wilmore all, and on 11 September 1874 she spent hours over her appearance, before leaving the house to go to 'Edward Frieke'. All she took with her were her night clothes wrapped in a paper parcel. She was never seen alive again.

Ellen Wilmore was to testify: 'Harriet left home carrying nothing more than her night clothes ... On the Tuesday following her disappearance I visited Henry Wainewright with the object of learning her whereabouts. He replied that he had sent her to Brighton for a day or two. I replied: "Why – she had no clothes!" He then observed: "I have given her some money, it's all right." I went home rather dissatisfied ... '

As well she might. Wainewright had made arrangements to pay her a weekly wage for looking after the two children. Three weeks later Ellen received a letter from Harriet, saying that Frieke had promised to marry her, but a condition of his proposal was that she should cut all contact with old acquaintances. Still later she received a telegram from 'Frieke' saying that he and Harriet were about to embark for the Continent. When she confronted Wainewright about this, he showed her an identical telegram which he himself claimed to have received.

The silence following the telegram did nothing to allay Ellen Wilmore's fears. She contacted Harriet's sister, communicating her suspicions, and later involved Harriet's father in the search for the missing woman – with the description 'frizzy golden hair, of slight build, and about five feet in height'. A private detective was hired, but all he discovered was that the 'Frieke' who had spirited Harriet away was not the same Frieke who was a respectable auctioneer. Finally, Harriet's father visited Wainewright, begging him to tell him whether Harriet was alive or dead. Wainewright coolly replied that he did not know.

In June 1875, Wainewright was declared a bankrupt, and his premises at 215 Whitechapel Road passed into the possession of a new owner. Wainewright had to act fast. Harriet lay buried on the premises, her body covered with quicklime. Her remains had to be moved to another resting place before the new owner discovered them. A terrible sickening smell had hung over the premises all summer, causing the tenants who lived above to complain. Wainewright did nothing, and the tenants moved out.

Acting in panic, Wainewright exhibited his basic stupidity. He recovered the remains and wrapped them in two parcels of American cloth, tied around with string. He then asked a local youth named Stokes, who had once worked for him, to help him carry the parcels. When Stokes complained of the weight, Wainewright asked him to keep an eye on the parcels while he went in search of a cab. While he was away, Stokes looked in one of the parcels and was horrified to discover a decapitated human head. (Obviously *Stokes* should have been sent for the cab while Wainewright guarded the parcels.) Wainewright returned with a cab and loaded the parcels aboard. Then came a scene worthy of a Mack Sennett silent comedy. Stokes ran after the cab, calling to two policemen to stop the vehicle. The officers merely laughed at him. Stokes continued his panting chase. Spotting a ballet dancer friend in the street, one Alice Day, Wainewright calmly ordered the cabbie to stop so that he could offer the woman a lift, which she accepted. Once more the cab resumed its journey, the indefatigable Stokes jogging behind.

Finally the cab stopped at the Hen and Chickens, where Wainewright unlocked the premises and carried one of the parcels inside. By this time Stokes had arrived on the scene and breathlessly persuaded two police officers to examine the parcels. When they approached Wainewright, he first tried to bluff his way out: 'Why do you bother me?' and then offered each officer a bribe of fifty pounds to let him go. Sternly they insisted on looking into the parcels, and there discovered the human remains.

Wainewright was initially charged with the murder of 'a woman unknown' – since he had, after all, been discovered in possession of the mutilated remains of a female. However, within twelve hours of his arrest he had been formally charged with the murder of Harriet Lane. What had happened was that Harriet's brother-in-law, a man named Taylor, read in the evening newspaper an account of Wainewright's arrest in connection with a female corpse, and was immediately convinced that the remains were those of Harriet. He went to the police station where Wainewright was being held and said that he could identify the body. When the police told him that the body was so badly decomposed as to be unrecognizable, he replied that he would be able to identify it by the hair, and by a decayed tooth in the upper jaw on the right side. The remains were thus duly identified as being those of Harriet Lane.

Ellen Wilmore was traced to Stratford, where she was living with Harriet's children. And the genuine Edward Frieke went to the police to tell them of the link between 'Mrs King' and Henry Wainewright. Thus on 21 September 1875 the police had enough to charge Wainewright with the murder of Harriet Lane some twelve months previously. His brother Thomas was charged with being an accessory after the fact.

The trial was the sensation of the day. As Henry stood in the dock at the Old Bailey, one newspaper reported: 'His appearance and facial expression is rather pleasing . . . When under examination, a pensive, grave, thoughtful, anxious look gave, perhaps, a melancholy cast to his well-chiselled features. Nevertheless, throughout the whole of the protracted and painful inquiry he maintained his firmness and self-possession.'

The trial began on Monday, 22 November 1875. Models and plans of the premises in Whitechapel Road and the Hen and Chickens were introduced into evidence by the surveyor for the Metropolitan Police. Then Alfred Phillip Stokes went into the witness box. He stated that he had once worked for Henry Wainewright, and on 11 September he asked him to carry a parcel for him. Wainewright also asked him to sell a chopper and a shovel. When Stokes asked what the substance on the chopper was, Wainewright said: 'Dog dirt', and wiped it off with a newspaper. Stokes told Wainewright he would carry the parcel – 'with the greatest of pleasure ... I accompanied him to 215 Whitechapel Road, where he unlocked the door ... I saw two parcels wrapped in American cloth and tied around with a rope. I lifted them up and said they were too heavy for me ... The prisoner then said he would carry one of the parcels. We walked together about a quarter of a mile. As we were going along I told the prisoner the parcel was too heavy and I must have a rest. He replied: "For God's sake don't drop it, or you will break it." '

Stokes then described being left to guard the parcels, and how he had peeked into one of them. 'The first thing I saw was a human head ... ' Wainewright arrived with a four-wheeled cab and drove off with the parcels, telling Stokes he would see him at seven that evening. Stokes ran after the cab. 'When the cab reached Leadenhall Street I was nearly exhausted and called to two constables to stop the cab, and they only laughed at me. I could only say: "Stop the cab for God's sake!" ' Stokes described how he had grimly plodded on after the cab, catching up with it when it stopped at the Hen and Chickens. 'I then spoke to two constables named Turner and Cox and asked them to go after the prisoner and see what he had in the parcels.'

Constable Turner then gave his evidence. 'I was on duty in the High Street about five o'clock on the evening of 11th of September, when the last witness called my attention to the cab in which the prisoner Henry Waine-wright was.' He watched Wainewright carry one parcel into the Hen and Chickens, then accosted him. 'I asked him what he had got there and he replied: "Why do you interfere with me?" and walked towards the Hen and Chickens with the parcel. I enquired if he lived there. He replied that he did not. I asked him to go into the build-ing. He hesitated, and I and Cox pushed him inside. The prisoner then exclaimed: "Pray, don't open it; don't touch

137

it whatever you do." I pulled the cloth open and my fingers came across a skull . . . I took hold of the prisoner while Cox went for a cab, and he then said: "I will give you two hundred pounds and produce the money in twenty minutes if you will let me go." Wainewright was then taken to the police station at Stones End Street, and examination revealed that the parcels contained 'portions of a female body very much decomposed and the features not distinguishable. The hair was clotted with blood and dirt.' Both Wainewright and poor Alice Day were charged with having in their possession a human body, supposed to have been murdered. Alice Day exclaimed bitterly: 'Mr Wainewright, you have done a fine thing for me!' The mystery remains as to why Wainewright stopped to pick up Alice Day when he was engaged upon such a desperate mission. Was it that he thought a female companion would make him look less suspicious, or was his over-active libido at work again?

The next witness was Alice Day. She admitted having known Henry for some twelve months, but denied that they had ever been intimate. She had not noticed any smells from the parcels in the cab. The Lord Chief Justice questioned her himself, curious and rather reproving about her habit of taking drinks with strangers. He obviously knew little about theatre-folk.

Ellen Wilmore was the next witness. She said: 'I knew the prisoner by the name of Percy King. He was introduced to me in the year 1872 by Harriet Lane, who then represented herself to be Mrs King. I took charge of her first child at the request of the prisoner, and he undertook to pay me one pound a week for doing so.' She spoke about the birth of the second child, and then: 'In May 1874, Harriet went to live at 3 Sidney Square with her two children, and I remained with her until 11th of September . . . At the end of August she was visited by a man who gave his name as Edward Frieke. An arrangement was made with me and Mrs King that I was to live at Stratford and have charge of the two children, and I

138

was to be paid five pounds per month for doing so by the prisoner.'

She then spoke of Harriet's disappearance on 11 September, when she had seemed to be 'in good spirits', and of how she later visited Henry Wainewright in his shop at Whitechapel Road to ask about Harriet's whereabouts and was given the 'Brighton' explanation. Wainewright had added that he thought Harriet had gone off with his friend Frieke, an auctioneer who had come into a fortune. Later the letter and telegram arrived. She gave evidence of identifying Harriet's clothing and distinguishing physical marks on the human remains.

Mrs Taylor, Harriet's sister, told of going to see Wainewright about her sister's whereabouts. 'He said he had received a letter and a telegram, and he read them. They were represented to come from Mr Frieke, and in it he "dared anyone to interfere with them", and said they were going off to Paris for a "jolly spree".' She said that Wainewright tried to pacify her by suggesting that he was sure the couple would return, once they had had their 'frolic'. Mrs Taylor said she felt sure that the remains she had viewed were those of her sister.

A procession of relatives followed her into the witness box. William Taylor, the brother-in-law, said he had recognized the remains as being those of Harriet 'by the small hands and feet, and the projecting teeth'. Harriet's father, John Lane, said he saw the remains at St Saviour's dead-house and recognized them the moment he looked through the glass. The private detective told of having traced the real Edward Frieke, and of the telegram he had seen. It was from 'Frieke: Dover, to Miss Wilmore at Stratford, and read: 'We are just off to Paris and mean to have a jolly spree.'

Edward Frieke went into the box to say that although he had known Henry very well, he had never met Thomas – or Harriet Lane. Telegraph clerks gave evidence about the telegrams. Record books for the relevant period were examined and produced. Although ostensibly the telegram had come from 'E. Frieke', the London telegraph office had recorded 'Wainewright: Dover Pier'. That meant that the message had come from a person named Wainewright.

Harriet's landlady, Mrs Jemima Foster, told of renting an apartment to Mr and Mrs King, and of the disturbance in the street which caused her to give Harriet notice to quit. She added that she was 'almost certain' that the prisoner, Thomas, was the same person who had once been introduced to her as 'Edward Frieke'. Other witnesses identified Thomas as being 'Frieke'.

John Baylis, of 149 Whitechapel Road, testified that he had sold Henry Wainewright a half-hundredweight of chloride of lime the previous year. Perhaps the most damaging evidence came from Wainewright's own foreman, George William Rogers. He told the court that Wainewright had asked him on 10 September 1874 – the day before Harriet Lane disappeared – about the price of lime. Rogers added: 'We had no use for it in the business.' He also stated that Wainewright had asked him to pawn a six-barrelled revolver for him, saying he was short of cash, but since Rogers could not get the two pounds for the revolver which Wainewright wanted, it was returned to him.

Three witnesses – James Kay, William Kay and James Wiseman – told the court that on 11 September at about six o'clock they heard three shots fired in rapid succession coming from the direction of Wainewright's premises. (It is indicative of the nature of the times that no particular attention was paid to these gun-shots. Evidence was given to the effect that Wainewright often indulged in shooting at targets. It was not necessary to have a firearms licence.)

Friday, 26 November – the fifth day of the trial – saw William Gregg testifying to having sold Wainewright some American cloth on the day before Harriet disappeared. The following day both Wainewright brothers were seen together between ten and eleven o'clock by a livery-stable keeper named Henry Young. The sheer amount of evidence was accumulating in sufficient quantity to ensure that Wainewright hanged.

But the statements made to the police by both Henry and Thomas Wainewright were enough in themselves to ensure conviction. In his statement Henry had tried to excuse his brother, saying: 'He's a good fellow, and only did for me what one brother would do for another.' The statement of Thomas, dated 2 October, was more explicit as to what 'one brother would do for another'. He said, in part:

> On Friday the 10th of September I called on my brother Henry. He asked me to buy him a garden spade and a chopper. I went to Mr Pettigrew's at 181 Whitechapel Road and got the articles, for which I paid three shillings, and charged my brother five shillings for them.

His profit for murder was just two shillings . . .

The many women in the court were asked to leave when the medical evidence was presented. Mr F. G. Larkin, surgeon, described the condition of the remains he had examined. They were of a young woman who had given birth at some time, and had been cut up unskilfully. There was dirt upon the remains, and chloride of lime – *the influence of which would be to arrest decomposition*. There was a fracture behind the right ear of the skull. This had been caused by a bullet wound. In fact, he had found two bullets in the skull. One had entered during life, the second when the first bullet had so far produced its effects that life was fast ebbing. Death was not necessarily instantaneous.

The Lord Chief Justice interjected at this point. 'Could a person live at all with a bullet in the brain?' he asked.

The surgeon replied: 'There was a remarkable case of a person living for some time with a bullet in the brain . . . The first bullet, in this case, was quite sufficient to cause death.' He added that the victim's throat had been cut either immediately before or just after death.

141

James Squire, a gun-maker of Whitechapel, testified that the bullets found in the skull had been fired either from a centre-fire or rim-fire revolver. (The vagueness of this 'expert' testimony would have infuriated the famous ballistics expert Robert Churchill.)

The prosecution had finished its case, and on Saturday, 27 November, the defence began its vain task. Mr Besley rose to address the jury on behalf of Henry Wainewright. He began by remarking that no one could envy the principal actors in a trial of this kind: they had had six days of mental torture. Upon the outcome of the trial depended their existence or non-existence. He then went on to say that it was a pity that the case had attracted so much public attention and indignation, but he begged the jury to put anything they had read about the case out of their minds. 'It is an undoubted disadvantage for prisoners to come before a jury when so much public attention has been directed towards the trial.'

The defence counsel heavily underlined the fact that all the evidence in the case was circumstantial. There was no *proof* that Henry Wainewright had deliberately premeditated the death of Harriet Lane. Or that there did not exist another person named 'Edward Frieke'. He went on: 'The questions to be decided are whether Harriet Lane died on 11 September, and whether Henry Wainewright caused her death. But was his conduct compatible with the latter act? If he had been conscious of crime, he would not have multiplied witnesses against himself by allowing Alice Day to ride in the cab . . . or would he not have sent Stokes for the cab? His conduct was inconsistent with a man whose hands were imbued with blood.'

His offering of a bribe to the police officers who arrested him was dismissed as the act of a man in an awkward position – had the jury not heard often of gentlemen offering bribes to the police when they found themselves accused of some trifling misconduct? (These lines alone speak volumes about the nature of the police force in Victorian England.)

Mr Besley then turned to the main thrust of his argument: there was no proof that the remains found were those of Harriet Lane. If the body was not that of Harriet Lane, then the charge against Henry Wainewright failed. And if the alternative was considered – that of murdering a woman unknown – then the jury must consider what evidence they had of her death, and 'the whole fabric of evidence about Harriet Lane fell to the ground'. Then they had to consider the probability that the person had committed suicide, a theory not incompatible with the condition of the remains.

This was too much for the Lord Chief Justice. With a note of acerbity, he remarked that persons who had committed suicide could not bury themselves . . .

Mr Besley hurried on. He called medical experts to testify that the remains found could not be those of Harriet Lane. Dr Alfred Meadows, an obstetrician at St Mary's Hospital, said that his examination tended to show that the woman had never given birth. Mr Besley finished his final address to the jury by imploring them to remember the awful issues involved, and to reflect that their verdict would be one from which there was no appeal.

Mr Moody then made his closing speech on behalf of Thomas Wainewright, arguing that there was no proof of a plot between the brothers, and that even if Henry was guilty of murder, this did not mean that Thomas had been aware of the fact.

The Attorney-General rose to make his reply on Tuesday, 30 November. He gave a digest of the defence of Henry Wainewright. There was no proof that the body was that of Harriet Lane, and even though found in possession of the remains of a dead woman, she may well have committed suicide, and Wainewright was induced by the horror of the moment to conceal the body. He went on: 'Just consider for a moment whether this theory is tenable. Can you imagine all those injuries to have been inflicted by her own hand? Supposing the cut in the throat was inflicted during life, how would it be possible for her afterwards to discharge these three bullets with such deadly and certain aim? Reverse the case, and suppose the bullets were first discharged, how was it possible for the woman afterwards to inflict the wound in her throat?'

He argued that, in any case, a woman wishing to commit suicide with a pistol would fire it into her mouth – not into the back of her head. 'I will not insult your reason and outrage your common sense by asking you to assume that the woman committed suicide.' The facts were simple, he maintained. 'There is a woman buried under the floor at 215 Whitechapel Road: on the 11th of September he is dealing with the remains. Can anyone doubt from the evidence that his hand severed the remains in a number of pieces? On the 11th he is taking them to the Hen and Chickens. He is arrested and gives an explanation which is utterly incredible . . . '

Sir John Holker, the Solicitor-General, had just one pertinent question. If the remains were those of a mystery woman, then: 'Where is Harriet Lane? How is it that she has made no enquiry after her children? Why does she not come forward to clear from peril one she once loved so tenderly?' He ended with a firm declaration that there could be no doubt that a combination had existed between the two prisoners, and that the younger man was a party to the scheme which Henry had prepared.

On Wednesday, 1 December, the court was packed to hear the summing-up. The Lord Chief Justice was brief and to the point. 'On the 11th of September the prisoner Henry Wainewright was found in possession of the mangled remains of the body of a woman. It was found that those remains had recently been severed by a blunt instrument. It was discovered that they had recently been taken from a grave dug for the purpose of concealment . . . There can be no doubt that the woman had been murdered. Was it by the hand of the prisoner in the dock that life was taken?'

He turned to the question of the identity of the murdered woman. 'It is not necessary, in a charge of murder, that the identity of the person killed should be established. The law throws its protection around the known and the unknown . . . ' He passed on to the question of motive. 'There can be little doubt that she was, in his estimation, a constant source of danger. He had not the money to satisfy her, and she was apt to be ill-tempered . . . Thus he lived, as it were, on the edge of a volcano that might at any minute have exploded and led to disastrous consequences as regarded both his domestic and his public life as a respectable tradesman . . . '

The jury retired for a bare fifty minutes, returning with verdicts of guilty of wilful murder against Henry Wainewright, and guilty of being an accessory after the fact against Thomas Wainewright. The Lord Chief Justice donned the black cap and sentenced Henry to death. Thomas received seven years' penal servitude.

Henry Wainewright was publicly hanged at Newgate on 21 December 1875, after growling at the spectators: 'Come to see a man die, have you, you curs?' Stokes, the cause of his undoing, was awarded thirty pounds for his 'public services', but the amazing sum of twelve hundred pounds was collected for the hanged man's widow and children.

It was a typically Victorian case, sin lying hidden behind a respectable façade. Henry's attempts to save his life were absurd, the evidence overwhelming. On 11 September 1874 Harriet Lane had vanished. Twelve months later a female body, which had been buried for a year, was recovered from Wainewright's premises. Wainewright was arrested trying to move those remains from one resting place to another. While it is true that he was not caught exactly red-handed, then surely he must remain the nearest thing to it. Above all, he remains an example of what can happen to even 'remarkably

145

intelligent' men when they are caught in an impossible situation and choose the impossible solution to the problem. If life is full of choices, then the criminal is the man who unerringly selects the wrong one – and pays the price.

10
THE LAWMAN WHO TURNED OUTLAW
1986

It will have been noted that I use the term 'crime of passion' in a very elastic sense. It could be argued that Wainewright's was no crime of passion, but simply a cold matter of elimination. But it was passion which had led him into the situation and, in a sense, most crimes are crimes of passion. What can demonstrate passion so terribly as the suicide? Quite rightly we say these crimes are the acts of people 'out of their minds', people who suffer from such distorted emotions as to render the balance of their minds unstable.

Love itself has been the subject of much debate over the centuries. Is it lust disguised? Is it an emotion which renders the victim temporarily incapable of rational thought – like a bad dose of flu? Certainly many crimes have been committed in its name.

The next case is not an exact parallel to that of Wainewright. The killer made no attempt to hide his victim's body, for example, but there are certain features in common. Both were 'gentlemen' – reminding us of Shakespeare's line from *King Lear*: 'The prince of darkness is a gentleman.' Both were driven to murder by financial problems, and both exhibited a remarkably calm and normal appearance after the act of murder. More importantly, both were intelligent men with monstrous egos to protect. They killed to preserve the integrity of their self-images.

This preamble is no 'cop-out'. I could easily have selected a case of a man disposing of an unwanted mistress, but such cases are suffocatingly banal. If, as De Quincey suggested with tongue in cheek in his celebrated essay 'Murder Considered as One of the Fine Arts', we were to present a prize for the best murder of the year, an 'Oscar' for the most imaginative homicide, it would rarely be awarded. Murder is by its very nature a messy and unstructured business which displays no art, and in its execution is usually horribly botched. This case is no exception. It was a deliberate and premeditated murder by a clever man, but it displayed no cleverness; just the savage vandalism of a mind in the process of disintegration.

Ughill Hall, an eighteen-room mansion high on the moors above Sheffield, was bathed in weak September sunlight. At noon on Sunday, 21 September 1986, the well-groomed man who was master of the hall took his beautiful French mistress to one of the bedrooms and made love to her. If it lacked the usual passion of their love-making, it was marked with a curious tenderness, an air of regret as he kissed her for the last time. Afterwards the mistress, who was ten weeks pregnant with his child, sat in a swivel chair worrying about the future.

Her lover, a solicitor, had confessed to her that evening that he was a thief. He had stolen £180,000 of his clients' money. But he promised to go to the police on the following day and confess everything. The woman's mind was full of conflicting emotions, torn between fear of an uncertain future and love for her unborn child. She sat in the chair, wearing a newly bought maternity dress, her face still showing a half-smile. She had enjoyed the love-making, despite the strange air of finality about the act, and her brow still glistened with the perspiration of passion spent.

Without warning her lover crept up behind her and fired a bullet from an Enfield army pistol into the back of her head, using a cushion to muffle the noise. She let out a faint cry, and he blasted her with another bullet.

148

The dead woman's two children, two-year-old Stephanie and Christopher, aged five, were watching television in another room in the mansion and were unaware of anything out of the ordinary. The man led the girl into an upstairs room and pretended to play a game of hide-and-seek with her. As the child giggled, the man covered her face with a duvet and shot her through the head at point-blank range. She fell on to the floor, her eyes still wide open. He shot her once more to make certain. Four bullets gone, two to go... Then he fetched the boy, Christopher, telling him he had a surprise in the bedroom for him. The boy was told to lie on the floor and cover his face with a towel so that he could not 'peek'. Then the man fired the last two bullets into the boy's skull. Miraculously, the boy was not dead...

The man was busy packing his suitcases, and as he passed the bathroom he heard the boy moaning. He took a heavy stick and beat the boy over the head until the stick broke and the moaning ceased. He turned away, satisfied that the boy was dead. The gun was dropped, abandoned, having done its work. That revolver had been used by the killer's father to commit suicide two years previously. It had been returned to the killer, along with eleven bullets, by the police. There must be cosmic humour at work in the universe.

The killing done, the man changed his clothes, picked up his bags – which contained £20,000 of his clients' money – and drove into Sheffield city centre, calmly stopping at his favourite pub for two glasses of wine – just as Wainewright had so calmly stopped his cab to pick up the ballet dancer. Then he picked up a hire-car which he had rented a week earlier in an attempt to lay a false trail, drove to Dover, and took the ferry to France.

He left behind little mystery for the police. They knew who the killer was; it was simply a matter of tracking him down. They were to learn of his whereabouts in dramatic fashion when, a week later, television news showed the killer perched high up on a gargoyle on

Amiens Cathedral, threatening to jump. French police managed to talk him down, and then it became a routine matter of extraditing him back to England to face trial for murder.

The killer was thirty-seven-year-old solicitor Ian Wood, on the surface a successful man enjoying the prosperous lifestyle of his chosen profession. The law had been good to him. After qualifying as a solicitor – graduating from Sheffield University with a third-class honours degree in law in 1968 and then working for a Sheffield law firm – he set up his own practice in 1983. It was to prove highly profitable. Wood spent the next few years building up a 'Mr Clean' image in Sheffield. He became secretary to the local law society and clerk to the city's tax commissioners, a position which paid £26,000 a year for the part-time job.

Ian Wood had found it easy to make the grade, having been born into a wealthy middle-class family. His father was a director of a thriving Sheffield steel firm. From the moment of his privileged birth, Wood began to reap the benefits. He went to an expensive public school, Haileybury. He was brought up in the fashionable West End area of the city and spent school holidays abroad. Then came university.

Wood was always expected to be a high-flier. While on holiday in the South of France he met a Newcastle girl, Margaret, whom he married in July 1976. The marriage lasted ten years and produced three children: an eight-year-old daughter and two sons aged six and two. Wood rented Ughill Hall in the Bradfield area and housed his family in style in its eighteen rooms. In time he was to develop almost as many facets to his personality as the house had rooms . . .

The point at which an honest man turns rogue varies with every individual, and the exact moment of change can almost never be determined afterwards. But the evidence suggests that Ian Wood's smooth façade began to crumble when a beautiful thirty-eight-year-old French

150

woman, Danielle Lloyd, walked into his office to ask him to institute divorce proceedings against her husband, Colin. Wood fell in love with her on sight and became obsessed by her.

Danielle was born in Camon in the Amiens region of northern France. She was always close to her parents, Robert and Térèse Ledez, and actually spoke to them by telephone just an hour before she was shot dead. Danielle had a tragic background. Her first husband was killed in a plane crash in 1972, on her birthday, and less than three years after the wedding. Later she moved to Vichy and bought her own home there. Then she met an English school-teacher, Colin Lloyd, whom she married in 1975. They set up home in Sheffield, where the husband taught; but with Christopher already born and Danielle pregnant with Stephanie, the marriage came under strain when the husband began an affair with a fellow-teacher fifteen years his junior. Danielle was distraught: just two days after the birth of Stephanie, her husband finally left her to live with his new love. Danielle kept visiting her husband, shouting abuse at the 'other woman', and on one occasion she poured motor-oil over her rival's car. Then she decided on divorce – only to meet another man who would mistreat her.

Ian Wood knew all about adultery; he had been unfaithful to his wife on many occasions, despite his air of respectability. Behind the façade of the lawyer lurked a Casanova. But Danielle was the rare woman he was determined to make his own. He bought her expensive presents, wooing her, finally making her his lover within a year of their first meeting. Then he deserted his wife and children to live with her and her two children. When the abandoned wife found out that she could no longer afford the upkeep of Ughill Hall, she moved out – and Wood and Danielle moved in.

But the new life Wood had made for himself did not work out. He detested Danielle's children, often referring to Christopher as 'the brat', and his business was in trouble. He was simply living beyond his means, unable to afford the large maintenance payments to his wife as well as the expensive presents for his mistress. He was trying to keep two families on the proceeds of his one-man business; and if that was not enough, he took another mistress, whom he installed in an expensive Sheffield hotel.

Wood was determined to live up to his image of the big spender. A typical gift was a £1,500 ruby and diamond necklace bought for Danielle with one of his many credit cards. He was living in a fantasy world, with debts piling up around his ears, and he tried to blot out reality by drinking himself into oblivion. And so his work suffered – it was a vicious circle. To pay for all this: the abandoned wife and children, the new mistress and her children, the third secret woman in his life, and the booze, Wood began stealing money from his clients.

His own family were not immune from his swindling. He embezzled £20,000 from his brother, and tricked his mother into underwriting his vast debts. As the business spiralled downwards out of control, Wood was forced to steal more and more money – in fact he could not steal it fast enough to cover his debts, having to rob Peter to pay Paul. It all became too much. In a desperate attempt to retrieve the situation, Wood took out a £20,000 loan from a bank based in Paris but registered in the Bahamas. He had to pay the loan with fifty per cent interest within a year. It was impossible, and Wood must have known it. He had to steal even more, robbing the account of one client to repay money stolen from another. By the time of the murders he had stolen some £180,000.

He had taken Danielle and her children on a holiday to France to visit her parents. There they bought wedding rings for one another. Then Danielle sprang the news on him that she was pregnant. She was delighted, buying two new maternity dresses a couple of days before she was murdered. But to Wood, the added burden of the pregnancy must have seemed like the last straw. The relationship with Danielle was under strain because of the bitter legal row with her former husband over custody of Christopher. Wood urged her to keep the boy, and on the day of the murders he had a violent row with Colin Lloyd, when he turned up at Ughill Hall to take Christopher out for the day. Wood refused to allow the boy to go out.

Wood knew that time was running out; that his thefts and deceptions would soon be found out. From the 'Mr Clean' lawyer, he had become an adulterer and a thief. Now he was contemplating adding murder to the list. In early September 1986 he made one last desperate bid to save the situation, flying to Paris to borrow more money. The deal fell through, and it was on his return to England that he confessed to Danielle about his thefts, which would mean a lengthy prison sentence.

Precisely why he determined to kill Danielle and her children will never be known, but the most likely explanation is that he could not bear to be exposed as a fraud, as a liar, thief and cheat. For her to be left to survive on social security while he spent years in prison – that was a picture his ego could not allow him to live with. In order to protect his self-image, he turned killer. Paradoxically enough, it was meant to save him from disgrace . . .

The day after the shootings, alerted by worried relatives, police broke into Ughill Hall. They found Wood's three victims lying in separate rooms, but incredibly, Christopher was still alive – if only barely. For twenty-one hours he had lain in the bathroom, slipping in and out of consciousness, his skull shattered by two bullet wounds, his scalp bleeding from the blows with the stick which had been used to bludgeon him. He staggered to his feet as police approached him, a tiny figure masked in blood. When an officier tried to loosen his clothing, Christopher cried out: 'No! No!' He was rushed to hospital, where neurosurgeons feared at first that he would die. Doctors, relatives and policemen were amazed at the tenacity with which he clung to life. Even after delicate microsurgery the boy was left blind for months and without his power of speech. Police recovered the two bullets fired into him from the floor in which they were deeply embedded. One had actually penetrated his brain, but their passage had caused massive shock-waves through his skull, which bruised his brain badly. As the bruise faded, his sight slowly returned. He was to make a full recovery, apart from slight tunnel vision. Today he is a normal and happy child, back with his father. The boy Wood tried so hard to kill, the boy who refused to die.

After the bodies of mother and daughter had been removed from Ughill Hall, and the only survivor of the carnage taken to hospital, police began the manhunt for Wood. They knew the murder weapon was his. They had given it to him, and had twice removed it from him for various reasons, but returned it again. At first police thought Wood was still in Britain, but during his week on the run, Wood made many telephone calls to friends and colleagues in England, telling them that the killings had been part of a bizarre suicide pact which had gone wrong. He promised to kill himself before being recaptured. 'I shot out of love,' he insisted during one of the calls. 'I couldn't kill in hate.'

The police were embarrassed by this stream of telephone calls. It was as if Wood was taunting them, and certainly they had an inability to trace his whereabouts, even though they tapped one of his calls, which lasted for thirty-five minutes. And he sent three cassette recordings – two to legal colleagues, one to the South Yorkshire coroner – in which he talked about the killings. He was preparing his defence: that the killings had been a suicide pact; that he knew the Law Society would compensate the clients whose money he had stolen; and most importantly, he claimed Colin Lloyd had hounded him and Danielle over custody of the children. The suicide pact was all his fault . . .

A week later came the television pictures of Wood clinging to a gargoyle two hundred feet up Amiens

Cathedral, threatening to jump. The crowd below were calling for Wood to jump, but after six hours the police talked him down. He surrendered himself to police, saying that for him to jump in front of a crowd howling for his death 'would have been like the last act of a circus clown'. Certainly Wood had no friends in France. Danielle's family, and the French people in general, felt detestation for a man who could so callously kill a woman and her children.

Wood was eventually extradited to England, where he told police his well-rehearsed story. He was word-perfect by the time he stood trial on 21 July 1987 at Sheffield Crown Court. The trial lasted eight days and was dominated by the sinister-looking man in the dock, who looked gaunt and haggard. He had lost several stones in weight during his ten months in custody, and his expensive, well-cut suit hung badly on him, giving him the appearance of a well-dressed scarecrow.

Mr Geoffrey Rivlin, QC, prosecuting, told the jury of eight men and four women that Wood was guilty of the deliberate murder of Danielle Lloyd, although he pleaded not guilty to the charge of murder but guilty to manslaughter. Wood did plead guilty to the murder of Stephanie and the attempted murder of Christopher, and the theft of monies belonging to his clients. So Wood, while admitting the murder of a two-year-old girl, was anxious not to be convicted of the murder of her mother. It could only be for reasons of vanity. The sentence would be life in any event.

Mr Rivlin told how Wood had shot his three victims 'in a calculating manner'. Not the impulsive actions of a man driven by passion, but the deliberate, cold-blooded moves of an executioner.

The prosecution read out the statement which Wood had made to the police, in which he claimed that he and Danielle had made an agreement to die. 'He says he and Danielle entered into a suicide pact – what he described as a suicide-tryst – and that is why he shot her,' said Mr Rivlin. 'He claims that although he shot her dead, he should not be convicted of her murder because when he shot her he did so as the result of an agreement between him and Danielle that he should shoot first Danielle and her children, and then himself.' Mr Rivlin said that the law was clear on this point: when one person kills another in pursuance of a suicide pact and he survives, he should not be convicted of murder but of manslaughter. He went on: 'But that is only if there is a *genuine* suicide pact. In the circumstances of this case it means that the defendant has to prove two things: that there was at the time a genuine suicide pact, and that he had a genuine intention to kill himself. Little children cannot, in law, agree to die, and these little children did not agree to die. In relation to them there is no such defence available to the defendant, and he has pleaded guilty to murdering Stephanie and attempting to murder Christopher.'

Mr Rivlin said that the prosecution did not accept that Danielle had agreed to die, or that Wood had any intention of killing himself. The whole story of a suicide pact was a 'tissue of lies'. In his statement to the police, telling of how he shot Danielle, Wood had said: 'I took her by the hand and led her into the end bedroom . . . I made love to her . . . then shot her.' After the shooting Wood had made several telephone calls to people and had made tape-recordings, which were played to the jury, in which he repeated his claim of a suicide pact, but said it had never been part of the agreement that he should die there and then. There were five things he had to do before he ended his life: light candles at various places in France, including Amiens. Try to explain their story to the press to counter adverse publicity. Kill Danielle's husband. Ensure that Danielle and the children were buried in France. Finally, visit the graves and put flowers on them. The prosecution said that the alleged agreement was a nonsense and had never existed. 'Witnesses will say that Danielle loved life and simply adored her children.' He asked the jury to give serious thought as to whether there could ever have been such an agreement as that described by Wood, and said that the story of a suicide pact 'does not have the ring of truth about it'.

The prosecution then related the background to the case. How Wood set up his solicitor's practice in 1983, and the following year his ailing father committed suicide with the very gun which Wood used to commit murder – a six-shot Enfield service revolver. That he met Danielle in 1984 and by 1985 they were lovers. He began stealing his clients' money shortly afterwards, and by September 1985 had stolen a huge amount to finance his double life. In November 1985 he confessed to his wife that he loved Danielle and moved out of Ughill Hall. Later, after his wife had moved out, he and Danielle, together with her children, moved in. In February 1986 Wood began another illicit affair with a married woman, spending nights with her at a Sheffield hotel. The last night they spent together was 12 September – just a week before the killings. He told his new lover that he was drinking too much because of 'problems', but said that he would not do anything drastic, like killing himself.

During interviews with the police Wood said: 'Danielle was the lady I loved. She was my eyes, my life and my lover. She was everything.' But, the prosecution emphasized, 'it is plain that the defendant did not have eyes only for Danielle . . . there was this other woman'. As for the claim that Danielle had agreed to die, she had spoken to her mother by telephone on the very day she died, sounding cheerful and happy, and promising to call her mother back on the following Sunday. Yet, according to Wood, before that telephone call was made, Danielle had already agreed to die. Witnesses would say that Danielle had appeared to be happy right up to her death.

On Sunday, 15 September, Wood hired a car and drove to Paris, where he spent a week trying to borrow money and avoid his creditors. On his return, on 19 September, he admitted to Danielle for the first time that he had been stealing money from his clients and promised to see the police on the Monday to make a clean breast of it. He did not go to the police, of course. At noon on the Sunday the massacre began.

The prosecution described the carnage, the hail of bullets, and read out Wood's account of it. 'We went upstairs and made love for the last time. The children were downstairs ... I used a cushion to stop the noise and shot her. She made a cry ... I fumbled with the gun and shot her again.' Then came the killing of the children. 'I went downstairs for Stephanie. I took her up to the bedroom to play "hide-de-boo". I covered her head and shot her twice. At first she was looking straight at me. Her eyes were open. I had to be sure she was dead, so I closed my eyes and shot her again. Then I went downstairs to Christopher, who was eating a tomato salad. I told him I had a surprise for him and to close his eyes and not to peep. I told him to lie down on the floor and I put a towel over his head and shot twice. I went down to the kitchen and then upstairs to pack. As I went past the bathroom I heard a low moan. Christopher was not dead. I picked up a thick pole and hit him four or five times until the stick broke.'

Wood's 'other woman' went into the witness box to tell of her love-sessions with Wood. Speaking almost in a whisper, she said she and Wood made love on about four or five occasions and she became very fond of him. Wood did not look at her as she testified. She was followed into the witness box by a fellow-solicitor whom Wood had telephoned the day after the killings to say that Danielle and the children lay dead in Ughill Hall. On the phone he said: 'Once I was nice, but not now ... To kill Danielle and the children was most appalling, but I did it because I loved them. It is a nightmare ..."

A French police chief, Superintendent Robert Canonge, told the court that he had joked with Ian Wood at the top of a French cathedral while a baiting crowd below called for the fugitive's blood. The police officer used light banter to prevent Wood throwing himself off the cathedral, and said: 'A large crowd had gathered below, and some people were shouting "Jump! Jump!" When he was taken from the cathedral the car was kicked and people were shouting "bastard".'

When Wood went into the witness box he used all his lawyer's skills to try and win the jury over and gain their sympathy – without success. He broke down and wept, pleaded, begged for understanding. He persisted in the story of the suicide pact, saying it had been Danielle's idea that all four of them should die. He said the decision came to her as she listened to him having a row with her estranged husband, Colin, over custody of Christopher. Wood claimed that Danielle decided there and then that she could not face her husband alone if Wood were jailed for theft. His voice trembling with emotion, Wood told the jury: 'It was Danielle's idea, and it never occurred to me that the children would have to die. She said that the children were going with her and that they would take sleeping pills. I said we couldn't do that because Stephanie was only two and it would be difficult for her to take the tablets. I said the best way would be if I shot them. Danielle asked if it would hurt and then agreed. I said I would commit suicide after shooting them. The children were not dying but were going somewhere better. It was inconceivable that she could leave them to Colin because he only wanted to use them against her. We truly believed that we were leaving the pain and suffering behind.' He told the horrified jury about the moment when he killed his lover. They had made love for the last time. Then his mistress murmured: 'Je t'aime, my man' – I love you – just before he shot her. Weeping, he continued: 'She made a noise and it was horrible. The cry stopped almost as soon as it started. I knew she was dead but I could not touch her. It was all so unreal, almost as if it was not me there, or that I would wake up.' He then related how he had killed the children – and failed, in Christopher's case. He told of his debts. 'My financial difficulties became a greater and greater burden and were one of the reasons my marriage broke up. It will sound like the old story of the fool, but I truly believed that they would come right. This didn't turn out to be the case, and I had to borrow money from extremely dubious sources and then face up to them making threats against my family.'

Wood spent five hours in the witness box. The most telling time was during his cross-examination by the prosecution. He denied having told a 'pack of lies' but admitted that neither he nor Danielle had kissed the children goodbye before they were shot. Mr Rivlin told him: 'There is absolutely no question of this woman agreeing that she and her children should die. You shot the woman you loved and her two children and didn't harm a hair on your head. You are telling a pack of lies. You gave yourself up in the most dramatic circumstances you could imagine, knowing the press and television cameras would be there and it would be a great performance.' Wood denied all the allegations, and as for his affair with the married woman, he claimed that Danielle knew all about it and did not mind him sleeping with other women.

Ian Wood's mother went into the witness box, mouthing the words 'I love you' at her son as she did so. She told the court that Danielle had been contemplating suicide eight months before her death because of the stress she was under from her ex-husband over custody of the children. 'Her depression was so overwhelming,' Mrs Barbara Wood told the court. 'I had never seen such sadness and despair. That is when she first told me of her intention to kill herself and the children. I couldn't believe it. She said there was no point in living because her husband, Colin, would never leave her alone.' Mrs Wood said that Danielle had mentioned suicide on at least ten occasions between February and May 1986.

Wood's doctor told the court that he had warned the police that Wood might use his firearms to harm himself or those around him. He said that on his first visit, on

11 November 1985, Wood had been extremely depressed. 'I felt there was a genuine danger of suicide. I felt there might be a danger to his former wife with one of those guns.' Later that day Wood left his wife, and visited his doctor again on 13 December.

'He was totally changed, a totally different character,' the doctor said. 'He was quite ebullient, quite excited. There was none of the earlier despondency. He told me of his relationship with a French lady . . . He had fallen in love with her and his only objective now was to divorce his first wife and set up home with this lady. But I was still concerned about the guns, because of the family history and his previous history of heavy drinking.'

Alcohol plays a prominent role in many crimes, such as lubricating the act of murder . . .

On 29 July both prosecution and defence counsels made their final submissions to the jury. Mr Rivlin told them: 'This was an utterly ruthless and cold-blooded killing in unimaginable circumstances. There is undoubtedly scope for the killings to be done in hatred and jealousy. The defendant had an obsessive hatred for Colin Lloyd, and on the day of the killings he faced disgrace, humiliation and prison for what he had done to clients. Given his hatred for Colin Lloyd, it may have run through his mind that Mr Lloyd would never, ever get the better of him. There was not a shred of concern or compassion in the defendant's voice when talking about Christopher on the telephone to his brother-in-law. The suicide pact is nonsense. Danielle certainly did not intend to die and the only witness who supports the defendant is his mother, and if she is right then Danielle managed to deceive her family, friends and doctor.'

Mr Gilbert Gray, QC, defending, told the jury that there was no other explanation for the killings but the suicide pact. He claimed that Wood had gone to France to carry out tasks he had promised Mrs Lloyd on her death-bed. He said: 'There was no greed, or sadistic pleasure in inflicting pain. This was a genuine suicide pact and into this pact two normal, rational people pooled all their tensions and their extraordinary personalities with all their weaknesses. The only answer to the anguish and agony of this situation could be a suicide pact.'

In his summing-up the trial judge, Mr Justice Taylor, urged the jury to cast aside all emotions when considering their verdict. 'What you have heard in this case may create horror and indignation in the minds of ordinary decent people. It would be hard not to have strong feelings, but it is important to put emotions aside. Do not be seized by feelings of revulsion. It is a question of murder or manslaughter.' The judge continued his summing up on the following day, going through each point of the evidence meticulously.

On 30 July the jury returned a unanimous verdict of guilty of murder against Wood. He remained impassive as the judge told him: 'These were cold-blooded killings of your mistress and her innocent children. You were prepared to kill all three of them, and afterwards you packed methodically, dressed smartly, had a drink at your favourite bar and set off for France in a hired car for which the police would not be looking. To try and put a better complexion on what you had done you sent a stream of messages claiming Danielle had agreed to die.'

He sentenced Wood to two concurrent life sentences for murder, twelve years for the attempted murder of Christopher, and a further three years for the theft of clients' cash.

After the case, Wood's relatives claimed that he had not had a fair trial and lodged an appeal. They were particularly upset by the judge's summing-up. Wood's brother Mark declared: 'We will stand by Ian. After the events of this morning we do not believe that justice has been done.'

A Home Office spokesman said: 'There is some concern about this case. We have asked for a transcript of the trial and have asked South Yorkshire Police to supply us with their explanation of what occurred.'

The cause of concern was how a man like Wood had been granted a firearms certificate. It transpired that it was due to bureaucratic blunders between two police forces. Following the suicide of his father, Wood had been given the death weapon by Sussex Police, together with eleven bullets. Having been warned by a doctor and a gun-dealer that Wood was mentally unstable, South Yorkshire Police swooped on Ughill Hall in November 1985, confiscating all his shotguns. But they returned them to him in January 1986, after his behaviour had improved. It was then discovered that he was illegally in possession of an Enfield revolver, but he was allowed to keep it on a technicality. Police were unaware that he had ammunition for the weapon. Detective Chief Superintendent Robin Herold, head of South Yorkshire CID, said later: 'It was an administrative slip-up between two forces. Sussex Police should have told us that he had collected the gun and ammunition, but didn't. We found out about the gun when his licence was renewed but did not know about the ammunition.'

Despite calls for the gun laws to be tightened up, it is difficult to see how any police force could have refused to grant a prominent member of the local community – a lawyer at that – a firearms certificate. They could not have known that he was about to turn killer.

A teacher at Wood's old school, Haileybury, said of him: 'He had quite a high academic ability and was a prefect here. The current circumstances he finds himself in have come as a shock to the entire school.'

Ian Wood was a man who became enmeshed in a web of passion which turned him from being a man of the law into an outlaw. The case shocked the legal establishment in Sheffield, proving that even lawyers can be poor judges of character. But this was a tragedy which left a beautiful young woman and her daughter dead.

11

THE SNYDER AND GRAY CASE, 1927

All crime is a product of its prevailing socio-historical conditions. This concept was first advanced by Lambert Quételet in the nineteenth century and means, in short, that we get the criminals we deserve. A greedy, success-at-any-cost society will tend to produce a rash of large-scale frauds; a society which peddles sex as a commercial commodity will experience a corresponding rise in sex crimes. The equation is that simple.

However, crimes of passion do not always obey this general rule. They are the odd and irrational acts of individuals possessed by ancient passions they are unable to control, and have occurred throughout history in good times and bad. Greed played its part in the Snyder and Gray case – at least on the part of Ruth May Snyder – and greed is a classic motive for murder. But Henry Judd Gray was under the influence of a dominant woman, a condition psychiatrists call *folie á deux*, which translates literally as 'the madness of two'.

Briefly, it is a condition in which a couple support one another's fantasies or delusions. Two people come together by accident. Separately they would be harmless, but in combination it is like bringing a detonator into contact with gelignite – the result is explosive. Examples of such couples include Bonnie Parker and Clyde Barrow, Bywaters and Thompson, Leopold and Loeb, Fernandez and Beck, Hulten and Jones, Juliet Hulme and Pauline Parker, Brady and Hindley – and Snyder and Gray.

What happens is that one partner is dominant and

infects the other with his or her madness – a madness born of long hours of fantasizing about the desired end. T. E. Lawrence in his *Seven Pillars of Wisdom* wrote with acute insight: 'Beware the dreamers of the day . . . for they are dangerous.' The majority of us – the dreamers by night – are harmless.

Incidentally, psychiatrists have found the condition of *folie á deux* to be curable; if the infected partner is removed from the dominant one the malign influence wears off in due course. When Judd Gray was removed from Ruth Snyder, and incarcerated, he quickly came to denounce her. By then it was too late. He was to share her fate in the electric chair . . .

What were the social circumstances surrounding this celebrated case? The crime took place in Queens, New York City, in 1925, the sixth year of Prohibition. It was a law generally ignored by the public, and bad law leads to lawless people. Prohibition was a disaster, causing the rise of such gangsters as Al Capone, who earned a fortune peddling bootleg liquor in seedy dives.

It was in 1925 that Ruth Snyder and Judd Gray first met and began their fatal liaison, brought together by mutual friends on a 'blind date'. They had dinner at Harry's Swedish Restaurant in New York City, drinking bootleg gin and swapping hard-luck stories. While they talked, Judd Gray, a meek corset salesman, gazed at the thirty-year-old blonde Ruth Snyder, an exotic woman of Swedish-Norwegian extraction, and fell instantly in love.

During the four hours they spent over that meal they exchanged life histories. Both, it seemed, were trapped in unhappy marriages. Ruth Snyder sighed as she pointed her shapely bosom at Gray, fiddling with her thick blonde hair as she told of how her husband Albert, who worked as a magazine editor and was thirteen years her senior, had taken advantage of her naivety and swept her off her feet when she was a mere nineteen-year-old girl in the typing pool. He was so mean, she said. But she was wearing a gray fox fur . . .

She was undoubtedly an attractive woman, her prominent thrusting jaw detracting little from her appearance. But if the face reveals the soul, that thrusting jaw was a sign of dominance.

Judd Gray was a thirty-two-year-old commercial traveller who earned just five thousand dollars a year – in a good year. He was slightly built, constantly blinking behind his wire-rimmed spectacles, and looked weak. But he was perfect slave material. He could be moulded. And he could never get over his luck at attracting such a glamourous woman. But maybe he thought he *deserved* something better from life. It was, after all, the Jazz Age, when the music promised 'anything goes'.

Mrs Ruth May Snyder chewed gum incessantly as she spoke about her unhappy marriage. Slipping her hand into Gray's beneath the table, she confided: 'He was so mean, that guy. He took me out dining and dancing then got real angry when I wouldn't come across and get in the sack with him. I was a self-respecting girl, so he changed his line. He bought me a box of chocolates with a diamond solitaire in them. Picture that! I was all of nineteen then . . . and he had this good job . . . On the day we got married I was too weak and faint to go to bed with him. He had to wait until I was better until he got his way. But to him I was never any better than an ex-switchboard operator who worked in the typing pool.' She spoke of frequent blazing rows followed by icy silences. Her husband did not love or respect her and she lived in a house of despair. It was a role Bette Davis could have played to perfection, and it never entered the mind of Judd Gray to doubt that this big strapping girl – even at age nineteen – could have been forced into a marriage she did not want.

For his part, Gray confessed that his wife Isabel was an 'invisible woman'. There were no rows in his home, just an insufferable boredom. His wife kept house well, cooked for him, looked after their child, but there was never any excitement in their drab relationship. He mourned the lack of 'romance' in his life. It was just a dull featureless terrain that he was forced to traverse every single waking day. And under the influence of the gin, he felt emboldened enough to say that he was 'damned sick' of it.

Ruth Snyder was more than willing to supply the romance – for a price. The price was that she wanted her husband killed. She had taken out an insurance policy on his life, without his knowledge, for fifty thousand dollars. It was double that in the event of accidental death . . . It was almost the plot of the later film *Double Indemnity*.

Ruth Snyder was due to go on a boating holiday with her husband and seven-year-old daughter Lorraine, so as they left Harry's Swedish Restaurant she arranged to meet Judd Gray again in August. 'Give me a ring,' she said. She played it casual, but with just enough barely concealed smouldering passion to keep Gray interested. What Gray did not know as he walked home that night, feeling ten feet tall, was that he was just another one of Ruth's 'men friends', the latest in a line of conquests with whom she danced, went to bed and drank beer. She could twist men around her little finger, but twisting one to kill was another matter. Gray seemed perfect, as malleable as plasticine . . . He was a weak character with a mother complex – ideal for her purposes.

Gray phoned her at her three-storey clapboard house at 9327 222nd Street, Queen's, New York City, on the night of 4 August, asking her to meet him at 'their place', Harry's Swedish Restaurant. After a meal of smörgasbord and several glasses of bootleg rye whiskey, Gray plucked up the courage to ask Ruth to come back with him to his office on 34th Street at Fifth Avenue, in the building belonging to the Bien Jolie Corset Company. Gray said he had to collect a case of samples – 'the latest thing in corselets'. He could never bring himself to utter the word 'corset'. It was too immodest.

Once inside his empty office, Ruth took off her scarf,

complaining of sunburn on her neck and shoulders. Gray was tender and solicitous, fetching camphor oil and rubbing it over her sore skin. 'Oh, that feels good,' she said. 'No one has ever been this kind to me.'

Gray was overcome. 'I've something else for you,' he muttered thickly. 'A new corselet. Please let me fit it on for you.'

'Okay,' Ruth smiled brightly. 'You can do that. And from now on you can call me Momsie.' And the couple then made love in that office, the first embrace in an affair which was to burn until March 1927. That first act of sex set the pattern for all that followed. He called her 'Momsie'. She called him 'Lover Boy'. They spent nights in Manhattan hotel bedrooms, sometimes even taking along little Lorraine Snyder to confer an air of respectability to their indiscretions. She stayed in the hotel lobby while the adults went upstairs to conduct 'business'. Gray was hooked, worshipping Ruth's naked body, showering her with caresses and calling her 'Momsie' or 'Queen'. She called him 'my baby'.

During the two-year affair, Ruth told Gray about the strange series of accidents which had befallen her husband, starting shortly after she began seeing Gray. He was once jacking up the family car to change a flat tyre when the jack slipped and he was nearly crushed under the vehicle. A few nights later, while cranking the engine, he hit his head and fell unconscious. Later that month he was in the garage at his home, lying under his Buick car tinkering with the accelerator controls with the engine running. Ruth brought him out a glass of whiskey, praising his skill as a mechanic. After drinking the liquor Mr Snyder felt very drowsy. He was almost asleep when he noticed that the garage doors had swung shut and he was trapped inside, inhaling deadly carbon monoxide fumes. He just managed to crawl out to fresh air before passing out. It appeared that Albert Snyder had survived several narrow escapes, including two poisonings and one gassing.

Ruth related all these accidents very innocently, but despite his passion Gray was no fool. He recognized what he was being told. 'What are you trying to do – kill the poor guy?' he asked.

'Momsie can't do it alone,' Ruth said demurely. 'She needs help. Lover Boy will have to help Momsie.' And, God help him, he did. Ruth told Gray that her husband had turned into 'a brute – a killer' and deserved to die. To sweeten the plan, she told Gray about the insurance money. In actual fact Albert Snyder was a quiet and inoffensive man who enjoyed outdoor activities like boating and fishing. He was a simple and honest soul, completely unaware that he had married a demon.

Perhaps Gray thought the talk of murdering Albert was just the result of too much drink, but when he next met Ruth she announced triumphantly that she had tricked her husband into taking out an insurance policy. 'He thinks it's only for a thousand dollars, but it's really for ninety-six thousand – if he dies by accident. I had him sign the policy without reading it.'

Albert Snyder survived three more near-fatal 'accidents'. In July 1926 he was nearly gassed while asleep on the living-room couch; in January 1927 he was taken violently ill after Ruth had given him 'medicine' for an attack of hiccoughs, and in February Ruth 'accidentally' turned on the gas tap in the living room. Luckily Albert detected it and switched it off. Albert never had a clue that attempts were being made on his life.

By now, through a mixture of sex and sweet talking, Gray had entered into the plot to kill the husband. It was during a night of love-making in a room at the Waldorf-Astoria Hotel in New York in February 1927 that Ruth outlined the details of the murder and gave Gray his instructions. When he was next out of town on business, he was to buy chloroform, some picture wire and a sash weight. 'That way we have three means of killing him,' she explained earnestly.

When Gray expressed reservations about the deed,

Ruth warned him sternly: 'If you don't do as I say, then that's the end of us in bed. You can find yourself another "Momsie" to sleep with.' Gray immediately caved in.

To prepare Gray for what he had to do, and make him familiar with her house, Ruth invited him home one evening when her husband and daughter were away. They got drunk together and – as Gray later testified – 'We went upstairs to her daughter's room where we had intercourse.' Even as she aroused him with erotic foreplay, Ruth was telling Gray what he had to do, step by step. The plan was to make it look as if the husband had been killed by a burglar he had disturbed. Ruth and Gray continued to meet, often with the daughter there too, and as new ideas came to her, Ruth would pass notes across the table to Gray. The daughter witnessed all this, but was unaware that she was listening to a plot to kill her father.

In the early hours of Sunday, 20 March, Gray entered the Snyders' house through an unlocked side door. He had taken a bus from downtown Manhattan to Queens, taking nips from a whiskey flask to fortify his courage. It was just after midnight. Ruth and her husband were out, playing bridge with a neighbour. They returned home at about two o'clock. Gray was hiding in the spare bedroom. The chloroform, picture wire and sash weight were lying on the bed, together with an Italian newspaper and a blue 'immigrant's' handkerchief which he had brought along to plant as false clues for the police.

Albert Snyder had been drinking heavily and lurched upstairs to bed, falling heavily across the mattress. Ruth slipped into the spare bedroom to warn Gray to be ready. After kissing him she went to her husband's bed. At three in the morning she crept out to join Gray again, taking a hefty gulp of his whiskey. 'Okay,' she whispered. 'This is it.'

Gray pulled on long rubber gloves to avoid leaving fingerprints, and carried the sash weight in his hand. Ruth Snyder carried the chloroform and picture wire.

They entered the bedroom and Gray stood gazing down at his sleeping rival – the only time he had ever seen the man. Then he raised the sash weight and brought it crashing down on the head of Albert Snyder.

Like some horrible nightmare the sleeping man woke and started to fight violently for his life, striking out at his unseen attacker and grabbing him by his tie. The sash weight slipped from Gray's nerveless hand, and the husband cried out piteously: 'Help me, Momsie! For God's sake help me!'

Ruth Snyder picked up the sash weight and swung it down on her husband's skull with all her force. Albert remained alive, his body twitching as Ruth stuffed chloroform-soaked cotton wool into his mouth and nostrils, and then neatly tied his hands and feet, before strangling him with the picture wire, her strong muscular arms performing with effortless grace. She hadn't needed Gray at all; she had simply wanted a patsy.

It had been a brutal murder, a scene reminiscent of *Macbeth*, save that Ruth Snyder would never have been troubled by conscience or plagued with invisible spots of blood.

There was blood everywhere: it had been quite literally bloody murder. Ruth's nightdress was soaked with it, as were the gloves she had worn. Gray's shirt and trousers were also soaked with the victim's blood.

For the next hour the murderous couple busied themselves in cleaning up, washing the blood from their bodies and changing their clothing. Gray put on one of Albert's shirts. Then they proceeded to set the scene to look like a burglary gone wrong. Gray hid the sash weight in the cellar. Ruth took her jewellery and furs and hid them. They disarranged the furniture on the ground floor to make it look as if the house had been ransacked. Then, after a final kiss to seal their bloody deed, Gray tied up Ruth and fastened a gag over her mouth, leaving her lying in the spare bedroom. He carefully placed the false clues in the room – the Italian newspaper and handkerchief.

Before leaving to book into the Onondaga Hotel in Syracuse, Kansas, to resume his corset-selling trade on the Monday, Gray took one final look at his mistress. We cannot know what thoughts went through his mind. Perhaps it was revulsion at what they had done together, or even a feeling that they were now inextricably bonded. But he said: 'It may be two months, it may be a year, before you'll see me again.' Then he left.

Ruth Snyder lay tied up all night, until found by her daughter Lorraine next morning. When the daughter untied her mother and removed the gag, Ruth told her to run to get help. Lorraine ran to the next-door neighbours, and within a minute or so Ruth was babbling out her well-rehearsed story to Harriet and Louis Mulhauser.

'It was dreadful!' she cried hysterically. 'Just dreadful! I was attacked by a prowler . . . he tied me up . . . He must have been after my jewels . . . ' And then last of all: 'Is Albert all right?'

Mr Mulhauser went to the main bedroom and took one look. In that vividly etched moment he saw the blood, the two gaping wounds to the head, and knew that Albert was dead. White-faced and trembling he returned to the 'victim', shaking his head sadly. Then the police were called.

Neighbours were one thing, but hard-nosed detectives were another, not so easily impressed or so quick to believe. They listened to Ruth Snyder's story with growing scepticism. They made her repeat it many times, and it sounded weaker with each telling.

Asked to describe her attacker, Mrs Snyder said: 'He was a big, rough-looking guy of about thirty-five with a black moustache. He was a foreigner, I guess. Some kind of Italian.' She first told her story to the doctor called to the house by the police to examine the corpse and treat the surviving victim. After examining the woman and finding no signs of assault – no bruises or abrasions of any kind – Dr Harry Hansen reported to the police that he felt that Mrs Snyder's account was 'a fabrication of lies'.

Over sixty policemen were at the Snyders' house by now, taking photographs and searching for clues. Police Commissioner George McLaughlin questioned the pale and trembling Ruth Snyder, together with his assistant, Inspector Arthur Carey. The questioning went on for twelve hours and was a good old-fashioned 'grilling'.

'This doesn't look like a burglary to me,' the policeman said bluntly. 'I have investigated hundreds of burglaries, and they just aren't done like this. Burglars don't kill, either, as a rule. They might hit out in panic, but why tie the hands and legs? Why the gag? All this furniture disturbed like this – it doesn't make sense. It would have made the job of finding valuables harder, not easier . . . '

'What do I know about burglars?' Ruth Snyder retorted defensively. The policemen thought it was an inside job; they made no secret of their suspicion. And when the missing jewels were found under a mattress and the missing furs in a closet, they were certain.

An address book belonging to Ruth Snyder had been examined and the names of twenty-eight men noted. The name of Judd Gray stood out because police also found a cancelled cheque made out to him for two hundred dollars. Mrs Snyder was taken to the nearest police station for questioning, and was tricked into making a confession. Under modern rules relating to police questioning of suspects, her confession would have been ruled invalid by the court and thrown out. Then it was accepted practice, as was quite brutal 'third-degree' questioning.

The Commissioner glared sternly at Mrs Snyder and told her: 'We have arrested Judd Gray and he has told us everything, so you might as well come clean . . . ' He had not been arrested, of course, or even traced at this point.

Ruth Snyder immediately broke down. Admitting the plot to murder her husband for the insurance, she said

173

the plot had been all Gray's idea. 'I didn't aim a single blow at Albert,' she protested. 'It was all Judd's doing. At the last moment I tried to stop him – but it was too late.'

By now the bloodstained sash weight had been found in the basement of the Snyder home, as had the insurance policies which made Albert Snyder worth more dead than alive. The order went out to apprehend Gray, and the corset salesman was arrested within hours at his Syracuse hotel. In a state of total moral collapse, he was taken by train to New York City under police escort. Officers told him that Albert Snyder had not died from the blows to his skull, but had been rendered unconscious with chloroform and then strangled while unconscious. By the time he was taken from the train and placed in a police car in New York, Judd Gray had already made a statement admitting his participation in the crime.

He made no attempt to shield his lover, detailing all the plans she had made for the killing. 'I would never have killed Snyder but for her,' he wept. 'She had this power over me. She told me what to do and I just did it.'

The sensational trial of the pair the press had labelled 'Granite Woman' and 'Lover Boy' began in Queens County Courthouse on 18 April 1927 and lasted eighteen days, filling the tabloid press with lurid accounts of the 'diabolical duo'. Ruth Snyder dressed in black – as if in mourning – a large crucifix prominent on her breast. Gray wore a double-breasted blue pin-stripe suit. He looked drab.

Peggy Hopkins Joyce, queen of the sob-sister reporters, was reporting from her seat in the press box in the court for the New York *Daily Mirror*. She wrote: 'Poor Judd Gray! He hasn't IT, he hasn't anything. He was just a sap who was kissed and told on! . . .

'This putty man was wonderful modelling material for the Swedish-Norwegian vampire . . . She was passionate and she was cold-blooded, if anybody can imagine such a combination. Her passion was for Gray; her cold-bloodedness for her husband . . . You know women can do things to men that make men crazy. I mean, they can exert their influence over them in such a way that men will do almost anything for them. And I guess that is what Ruth did to Judd.'

But the real delight of this case was the fact that Damon Runyan also reported the trial, and his account makes fascinating and hilarious reading, worthy of Mark Twain himself. In his report he penned the classic definition of the good liar.

Relating how she performed under cross-examination by the prosecutor, Runyon wrote: 'She is a magnificent liar, if she is lying. You must give her that. And if she is a liar she is a game liar, one of those "that's my story and I'll stick to it" liars, which is the mark of the able liar.

'And I regret to report that she seems to impress many of her listeners in the light of a wonderful liar rather than as a poor widowed soul falsely accused. The men were rather softening up to the blonde woman at the close yesterday in sheer admiration of her as a possible liar, and even the women who leer at her all day long had stopped hating her. They seemed to be commencing to think that she was reflecting credit to femininity just as a prodigious liar . . .

'Most of her answers were sharp yesses or noes. In fact, Froessel insisted on yes-or-no answers, though sometimes she whipped in a few additional remarks to his great annoyance. He hectored and badgered the blonde at times until her counsel objected and the Court admonished him. Froessel, a plump-built man of medium height, in his early forties, has a harsh voice and a nagging manner in cross-examination. He wears spectacles and is clean-shaven and persistent, and there is no doubt that Mrs Snyder at times wished she had a sash weight handy . . . '

On 9 May the jury found Snyder and Gray guilty as charged, and they were both sentenced to die in the electric chair at Sing Sing. While on Death Row both wrote their autobiographies, and Ruth Snyder received hundreds of proposals of marriage from men anxious to serve under her in the event that she was spared.

In his autobiography Gray wrote of his marriage: 'Isabel, I suppose, one would call a home girl; she had never trained for a career of any kind. She was learning to cook and was a careful and exceptionally exact housekeeper. As I think it over searchingly I am not sure, and we were married these many years, of her ambitions, hopes, her fears or her ideals – we made our home, drove our car, played bridge with our friends, danced, raised our child – ostensibly together – married. Never could I seem to attain with her the comradeship that formed the bond between my mother and myself.'

On 12 January 1928, their appeals having been rejected, Snyder and Gray went to the electric chair within four minutes of each other. A remarkable feature of the execution was that an enterprising press photographer, with a camera strapped to his ankle, managed to get a picture of Ruth Snyder at the moment of her death, a photograph which appeared on the covers of the tabloids and became a classic of the genre.

In death the pair were reunited when they were laid out side by side on the stone slabs in the prison's autopsy room. Gray had rejected 'Granite Woman' but she had undergone a religious conversion in the Death House and written him a fond poem. However, another of her efforts at verse attacked the public and the authorities:

> You've blackened and besmeared a mother,
> Once a man's plaything – a Toy –
> What have you gained by all you've said,
> And has it – brought you Joy?

She went on to record how much she was looking forward to going to heaven – which must be the triumph of religious hope over experience. She deserved hell for what she did to her husband. But gazing at the photograph of her, trapped forever in her final agony, it is impossible not to forgive her. If it was a crime of passion it was a cold and calculated one, but she paid for it. How she paid . . . But then, so did her patsy.

12
THE PUB 'PASSION' KILLING
1984

It was a murder case with a distinctly old-fashioned flavour; but then passion between a man and woman has long been a potent motive for murder. This case had the sleazy, humid atmosphere of James M. Cain's *The Postman Always Rings Twice* – that tough, gritty thriller, a surprise best-seller in the thirties, which brought a scorching slice of real life to the highly mannered novels of the time. The story is a terse, first-person account of how the passion between a man and woman drives them to murder the woman's husband. Frank Chambers is a drifter who arrives at a diner owned by Nick, a middle-aged Greek with a beautiful young wife. An affair begins between Chambers and the wife, and with grim inevitability they arrive at the decision to kill the husband. But the act of murder itself drives them apart; the world is not big enough for two people with their terrible secret, and they eventually turn on one another in their haste to lay the blame . . .

The Jones and Tillotson case followed this classic pattern, almost as if they were acting out a script. It was an old-fashioned location – a seaside resort – and even the policeman heading the murder inquiry had a name which might have come straight out of a Dorothy L. Sayers mystery: Detective Chief Superintendent Strickland Carter. And to add a further fictional allusion, the Superintendent sports an ornate waxed moustache like that of Hercules Poirot.

In 1972 attractive dark-haired Gail from Farnham,

Buckinghamshire, a girl just out of her teens, met Graham Jones on a holiday cruise. It was love at first sight, and a whirlwind courtship ensued. For Graham the attraction may have been purely physical, but for Gail it was probably because women in general are attracted to men who seem to know where they are going and project a sense of determination and purpose.

Graham Jones was a time-and-motion engineer in Coventry, and the couple lived in that city after they were married in 1973. Later, seeking better opportunities, Graham took up a similar position in Wetherby in Yorkshire. The couple seemed reasonably happy, and by now had two young children. For some reason Graham decided to change his career. He had always wanted to run a pub – a common ambition, but most who try it find financial ruin rather than success. However, Graham was a professional man; his risks were carefully calculated equations. The couple obtained a licence to manage the Belle Vue Hotel in Filey, a popular seaside resort. They moved into the pub in September 1981, and Graham soon showed his mettle. Northerners do not take easily to strangers, but as a keen sportsman Graham was soon running the local football team. The couple were popular in the town: an attractive young couple with two young daughters and a successful business.

In fact business *was* thriving, so much so that Graham felt he needed more help behind the bar. One of his regular customers was twenty-nine-year-old Rod Tillotson, who had a reputation for being a 'ladies' man'. Women were attracted to him because of his raffish nature, but men felt threatened by his display of macho virility. However, Graham felt secure enough in his marriage to offer Tillotson part-time work at the busy period over Christmas 1983. By the following March Tillotson was a full-time barman. An employee of the man he was to murder . . .

For all his time-and-motion expertise, Graham had not bothered to check into Tillotson's background, simply accepting him at face value. Had he researched a little he might well have saved his life. Tillotson was a drifter with an eye to the main chance. Born at Brookby, near Rugby, he left school aged fifteen and spent a year at an agricultural college. It was not to his liking and he left, working for his father's small domestic appliance business in between other casual jobs. At one period he lived in Manchester for two years and became a railway guard.

In 1975 he married, and lived with his wife and daughter in Manchester. The marriage went sour and they moved South, taking a farm labouring job with a tied cottage. The change of scene did not help and they separated. His wife finally divorced him for 'unreasonable behaviour' after seven years of marriage. It was after the break-up of his marriage that Tillotson went to live with his elderly parents in Filey. Their council flat adjoined the Belle Vue Hotel ... He was an unstable character with a touch of the chancer about him – not the kind of man anyone would want to bring into contact with their home and family.

Tillotson got on well with the family, making it his business to ingratiate himself with the children, Helen, aged five, and Karen, who was eight. He served behind the bar with his boss's wife and partnered her in the pool team. Soon he was making the odd flirtatious pass, and Gail was entranced. It was the old story of a woman finding a slightly villainous man more attractive than a stuffy, respectable husband. There were snatched kisses when nobody was looking, more serious embraces when Graham Jones had a night off or went to visit his elderly mother in the South. Some of the 'goings-on' would have shocked locals, had they known, and, far from being romantic, sex on the floor of a pub was merely a sordid coupling.

But it was a strange thing: at first, just like in the James M. Cain novel, Tillotson saw Gail Jones as just another conquest, someone he could manipulate. But then it all turned upside-down because *he* became the infatuated one – and the secret love triangle at the seaside pub made him crazy enough to kill for her.

Six weeks before his death, rumours of his wife's affair reached Graham Jones's ears. He challenged the guilty pair but accepted their denials, their claim that they were the victims of vicious tongues. On the night of his death he was upstairs in the flat above the pub, leaving his wife and Tillotson to clear up.

While Graham was relaxing, examining his stamp collection through a magnifying glass, Tillotson, just six months after starting work at the pub, was nerving himself to carry out the grim arrangement which he and Gail Jones had made. Graham was in the way. He had to be got rid of – and if Tillotson needed any inducement other than her body, Gail Jones could remind him of the £64,000 insurance policy on her husband's life.

It was a warm July evening in 1984, the day chosen for the murder after weeks of careful planning. The scheme was simple: to fake an armed robbery by unknown assailants which would leave Graham Jones dead. For all the planning, over countless cups of coffee at secret assignations, the actual execution of the murder was a botched and clumsy affair.

Long after the pub had closed for the night, at about 1 a.m., Tillotson lured Graham downstairs by shouting up to him that Gail had fainted. As Graham, who had run downstairs in alarm, bent over his seemingly unconscious wife, Tillotson hit him over the head with a pickaxe handle, raining blows on his skull. After five blows the killer paused. The sight of so much blood had unnerved him.

Gail Jones urged him to 'finish the job'. More blows struck her hapless husband, twelve of them in all, splitting his skull apart, before he was left dying in a pool of blood. Even then, his wife covered his mouth with her hand to ensure his suffocation.

The highly charged atmosphere of the killing left the pair feeling slightly hysterical, giggling over the fact that they had broken the ultimate taboo. But they calmly carried out the rest of their elaborate scheme. Tillotson changed out of his blood-spattered clothing, handing it to Gail Jones to wash later, while she removed the takings from the till to fake robbery. Then, on his signal, she struck Tillotson two blows with the murder weapon for the sake of realism, and threw a tray of glasses over him as he lay feigning unconsciousness.

With the scene set, a sobbing Gail Jones phoned for the police and ambulance, telling of a raid on the pub by two men whom she had seen running away. According to her story, they had killed her husband, attacked the barman, and stolen the night's takings.

The police initially accepted her story, putting out descriptions of the wanted men and launching a full-scale murder hunt. It was, after all, a case of murder – the first in Filey for a hundred years. The barman was taken to hospital and the grief-stricken widow was questioned gently. Her story was that she had been upstairs in the flat when she heard noises from downstairs. 'Thudding noises,' she said. She came downstairs to find her husband dead and the barman injured, with two men running away. She was able to supply detailed descriptions of both men.

Within days the police had become suspicious and started looking inside the case rather than outside. Questioning of locals revealed that the affair between Gail Jones and the barman was common knowledge, despite her attempts to be discreet. The main point of suspicion was that parts of the stories given by the barman and the wife did not tally. Once again, as is so often the case, it was forensic science which was to point to the solution.

Meanwhile there was an embarrassing police *faux pas*. Two days after the murder the flat above the pub was searched, in case the killers had left clues up there. Police were convinced that the murder weapon had been an iron bar, and when Detective Constable Stephen Ridley found a pickaxe handle under Gail Jones's mattress, he replaced it on the instructions of senior officers. Gail Jones was later to chop it up, burn the pieces in the kitchen stove and throw the ashes in the sea off Flamborough Head. Fortunately, there was sufficient remaining scientific evidence to convict the guilty pair.

The painstaking forensic examination at the scene of the crime alerted detectives to discrepancies in the story of a robbery gone wrong. Tillotson said he had collected the glasses from the *downstairs* bar and was on his way upstairs when he was attacked. He never saw who hit him, he said. Every single glass was fingerprinted and each customer who had used a glass eliminated. All had been in the *upstairs* bar: no one had been downstairs. Tillotson could not therefore have collected those glasses from downstairs, as he claimed, and must be lying.

His shoes bore traces of Graham Jones's blood, as did the blouse Gail Jones had been wearing. She claimed it came from having cradled her husband's head against her breast; what she did not know was that scientists had also found blood on the *back* of her blouse. The paper till-roll was also missing, which would have revealed exactly how much had been stolen. Gail Jones had inflated the real amount.

Four weeks after the murder Detective Chief Superintendent Strickland Carter arrested the couple, telling them bluntly: 'You have been telling us a load of rubbish.' Questioned separately, Tillotson soon cracked, telling of the *'femme fatale'* who had led him into murder. When each was confronted with statements made by the other, they rushed to make fresh statements to implicate the other further. It was left to a jury to untangle the web of lies and deceit.

The trial began at York Crown Court on Monday, 17 June 1985, with Jones and Tillotson, charged jointly with the murder of Graham Jones, pleading not guilty. It was significant that the former lovers sat as far apart from each other as possible in the dock. Gail Jones sobbed continously as she listened to Mr Simon Hawkesworth,

QC, open the case for the prosecution by telling the jury of a ruthless murder plot involving a fake robbery.

The jury were told of the affair between Jones and Tillotson, and how the lovers betrayed the husband at every opportunity then decided upon his murder. The prosecution said Tillotson had confessed to the police that the murder had been 'carefully planned' several days before the event. Tillotson had been obsessed with Gail Jones; she declared her love for him but said she could not leave her two children and did not know what to do. The husband was the obstacle . . .

Mr Hawkesworth said that Tillotson then suggested that Graham Jones could easily be killed 'accidentally' if he was knocked unconscious in the pub cellar and a beer barrel fell on his head. Mr Hawkesworth continued: 'Tillotson eventually hit on a plan which had been discussed earlier, when they met for coffee in the town.'

The prosecutor described the murder, the subsequent cover-up, and the charade of the fake robbery with a hysterical Gail Jones phoning the police to tell how she had come downstairs to find her husband lying dead in a pool of blood, Tillotson unconscious, and two men running away. He listed the forensic clues which had cast doubts on their story: bloodstains on their clothing, the wrong fingerprints on glasses, the hiding of the murder weapon under Gail Jones's mattress, and the washing machine running in the early hours of the morning – attempting to wash blood from Tillotson's clothing.

Tillotson told police that he had kissed Gail Jones as her husband lay dying, saying to her: 'I love you.' She had replied that no matter what happened, she would always love him. But that love did not even survive the moment of arrest, and it was love-turned-sour in the dock. Gail Jones, said Mr Hawkesworth, had admitted assisting an offender, knowing Tillotson was guilty of murder. But Tillotson had counter-claimed that the murder had been her idea and that she had put her hand over her husband's mouth to suffocate him.

184

Continuing his opening address the following day, Mr Hawkesworth spoke of the 'crocodile tears' shed by Tillotson after the killing. He had been interviewed in his hospital bed, where he was being treated for the injuries caused by the imaginary robbers. He told the police that he did not see who had hit him. When told Graham Jones was dead, he began crying, saying: 'Why Graham? He has not done anything wrong to anyone. He wasn't just a boss, he was a good friend. If I could help you I would, but I can't tell you anything.'

The first witness called was an ambulanceman who had gone to the pub in response to an emergency call. He said the sight which greeted him was the worst in his twenty-three years' experience. But he did recall one odd fact: when he helped Mrs Jones up to her flat above the pub, the washing machine was going, at after 2 a.m . . .

On the third day of the trial, Gail Jones went into the witness box to testify on her own behalf. Claiming she had been helpless to prevent her husband being clubbed to death, she said her lover, Tillotson, had told her that he had killed her husband so that they could be together. As her husband lay dying, she said, Tillotson looked up at her and said: 'I told you that one day I would prove how much I loved you – now do you believe me?' Gail Jones was playing the role of the intimidated wife, frightened of Tillotson but grieving for her husband. She claimed she had believed that Tillotson was joking when he spoke of 'possible accidents' which might befall her husband.

She had to admit to having had sex with Tillotson – 'about three times' – if only because she had been pregnant by the man, but she claimed she ended the relationship prior to the murder because it was getting too serious. She had never wanted to kill her husband, neither had she discussed such a terrible thing with her lover.

Her story was a neat reversal of the original plot. She had fainted while behind the bar. When she came to it was to hear 'thudding noises'. She saw Tillotson battering her husband with a pickaxe handle, and watched with horror as he struck her husband at least ten times. She claimed she tried vainly to stop him. She trembled in the dock as she spoke, the very picture of terrified innocence. Why, she was asked, had she gone along with the cover-up about a fake robbery? Because she was frightened of Tillotson, she said, and was also afraid that the police might think she had been part of it all.

She went on to tell the jury she had subsequently discovered the reason she had fainted that night was because she was pregnant by Tillotson. She went on: 'I didn't want to believe it. I took a second test. I couldn't believe I was carrying the child of the man who had killed my husband. I was going out of my mind and I got rid of it.' She added that she was worried the pregnancy might add weight to Tillotson's story that they had planned the murder together. Three weeks after her arrest she had an abortion in prison, while awaiting her trial.

Cross-examined, she said she was sure the baby was Tillotson's. Her husband had had a vasectomy. As for the £64,000 insurance policy on her husband's life, she said the suggestion that the policy was in her mind before the murder was 'completely untrue'. Mr Gilbert Gray, QC, defending Tillotson, attacked her in cross-examination, saying she had 'lied and lied again' to the police and was now lying to the jury. She shook her head in denial of the accusation. Mr Gray went on to suggest that she had 'wound up' Tillotson into taking part in the murder by telling him of how her husband beat her and wanted to have 'unnatural' sex. Mr Gray, looking directly at Gail Jones, said: 'You, with cold-blooded determination, plotted the slaughter of your own husband.' He turned his back in contempt at Jones's denial.

Mr Gray went on to say that although she had shown the 'tearful dejection' of a grief-stricken widow in the dock, she had in fact been laughing in the cells below the court. Jones indignantly denied this, saying her reactions in the dock were genuine. Mr Gray put it to her that she had once been caught by her husband having sex in the bar with a customer. Jones denied that sex had taken place. She and the customer had both been drunk and ended up with some clothing removed. When her husband found them, the man fled. Mr Gray suggested that she had encouraged the man's advances. Jones replied: 'I came on too strong. I didn't want intercourse with him. I wasn't prepared to let that happen.'

Tillotson followed her into the witness box to give a very different version of events. He said he had fallen deeply in love with Gail Jones and was disgusted to learn of her husband's sexual fetishes. They wanted to be together and Gail Jones suggested that they should kill her husband. He told the jury that just before the murder he had asked his lover if she could go through with the killing. She replied: 'Yes, I'm sure. I love you, and it's the only way we can be together.' He said he had told her: 'You realize we are talking murder?' She had replied: 'Yes.'

He said that Gail Jones first suggested murder; they had sex on the floor of the pub months before the killing, and slept together regularly when the husband was away. Gail complained that her husband forced her into sex by 'pushing her around', made her watch blue movies, and wanted to send nude photographs of her to contact magazines and perform perverted sexual acts with her.

He had thought Gail was joking when she first suggested killing her husband, but she persisted, saying: 'The only way we can be together is to get rid of him, to kill him.' The discussion went on for two or three months before he suggested a fake robbery as a cover for the murder. But, he added, it was she who perfected the details of the plot and chose the night of the murder. Describing how he had battered Graham Jones with the pickaxe handle, he said Gail Jones had said: 'He's still alive. Finish him off!' Tillotson said he had replied: 'I can't. I can't hit him any more. I can't go through with it.' But she had insisted firmly: 'Finish him off!'

187

On the Monday of the second week of the trial, all the evidence having been heard, dissected and challenged, it was time for the closing speeches from the prosecution and defence counsel. Mr Simon Hawkesworth invited the jury to find both defendants guilty of murder. He said that Gail Jones had been unmasked as 'a hard and callous woman' by a single remark. When the police put it to her that she was part of the murder plot, she had replied scornfully: 'I like to think if I had planned it I would have made a better bloody job of it.'

Mr Hawkesworth said that Jones had taken part in the laying of the false trail for the police for two reasons: 'Hatred for her husband and because she was determined that neither she nor Rod Tillotson would be found out.' He said that her account of having gone along with the cover-up because she feared implication in the murder 'defied common sense, because if he had been solely responsible, Tillotson would not have left to chance her cooperation in the cover-up of a fake robbery'. He said that Jones had been reminded of the insurance on her husband shortly before the murder.

Mr Gilbert Gray, for Tillotson, said that his client had been provoked into murder by Jones, and invited the jury to return a manslaughter verdict against him. He said that Jones had 'wept without a tear' in the witness box, and his client regretted ever getting involved with a *femme fatale* who could play a tune with his emotions.

Mr Barry Mortimer, QC, for Jones, said that Tillotson had been overwhelmed by hatred and jealousy and had seized his chance to carry out the killing, forcing his client against her will to become a reluctant accomplice.

Mr Gilbert Gray had earlier praised the police for their honesty in telling the court of their mistake when they found the murder weapon but allowed it to slip out of their grasp. He said it was 'the most embarrassing piece of evidence in the case' for the police, but it showed 'the chilling cynicism and hypocrisy' which led Jones to hide the murder weapon in the bed she had shared with her husband – and victim.

On Tuesday, 25 June 1985, the jury retired. It took them two and a quarter hours to conclude unanimously that both the accused were guilty. Jones stood pale and shaking as the verdicts were announced, then fainted into the arms of prison warders as the judge pronounced life sentences on them both. Tillotson remained impassive. A doctor was called to treat Jones in the cells, before she was taken by taxi to prison, where she will have plenty of time to reflect on the 'bloody job' she and her lover carried out.

After the case, Detective Chief Superintendent Strickland Carter had the last word. He said: 'Hers was a play-act from beginning to end. She was arrested because she overacted, and I had a gut feeling she was putting on a show. She maintained it to the end, even with the stage-managed collapse in the dock.'

It was indeed a very old-fashioned case . . .

13

ELVIRA BARNEY, 1932: DEATH AMONG THE 'BRIGHT YOUNG PEOPLE'

A scrap of memorabilia of one of the most sensational pre-war murder trials was sold at auction in Edinburgh in October 1989. It fetched just £190. Had I known about the sale, I might just have been tempted to put in a bid myself for the item, which was a sampler embroidered by Elvira Barney. Typically, it was a poem about a woman in love with two men, and contained the line: 'She is best who loves a lot.' Elvira died young, quite worn out by love, and the sampler remains an echo of a tragic and doomed young woman and a reminder of an unforgettable case.

Elvira Dolores Barney was a member of the 'Lost Generation' in the period between the two world wars known in America as the 'Jazz Age'. In England people like Elvira were regarded as 'bohemian' and were looked at askance because of their unconventional attitude towards life. Coming from wealthy privileged backgrounds, they rejected the values of their society and current morality. Elvira lived life to the full – and paid the price. She was 'lost' both spiritually and psychologically, and was to become her own executioner.

In many ways the 'Bright Young Things' – so savagely mocked by Evelyn Waugh in his novels – lived a seedy and dishonest kind of existence. Although they rejected their parents' values, they did not reject their wealth, and lived lives of conspicuous consumption, running about in smart little sports cars and playing practical jokes –

pinching a bobby's helmet was considered the height of fun – and drinking themselves into a stupor at Champagne parties at the most expensive nightclubs.

They were parasites, flaunting their extravagance in an England which was in the middle of a slump, with millions out of work and condemned to live on the 'means test'. Such was the economic crisis that the Government ordered all its employees – civil servants, policemen, teachers, members of the Armed Forces – to take a ten per cent cut in pay. Sailors in the Royal Navy refused to accept the cut in pay, and the Home Fleet mutinied at Invergordon in 1931.

Elvira Barney was the eldest daughter of Sir John Mullens, an Old Etonian and pillar of the Establishment. He was a Government stockbroker. The younger daughter married a prince. Elvira, undoubtedly a beautiful woman, flirted with the idea of becoming an actress and went on the stage as part of the chorus at the Gaiety Theatre under the name Dolores Ashley. Here she met John Sterling Barney, an American singer who was appearing in cabaret in London in an act known as the 'Three New Yorkers'.

Elvira, just twenty-two, fell in love with the handsome American and they quickly married – much to the shock and distress of her family. However, it was not a happy relationship and her husband soon left her to return to the United States. Elvira had a flat in Knightsbridge, at 21 William Mews, not far from the house of her wealthy parents in Belgravia. She continued to live there alone after her marriage had ended, and took part in a hectic round of parties. They were days of wine and roses; parties which lasted all night and ended only with the dregs of dawn.

By 1932 Elvira was beginning to lose her looks. Her debauched life-style showed in her features and her thickening waistline. She was certainly spoilt, and may well have been a nymphomaniac. Apart from the obligatory cocktail cabinet, her flat was furnished with a collection of instruments of sexual perversion and pornographic books. She had a preference for young lovers from the homosexual underworld, and in the course of her round of parties she met Michael Scott Stephen, a handsome young man who was the son of a well-known banker and who described himself as a dress designer. He was three years younger than the twenty-seven-year-old Elvira, and bisexual. Since his father had cut off his allowance because of his dissolute ways, he was content to spend the odd night with Elvira in her mews flat and, in effect, to live off her.

He had been living in a bedsit in Brompton Road, sponging off rich women when he could. His wild and abandoned love-making with Elvira was usually followed by violent arguments because of her jealousy over his other women, but finally he moved in with her permanently. The need for security overcame his aversion to screaming battles with his mistress.

The couple should have enjoyed an idyllic existence in a comfortably furnished flat replete with all the luxuries which money could buy; but the relationship was always a turbulent one, with a hint of viciousness never far from the surface.

On the evening of 30 May 1932, Elvira and her lover threw a party at the flat, and from seven o'clock onwards cars began arriving and parking in the narrow mews. The throng of socialites who came to the party kept the mews rocking all evening with loud music and shrill laughter. The last guests left shortly after ten, when Elvira and Michael Stephen left the flat to attend a Soho night-club – the Blue Angel Club in Dean Street – returning home at about four in the morning of 31 May.

Soon afterwards the neighbours were disturbed by a noisy argument coming from 21 William Mews. There was screaming and shouting, followed by the sound of breaking glass. Then they heard Mrs Barney pleading: 'Chicken! Chicken! Come back to me!' This was followed by a woman's screams and then a loud gunshot. The neighbours had by now abandoned any thoughts of sleep. Mrs Barney telephoned her doctor, Thomas Durrant, exclaiming frantically: 'Come at once – there's been a terrible accident.'

Mr Durrant, a prominent London physician, arrived on the scene and found Michael Scott Stephen lying dead on the landing, his legs draped down the stairs. He was fully dressed, and through the lapel of his jacket was a bullet-hole. The bullet, which had penetrated his chest, must have led to death within a very short time. Lying near the dead man's left wrist was a loaded revolver.

Mrs Barney was hysterical, screaming at the doctor: 'He can't be dead! I love him so . . . He wanted to see you to tell you that it was an accident . . . Let me die, let me die, I will kill myself.' Dr Durrant had to put his foot firmly on the revolver to prevent her from seizing it.

He tried to soothe the frantic woman, at the same time getting out of her, in disjointed sentences, an account of what had happened. She said she and Michael had had a quarrel. Michael had taken up a revolver from a chair, where it was hidden under a cushion. She grabbed for the gun and there was a struggle, during which the gun went off, killing him. As he lay dying he told her to call a doctor.

The doctor telephoned the police, as was his duty, and waited with Mrs Barney. Detective Inspector Winter arrived shortly afterwards from Scotland Yard. Having ascertained that the victim was indeed dead, he first examined the five-chambered revolver. Two cartridges had been discharged, and three live bullets remained in the weapon. He examined the scene of the incident, noting that the bed in Mrs Barney's room bore signs of having been occupied by two people, and he also noticed a bullet-hole in the wall. However, someone had dug the bullet out of the plaster.

A sign of how the upper classes could literally get away with murder was illustrated by the fact that when the inspector tried to question her, Elvira – who had been sitting in a chair near the body, sobbing and rocking backwards and forwards in extreme grief and agitation – suddenly flew in a rage at the officer, shouting hysterical abuse and slapping his face. She ordered him out of the flat, adding: 'I'll teach you to try and put me in a cell, you fat swine!' She was not arrested and taken to a police station, as would have been the fate of any ordinary woman. She was allowed to remain in her flat, waiting for her parents.

When they arrived she went with them to the police station and made a statement explaining how the 'accident' had occurred. There had been an argument over another woman. Then came the struggle for the revolver – 'and as we were struggling together it went off'. She telephoned for a doctor at her dying lover's request.

Her statement began:

Yes, I shall have to tell you sooner or later. I might as well tell you now . . . I know a man called Michael Scott Stephen, of Tenshurst, Kent . . . We were great friends and he used to come and see me from time to time . . . He always used to see me home; last night he did so as usual . . . Immediately we got in we had a quarrel over a woman he was fond of. He knew I kept a revolver in the house . . . last night it was under a cushion on a chair near the bed. He knew where it was and got it, saying: 'I am going to take it away from you for fear you will kill yourself.' He took it and went out of the room. I ran after him, trying to get it back . . . as we were struggling together it went off. He went to the bathroom and half-shut the door. He then said: 'Fetch a doctor.'

I rang up the doctor and no one answered. I went upstairs again and saw him sitting on the floor. I again tried to ring up the doctor. When I went back he said: 'Quickly. Quickly. Why does a doctor not come? I want to tell him it was not your fault.'

I again rang up the doctor and they said he was leaving . . . I again went upstairs and saw that he was dead. I don't remember what I did afterwards. I was so frantic . . . as far as I know there was only one shot.'

Having signed her statement, Mrs Barney was allowed to leave the police station and go home with her parents. Meanwhile the police acted swiftly, before the aristocracy could mount any cover-up. The famous pathologist Sir Bernard Spilsbury was roused from his bed, as was noted firearms expert Robert Churchill. They were asked to go and examine the scene of the shooting in the mews flat. Churchill examined the revolver, a Smith & Wesson .32, and came to the conclusion that it could not have been fired accidentally. It required too strong a pull on the trigger for that. Spilsbury agreed with the view that it could not have been an accidental death. There was no scorching or powder-burn on Stephen's clothing, as there should have been if the gun had been discharged during a struggle with the couple close together. The evidence was consistent with the view that the gun had been fired from some distance away. In other words, Mrs Barney deliberately shot her lover dead, making it a case of murder.

The police questioned the neighbours. One had heard Mrs Barney threaten to shoot Stephen, while another had heard more than one shot. They told of how, a few days earlier, a nude Mrs Barney had leaned out of her mews window and shot at her lover in the street below. The picture which emerged was one of a woman of strong temper who was used to getting her own way, and who had killed her lover when he threatened to leave her.

Events moved rapidly after that. On 3 June the inquest was opened before the Westminster coroner, and was adjourned until 16 June to allow the police time to complete their inquiries. At 5.30 p.m. on that same day the body of Stephen was cremated. At 6 p.m. there was a conference of senior officers at Scotland Yard, and at 8 p.m. Mrs Barney was arrested and charged with the wilful murder of Stephen. Her answer to the charge was: 'I didn't shoot him. I am not guilty.'

The following day a black-clad Mrs Barney, with two gardenias in her hat, appeared in the dock at Westminster

Police Court. She fainted and fell headlong to the floor when the magistrates adjourned the case, remanding her in custody. She appeared in the same dock on 18 June, when the Crown presented its evidence. Mr Reid, for the prosecution, said that Mrs Barney was charged with the murder of Michael Scott Stephen, and there would be a further indictment charging her with shooting at him on 19 May with intent to do him grievous bodily harm. He told of the events of the night of the shooting: the cocktail party, followed by a trip to the Café de Paris and a nightclub, after which Mrs Barney and the dead man returned to her mews flat.

Mrs Dorothy Hall, who lived at No. 10, facing Mrs Barney's flat, said that she had been awakened at about 4.30 a.m. on 31 May by shouting and screaming. She knew the prisoner and the deceased by sight and knew their voices well. She had heard Mrs Barney shout: 'Get out of my house! I hate you! Get out, get out or I will shoot you!' This was followed by the sound of a shot, and Stephen shouted: 'Oh my God, what have you done?' Then Mrs Barney cried out: 'Chicken, Chicken come back. I will do anything you ask me.'

She also told about the earlier shooting, when Mrs Barney had shot at Stephen in the street, shouting: 'Laugh, baby, laugh for the last time.'

Dr Durrant then gave his evidence. He said that Mrs Barney had telephoned him at about 5 a.m., saying: 'Come at once. There has been a terrible accident.' When he asked her what had happened, she said: 'A gentleman has shot himself.' He drove to William Mews, off Lowndes Square, and found Stephen lying dead. Mrs Barney was hysterical and said: 'He isn't dead, is he? If he is dead, I will die too.' When he told her that the police must be notified at once, she said: 'You must not do that.' She then lay upon the dead man's body and cried out: 'I love him so.'

Mrs Barney broke down while this evidence was being given, and her counsel, Sir Patrick Hastings, announced that she would reserve her defence. She was committed for trial at the Old Bailey on 28 June. A grand jury later found a 'true bill' against Mrs Barney. The evidence against her was, after all, very damning. She had been found alone with the dead man; it was *her* revolver which had shot him; she had shot at him previously; she had been heard to threaten to kill him. Then there was the evidence of Spilsbury and Churchill.

Fortunately for Elvira Barney, her family's wealth and influence could afford to hire the services of the most brilliant barrister of his generation. Sir Patrick Hastings was little short of a genius. He had the power, it was commonly believed, to convince a jury that black was white. He did not usually appear in criminal cases, but this time he made an exception. He would need every ounce of his skill to save Mrs Barney from the hangman.

The trial began on 5 July 1932 before Mr Justice Travers Humphreys. The prosecution team was led by Sir Percival Clarke, while Hastings led a team of three for the defence. The crowd outside the Old Bailey had to be held back by policemen with linked arms. It consisted of what seemed to be all the fashionable society ladies in London, come to see one of their own on trial for her life. They crushed into the courtroom, squeezing into the public seats and filling the air with their chatter.

Sir Percival Clarke made the opening speech for the prosecution, describing the circumstances of the case and outlining the facts behind it. He said: 'The jury will direct their attention to the question: was it Mrs Barney who caused this man's death? If she did, is she guilty of the crime of murder?' He went on: 'It is not the first time there has been a quarrel. You will hear there was *often* quarrelling, but if the defence is raised here that it was entirely an accident, then it becomes very material . . . '

Before he could call his first witness, Sir Patrick Hastings rose to his feet. Polite and urbane, a sophisticated man who was like a character from a Noel Coward play, he had thought out his strategy carefully. He knew that his real opponent was not the prosecuting counsel, but the formidable Bernard Spilsbury. He therefore made an unusual request: that Spilsbury should not be present in court except to give his evidence. The puzzled judge agreed to this. It seemed harmless enough.

In fact, Hastings was aware that if Spilsbury listened to the whole case and knew that the defence was one of accidental shooting, it would only take prosecuting counsel counsel to ask him: 'Do you think this was possible?' and for him to state 'No' for the whole defence case to be undermined. But if he was not in court he could not be asked the question. When Spilsbury was sent out of the court, Hastings had won the first round of the battle.

Now the various witnesses were called, prominent among them being Mrs Dorothy Hall. She repeated the evidence she had given before the magistrates. She had seen Stephen often at Mrs Barney's flat; had heard frequent quarrels, with him begging for money. He had often stayed overnight. Coming to the shooting itself, she said she had heard Mrs Barney shout 'Get out – I'll shoot', repeated twice.

'Did you hear any answer?' Mr Clarke asked.

'No, I only heard a shot,' she replied. She also told about the earlier shooting.

The judge intervened to ask her: 'You mean you saw Mrs Barney fire?'

'Yes, my Lord. She fired out of the window. That was in the early hours of the morning.'

'How was she dressed?'

'Oh, I don't think she had anything on.'

'How do you know she fired?'

'I saw her and heard the shot.' She said the shot had been accompanied by a puff of smoke.

She had heard only one shot on the morning of the killing. She was certain of that. But she had made a slight variation in her evidence. Before the magistrates she had said that Mrs Barney had shouted: 'Get out – I will shoot you', repeated twice. Now she had changed it to: 'Get out – I'll shoot.' A lesser barrister would have seized on that change of words immediately. But not Hastings: he wanted to save that for his final speech. After all, the prosecution had made much of the original words: 'I'll shoot you.'

When he rose to cross-examine Mrs Hall, Hastings did not refer to the change in words, for fear she would change them back. Instead, he concentrated on the earlier shooting incident. Mrs Hall had said: 'Mrs Barney was leaning out of the window, screaming at him to go away before she called the police.' He was outside Mrs Barney's door. He asked for money and was told to go away 'and fish for it'. He went away in the taxi he had come in, but he soon came back – 'walking'. After Mrs Barney shot at him, Stephen got into a greengrocer's van which was standing in the mews and spent the night there.

Hastings asked Mrs Hall to describe what she had seen when Mrs Barney fired at her lover in the street, while leaning out of her window. Mrs Hall said that Mrs Barney was holding the revolver in her left hand and had fired it. Mrs Hall had seen a puff of smoke come out of the gun. Hastings asked her, almost casually, if she was aware that modern cordite was smokeless, and that there-fore there would have been no puff of smoke? He had cleverly established two important points: one was that the witness had described Mrs Barney as being left-handed – when she was not. The other point – about the 'smokeless powder' – wasn't even true, since all firearms emit some kind of smoke, but it established early in the minds of the jury Hastings' exhaustive and expert knowledge of firearms. He had none, in fact, but had simply mugged up on the subject from books over the weekend.

After Mrs Barney had shot at Stephen, Mrs Hall had had words with him. Hastings asked her what those words were. The prosecution objected that this was inad-missible evidence. Hastings appealed to the judge, who allowed the question. 'What conversation passed between you and the young man?'

'I asked him to clear off, as he was a perfect nuisance in the mews,' Mrs Hall said.

'What did he reply?'

'He apologized and said he didn't want to leave Mrs Barney *because he was afraid she would kill herself.*'

It was round two to Hastings.

Another witness, the wife of a chauffeur, swore to having heard five shots fired on the night of the killing. Hastings cross-examined her. 'You say you heard five shots?'

'I heard five shots altogether, and a great many other people must have heard them too, but they are not public-spirited enough to come forward.'

The judge intervened to put a question to the witness. 'Do you think you are quite sure that what you heard were pistol shots, and not something else?' The witness was adamant: they were pistol shots – five of them. This too helped the defence, since it demonstrated how a witness at the same scene could be so hopelessly confused about what they had heard or seen. And after all, only two shots had been fired from that revolver . . .

The cross-examination of Dr Durrant brought out all those intimate little details designed to bring tears to the eyes of any juror with an ounce of romance in him. 'Did she appear to be passionately devoted to this dead man?' Hastings asked.

'Oh yes.'

'Did she kiss him after he was dead?'

'Yes, several times.'

'And did her actions appear to you, so far as you could judge, to be absolutely sincere and genuine?'

'Certainly.'

'Did you believe that she was telling the truth?'

'I haven't the slightest doubt that she was telling me what she thought was the truth.'

On the morning of the second day of the trial Detective

Inspector Winter entered the witness box. He described going to Mrs Barney's flat and how her behaviour had appeared to him. He then read out a love-letter he had found in the flat, from Stephen to Mrs Barney, begging 'forgiveness for all the dreadful, horrible things' he had done. A letter in reply from Mrs Barney read: 'You hand me the biggest thrills I've ever had, my sweet, and all I hope is that we can go on being thrilled endlessly . . . I feel like suicide when you are angry.'

Hastings even managed to score a couple of points off Inspector Winter when he cross-examined him. The first was that despite an intensive search of the mews, no trace of the bullet alleged to have been fired into the street was ever found. (It was the defence contention that Mrs Barney did not fire out of her window, but had fired into the bedroom wall to frighten her lover into thinking that she had killed herself.) The second point related to police sloppiness in the handling of the revolver. No pencil or handkerchief had been used to pick it up.

Hastings asked the Inspector: 'Was this revolver examined for fingerprints?'

'Yes.'

'Was it found that the marks on it were so blurred that no fingerprints were decipherable except one?'

'That is so.'

'Whose was that one?'

'Mine.'

Now came the 'expert' witnesses. Robert Churchill was a renowned gun expert whose testimony four years earlier had helped send Browne and Kennedy to the gallows for the murder of PC Gutteridge. Now Hastings was to succeed in the remarkable feat of turning him into a witness for the defence. Churchill began by saying that the weapon in question was one of the safest revolvers ever made and required a fourteen-pound pull on the trigger, with room for only one finger inside the trigger guard. He said that when discharged there would be a loud report but very little smoke.

Hastings began his cross-examination with a very theatrical trick. He picked up the revolver and pointed it at the ceiling, pulling the trigger rapidly, click after click echoing around the courtroom. 'It does not seem to require any terrific muscular development,' he remarked. 'It looks as though we are much stronger than one thinks, if we can pull it as easily as that.' Churchill agreed that it looked easy, but protested that it would require a stronger pull if held loosely. 'Would it?' Hastings said, changing his grip until he was holding the revolver almost negligently. Again he pulled the trigger rapidly, with no apparent effort. It had an effect on the jury, impressing them no end, although Hastings later confided to his clerk that it had made his finger very sore.

Hastings now concentrated on the fact that some of the cartridges had been fired, others not. Mr Churchill explained that the cylinder could be turned by hand. 'If two people were struggling to get possession of the revolver and the pressure exerted was not enough to fire it at first, the cylinder might be turned around?' Hastings asked.

'It might spin round,' Churchill agreed.

'If the struggling persons are close and one has the revolver in her hand and the other seizes her hand, would it go off?'

'It might,' Churchill conceded.

'When the finger, not of the person killed, is on the trigger?'

'Yes.'

Hastings had now effectively explained away the awkward question of why there had been no gunpowder blackening on Stephen's hand, as there would have been had he fired the revolver. It was Elvira who had fired the gun ... It was a risky thing to admit, but the safest way out of the dilemma.

Spilsbury now came into the witness box. He had heard nothing of the previous questions. Hastings rose to his feet. Everyone expected a clash of giants. Instead,

Hastings put three simple questions. In his evidence Spilsbury had said that Stephen's hands and wrists were perfectly clean, with no sign of powder blackening on his shirt or coat sleeves. He told of trying to fire the revolver when it was in the position it was said to have been in while Mrs Barney and Stephen were struggling for it. 'The revolver requires both a long and heavy pull,' Spilsbury said. 'The trigger has to be moved right back before it can be let off.' He demonstrated to the jury how he had tried to fire the revolver while in the position Stephen was said to have been in. 'I find it impossible to discharge it,' Spilsbury said. 'Holding it in this position, about three inches from the body, with the wrist bent back, as it must have been, I could not get enough room to fire it at all.'

But Spilsbury was unaware that it was the defence contention that Mrs Barney had been holding the gun, and that Stephen had grasped the cylinder and rotated it, causing her to pull the trigger. He could not know because he had not been in court to hear this. Finally, Spilsbury said that from the fact that one of the victim's ribs was fractured, he deduced that the bullet had taken a horizontal path.

Now Hastings asked his three simple questions, inviting only yes or no answers.

'The bullet took a horizontal path?'

'Yes.'

'Have you made tests on a skeleton?'

'Yes.'

'Would not the best way of testing the line of flight be a post-mortem examination?'

'Yes.'

'Hastings sat down abruptly, leaving Spilsbury open-mouthed and bewildered. He had expected far more questions and a much rougher ride. But Hastings had deliberately avoided a confrontation, managing to phrase his questions in such a way that Spilsbury agreed with everything he said, and added nothing which would contradict the defence theory of the shooting – as Hastings was to stress to the jury in his closing speech.

Had he in fact asked Spilsbury point-blank if it could possibly have been an accidental shooting, Spilsbury would have replied with a firm 'no', using his cool and precise grasp of logic and science to prove his case and so destroy the defence. But Spilsbury had not been allowed to do this. He had not been asked the question, and a witness cannot answer a question which has not been put to him. It was a lawyer's trick, but a very adroit one.

Having disposed of the expert witnesses, Hastings now called his only defence witness: Elvira Barney. She went into the witness box to tell her own story, trembling as she took the oath and looking vulnerable and tragic, a broken women. She told of her marriage to the American, of his brutal ill-treatment of her and her inability to get a divorce because of his American domicile. Hastings led her, getting her to tell of her first meeting with Stephen in the previous autumn and how she fell in love with him.

'Were you anxious to marry him?'

'Very.'

'And from the time you became devoted to him did you in fact become his mistress?'

'Yes.'

'And did you support him almost entirely?'

'Almost entirely.'

She said that Stephen had sometimes physically ill-treated her, and described him as a 'brute'. The main cause of the quarrels between them had been his obsession with gambling and the woman he used to take gambling with him. Mrs Barney had to give him money for this purpose.

She explained that the revolver had been given to her by a friend in Devonshire, who had used it for shooting rabbits. She claimed she had never called her lover 'Chicken' in her life, and her devotion to him had remained unbroken. 'I loved him, I adored him,' she said, her voice breaking.

Hastings asked: 'Why did you keep the revolver loaded?'

She replied: 'Because I was alone and the windows were near the ground and I was afraid of someone breaking in.'

'When Stephen came to your window, in May, what did you do or say?'

'I was so unhappy that I thought I could make him think I was going to commit suicide, so I got the revolver and fired it at random.'

'We know now that on the left-hand wall of your bedroom are the marks of a revolver bullet having been fired into the wall. When were those marks made?'

'On that occasion.'

'Was that the only day you fired a revolver shot?'

'Yes.'

She recounted how she and Stephen had returned to the flat on the night of his death. He had been kind to her at first, but then his mood had changed. 'He made love to me and he was very angry because I did not respond in the way that he wanted me to.'

Mrs Barney was obviously embarrassed at having to disclose these intimate details. 'He said that perhaps my feelings had changed and I told him it was only because I was unhappy and could not forget what he had said to me. Then he said that he was not pleased with the way things were going and he wanted to go away the next day and not see me at all. That made me very unhappy. He got up from the bed and dressed. I asked him not to leave me and said that if he did I should kill myself.'

'Did he say or do anything then?'

'He got up and took the revolver, saying "Well, you don't do it with this." '

'Where did he go?'

'He ran out of the bedroom towards the spare room.'

'What did you do?'

'I ran after him. We struggled for the revolver. He had it and I wanted it and I kept saying, "Give it to me." ' She went on: 'We were moving about in various positions . . . I was crying . . . I remember fighting and suddenly I heard a shot.' She broke down, weeping bitterly.

Hastings now had to convince the jury that the witness who said that she had seen Mrs Barney deliberately shoot at Stephen with the revolver in her left hand was mistaken. He decided upon another piece of theatre. He asked the usher to place the revolver in front of Mrs Barney. He turned to face the judge, as if to speak, then whirled around and commanded Mrs Barney: 'Pick up that revolver!' Mrs Barney was startled and automatically picked up the gun – with her right hand.

Hastings went on: 'Have you ever desired in your life to shoot Michael Stephen?'

'Never.'

'Has there ever been anyone in your life of whom you have been fonder than Michael Stephen?'

'Never.'

'Did you shoot him that night?'

'No.'

'Had you any motive for shooting him?'

'None.'

Hastings sat down. He had created an atmosphere of sympathy for the poor woman in the dock which was almost palpable. The only real question left was whether she could stand up to cross-examination.

The prosecutor began by suggesting that she had a very clear motive for shooting Stephen – jealousy of the 'other woman' whom she had admitted Stephen was fond of and liked going about with.

'When he said he was going to leave you, did you think that he was going to leave you for this other woman?'

'No.'

'Whom did you think was going to keep him?'

'I thought he would probably try to keep himself by gambling. He thought he was very successful at it.'

Mr Clarke asked: 'You loved him very much?'

'Yes.'

Mr Clarke alluded to her temper; she had admitted that she sometimes got agitated.

'Did you genuinely intend to commit suicide?' he asked.

'The last time I genuinely intended to do it.'

'Did you say to him: "Get out, I will shoot you, I will shoot"?'

'No, I said: "Don't leave me. If you do I shall shoot myself." I did not want him to go.'

The prosecutor was failing to shake the woman in the dock. He had one final question for her. 'In the course of the struggle the pistol went off. Whose finger was on the trigger?'

Mrs Barney shrugged. 'I have no idea,' she replied.

The case was virtually over.

The prosecutor made his closing speech, emphasizing Mrs Barney's jealous nature and the evidence that she had fired the fatal shot. He stressed the lack of scorching on Stephen's clothing; he had certainly not shot himself. Mrs Barney had the motive: jealousy. He finished his speech just as the court ended for the day.

Hastings had all night to think of his counter-attack, on the third day of the trial. He began by reminding the jury that Mrs Barney's words: 'I will shoot you', which had been used in the opening address by the prosecution and throughout the trial, had been shortened by Mrs Hall herself to 'I will shoot'. Could that not have meant: 'I will shoot myself'?

Hastings did not make any crude appeal to emotion – as Marshall Hall, for example, would have done – but relied on a careful analysis of the evidence, letting the facts speak for themselves. Mrs Hall had also told the court that Stephen was afraid that Mrs Barney might kill herself. This was a case of the victim and the chief prosecution witness combining to confirm the defence story.

If Mrs Barney had really tried to kill Stephen in the earlier incident, why had the police failed to find any trace of the bullet in the mews? Mrs Barney's story, from the arrival of the doctor on the scene of the shooting until the end of the case, had been consistent. It had been an accident. This was supported by the doctor, who said that in her hysterical condition she could not have invented a lie. Hastings criticized the police for their lack of forensic care in handling the revolver. The fingerprints on it would have cleared his client conclusively, he claimed.

He went on: 'I am not going to beg for mercy and for a lenient view of what has happened. I stand here and claim that on this evidence Mrs Barney is entitled, as of right, to a verdict in her favour. She is a young woman with the whole of her life before her. I beg you to remember that. I ask you as a matter of justice and right that you should say "not guilty".'

In his summing-up the judge referred to Hastings' speech as 'one of the finest' he had ever heard in his long career at the Bar. He concluded by telling the jury that there were three possible verdicts they could return: guilty of murder, not guilty of murder but guilty of manslaughter, and not guilty.

The jury deliberated for just under two hours, returning with a verdict of not guilty. Mrs Barney cried out: 'Oh!' and stuffed her handkerchief in her mouth. She left the court with her family and friends, and was enthusiastically cheered by the waiting crowd outside.

'She is a young woman with the whole of her life before her,' Hastings had said. But what did she do with the rest of her life? Spend it regretting past follies and determined to make something of herself? In mourning for lost love? In penance?

No, her self-destructive streak could not be denied. She was soon immersed in a life of sex and drink again.

208

Shortly after the trial she was at the Café de Paris with friends. Conscious of stares, she stood up and shouted defiantly: 'I'm the one who shot her lover – so take a good look!'

She changed her name and went to live in Paris. Four years later, after a round of parties, she collapsed and died on Christmas Eve 1936 of a cerebral haemorrhage due to excessive alcohol consumption. She was just thirty-one years of age . . .

That sampler was passed on down through the family until finally it was sent for sale in Edinburgh, the same city which had acquitted Madeleine Smith, and was the only reminder of a flame which burned too brightly.

14
RUTH ELLIS: A WOMAN DRIVEN
TO KILL
1955

Ruth Ellis was another mistress who shot her lover dead, but the outcome of her case was very different from Elvira Barney's.

Had she been born ten years later, Ruth Ellis might well have been a woman of her time, at home in the London of the 'Swinging Sixties'. But the date was 1955, when public morality was still pretty strict and a platinum-blonde prostitute had to fight to keep her head above water.

Not that Ruth Ellis had ever been a prostitute in the real sense of the word. She tended to give her favours away as often as she sold them. She lacked the calculating character of the harlot, and even fell desperately in love with one of her 'punters'. It was a mistake which the hardened professional would never make, and it was to prove a fatal one.

She was born Ruth Neilson in the Welsh seaside resort of Rhyl on 9 October 1926. She grew up there but got away as soon as she could, anxious to escape from the poverty of her family background and the narrow-minded chapel-going neighbours. Like most young girls she had dreams, dreams of somehow 'making it', of becoming a somebody in the world. And if it took a hard slog, or even a tooth-and-claw struggle, she was determined to succeed in her quest. 'If you don't like your life you can change it' was the message of H. G. Wells. Ruth certainly changed hers . . .

Like most star-struck provincials, she regarded London as her mecca and arrived there to take the rather mundane job of machine-minder in a south London factory. She left to become a waitress. There was a war on, and there were exciting prospects for anyone with their eyes open, but Ruth found London life rather messy and confusing. At the start of 1944 she had an affair with a French-Canadian serviceman, giving birth to an illegitimate son in September of that year. Life as an unmarried mother is never easy: then it was just that much harder.

Desperate to get on, to meet a better class of person, Ruth became a hostess in a clip-joint. There she met and bewitched George Ellis, a divorced dental surgeon from Surrey. They got married in November 1950, when Ruth was twenty-four and her husband forty-one. She tried to be a wife to him, and even bore him a daughter in October 1951, but the husband was an alcoholic and Ruth liked to play the field. Within a month of the birth of her second child the couple had parted.

Still Ruth persevered, determined to penetrate what she viewed as the desirable world of the middle class, and eventually became manageress of the Little Club in Knightsbridge. She served drinks from three in the afternoon until eleven at night to a crowd of regulars, many of whom were drifters, and not a few with links to the underworld. Here in this upstairs drinking room they gathered to ogle the smashing blonde who smiled from behind the bar. Which was exactly why Ruth had been given the job, of course. On a basic fifteen-pound-a-week salary plus a ten-pound-a-week entertainment allowance, with a rent-free two-roomed apartment and kitchen above the club, Ruth was well off. And it was at the Little Club she met up with young David Blakely again, one afternoon in 1953. Coronation year . . .

She had met him a couple of weeks previously in another club in the West End and had not been impressed. She had heard him making some unflattering remarks about the hostess there and bluntly told him that he was 'a pompous ass'. He had resented the public criticism and walked off glowering at her. Now she was serving him a gin and tonic in her own club, and the initial antipathy seemed to melt away.

David Moffet Drummond Blakely was born on 17 June 1929, the son of a Sheffield doctor, and he too had been anxious to escape from his provincial background. Lacking any desire to work for a living, he made use of his natural charm to woo people, and lived off his family. He tended to drink too much, and when drunk exhibited a nasty, aggressive streak. He hoped to succeed as a racing driver, but although he spent thousands of pounds on fast cars and raced at Le Mans, among other circuits, he lacked the necessary skill and perseverance to become any good.

He had received seven thousand pounds from his father's will in 1952, but soon frittered away what was then a considerable sum. He was a natural drifter, the eternal playboy, because of a lack of any real inner resources. Ruth was never able to see behind the façade and was attracted to Blakely because of his 'better-class' background and good manners. A bit of a snob herself, Ruth was probably impressed by his posh accent.

Soon she was taking him to bed in her apartment above the club, spending lazy sensuous afternoons with him. Not every afternoon, of course, because sometimes Ruth used those free afternoons before the club opened for the evening to promote her call-girl career, entertaining a few selected clients for money. It was always strictly cash – except for David Blakely. For him it was free. He had spent most of his life using his charm to such effect that he came to expect everything to come to him without charge. He expected to be able to use a woman's most valuable resource – her heart – free of charge as of right. But in the end Ruth was to make him pay dearly . . .

At the time of this affair, Blakely was engaged to the daughter of a wealthy businessman, but kept assuring Ruth he had no intention of marrying the girl. He was in it for the money. Then Ruth became pregnant by Blakely.

She was later to say in a statement: 'In December 1953 I had an abortion by him and he was very concerned about my welfare. Although he was engaged to another girl, he offered to marry me and he said it seemed unnecessary for me to get rid of the child, but I did not want to take advantage of him. I was not really in love with him at the time and it was quite unnecessary to marry me. I thought I could get out of the mess quite easily. In fact, I did so with the abortion.'

Despite her words, Ruth was hurt by the need to have an abortion, and afterwards began denying Blakely exclusive rights over her affections. In fact, she began encouraging the attentions of a thirty-three-year-old bachelor and company director, who fell deeply in love with her. Although continuing to see Blakely, she was cool towards him, and this had the effect of making Blakely desire her all the more.

Blakely grew jealous of the new man in her life, and Ruth fostered this feeling by her attitude. Perhaps she wanted to pay him back for his casual neglect of her, or perhaps it was her way of entwining him more deeply in her meshes. The strange thing was that Ruth never did take much pleasure in the act of sex. What she needed – and had a compulsive desire for – was the constant attention of men. She needed that false reassurance.

The atmosphere between her and Blakely developed into one of raging jealousy. Sometimes she needed him, sometimes he needed her, but these times never coincided. If he had toyed with her affections, then she now played with his.

If it was all a plan to trap the man she desired, it worked. Blakely begged her to marry him and, although she refused this offer, in February 1955 she and Blakely moved into a one-room flat at 44 Egerton Gardens, Kensington, living together as 'Mr and Mrs Ellis'.

It was not an idyllic existence. Ruth continued to see

her company-director lover, who was loaning her money to pay the rent. Blakely was playing around trying to raise money to build a new racing car. He named it The Emperor, but on its very first track outing it fell apart.

Life at Egerton Gardens grew grim. Blakely resented his failure, resented having to live off a woman. He began drinking heavily, and revealed his nasty streak by beating Ruth quite badly – certainly badly enough to cause severe bruising. She was pregnant again – she could not be certain of the father, given her other lover – and again had an abortion. Blakely beat her when drunk, but was remorseful when sober. These alcoholic reconciliations were not to last.

By now Ruth had her ten-year-old son living with her, and he slept each night on a camp bed in the bedroom she shared with Blakely. Ruth still demanded Blakely's sexual attentions, not to cure any sexual itch but to demonstrate her possession of him. Blakely resented having to share his bedroom with a child, to perform with the son in the room, to live without money. A brief affair with a vivacious tart was one thing; actually living with her quite another. Everything got on his nerves, and he drank even more, thus fuelling the vicious cycle.

Blakely was friendly with a young married couple he met in the Magdala public house, Anthony and Carole Findlater. One evening he met them in the pub in a despondent mood, telling them he was desperate to get away from Ruth but was worried what she might do if he left her. They soothed his fears and persuaded him to spend the weekend with them at their flat in Tanza Road, just a few hundred yards away. He agreed.

Ruth was expecting David to arrive home at 9.30 p.m., and when he failed to do so she promptly phoned the Findlaters, asking: 'Anthony – is David with you?'

Anthony Findlater lied. 'No,' he replied.

Ruth was nonplussed. 'Oh. I'm very worried because he should have been back to meet me. Do you think he is all right?'

Findlater replied: 'Oh, he's all right.'

Ruth put down the receiver convinced that she had detected a mocking note in Findlater's voice, and that David really was with the couple at Tanza Road.

She rang several more times that night, but as soon as her voice was recognized the receiver was replaced. Filled with anger, Ruth walked to the flat in Tanza Road and spotted David's Vanguard van parked outside. But when she rang the bell to the flat, she got no answer. Infuriated, she turned her rage on to the van, smashing in its windows. The noisy destruction brought Anthony Findlater to his doorstep in pyjamas, and Ruth demanded fiercely: 'Where is David? I want to speak to him!' Findlater persisted in saying that Blakely wasn't there, but Ruth shouted: 'I know he is there! Ask him to come down.'

The Findlaters had telephoned the police and an inspector duly appeared on the scene, trying to calm Ruth down and persuade her to go home. She retorted: 'I shall stay here all night until he has the guts to show his face!' The inspector tried again, but his efforts failed and, unwilling to interfere in a domestic dispute, he drove off, leaving Ruth alone on the field of battle.

Ruth did not in fact go home at all, but spent the entire night huddled in doorways keeping watch on the door to the Findlaters' flat, convinced that the couple were determined to break up her relationship with David. She was equally convinced that David must have found a new woman, and suspected that her rival was the nanny employed to look after the Findlaters' baby.

At eight the next morning Findlater and Blakely came furtively out of the flat and did not spot Ruth concealed in a doorway. They walked around the Vanguard van, inspecting the damage, before getting in and driving away. Ruth had to give up the hunt at this point. She went home and gave her son some money, telling him to spend the day at London Zoo. Then she persuaded her other lover to drive her to the Magdala pub in Hampstead, where she thought she might find Blakely.

He was not there. That night saw her back outside the Findlaters' flat, keeping watch from the shadows. It was a Saturday night, and from the flat came the sound of a party. Ruth was enraged to hear a woman's laughter ringing out, certain it came from her rival.

What her thoughts were during this time, how she managed to snatch any sleep, we do not know. But she must have been in the depths of bitter despair. The next evening, Easter Sunday, Clive Gunnell, another friend of Blakely's, arrived at the Findlaters' flat with his record-player, and the party sounds continued. At about nine that evening Blakely and Gunnell decided to pop out to the Magdala to get some beer and cigarettes.

Easter Sunday 1955 . . . Ruth Ellis had just arrived to keep vigil outside the Findlaters' flat once more when she noticed that the Vanguard van was missing. Surmising correctly that Blakely would be at the pub, she walked there, her handbag weighed down with a loaded revolver. She must have been raging with jealousy, and yet her subsequent actions seemed to be those of someone totally calm and self-possessed; she was cold and efficient in her movements. In reality she was suffering from what psychiatrists call 'dissociation', moving robot-like in a private nightmare. It wasn't happening to her, but was more like watching someone else . . .

It was just after nine in the evening of that Easter Sunday, 1955. The pub was packed with its regulars, who tended to be young men wearing sports jackets. The landlord, Mr Colson, was later to remember serving the twenty-five-year-old David Blakely. He cashed his cheque for five pounds.

After spending some time drinking with Clive Gunnell at the bar, Blakely bought three flagons of beer to take back to the party at the Findlaters' flat. The two men said a few goodbyes and then walked out of the pub, making for Blakely's Vanguard van, which was parked by the pub door. Gunnell waited by the passenger door, while Blakely walked around the vehicle and stood by the driver's door, juggling with his flagons of beer and trying to fish the car keys out of his pocket.

Neither man noticed the slight but determined-looking blonde walking down the hill towards them. Her eyes fixed on him, the woman did call out 'David!' but Blakely did not hear her. It was only when she was standing beside him that he noticed her presence – the woman he had been so studiously avoiding.

No words were spoken: it had gone too far for that. Blakely watched almost hypnotized as Ruth Ellis opened her handbag and took out a Smith & Wesson .38 revolver. Raising the weapon, she pointed it directly at Blakely. She did not say a word or make any other movement. For a moment the dramatic tableau, pregnant with menace, was frozen in time.

Then the spell was broken by Blakely turning and starting to run towards the back of the van in panic. The woman fired two shots in quick succession, both shots finding their target. Blakely stumbled, crashing into the side of the van, before stumbling forward again, screaming out 'Clive!'

Gunnell stood stock-still, frozen with disbelief and terror as he watched the woman walk with grim implacability after her victim, following Blakely around the van. She spoke just once. 'Get out of the way, Clive,' she warned. She walked the length of the blood-smeared van to find Blakely scrabbling desperately at the other side. She fired again. Blakely's body made a half-turn as it spun sideways, falling down full-length. The woman stalked up to the body relentlessly, firing more shots into it at point-blank range until the six-chamber gun clicked empty. The woman stood blankly, like a robot which had been switched off and robbed of purpose. She was unaware of the cry of pain from a bank official's wife who had been wounded in the hand by a ricocheting bullet.

Blakely lay dead in the gutter, a mixture of blood and beer from the smashed flagons coursing towards the drain. Customers had poured out of the Magdala, aroused by the sound of the shots, and surrounded the body in a state of shock. Such things belonged to gangster films: they certainly never happened in Hampstead . . .

One of the group looked towards the motionless woman who still clutched the gun, her green sweater and grey two-piece suit immaculate and free of any bloodstains, as she leaned against the wall behind her as if for support. 'What have you done?' he screamed. The woman made no reply.

A tall, well-built man came out of the Magdala and approached the woman cautiously. She glanced at him, then said calmly: 'Phone the police.' The man studied her for a moment, puzzled by her apparent lack of concern. 'I *am* a police officer,' he replied, taking the weapon from her hand. She made no effort to resist him, and stood quietly beside the police officer – Police Constable Alan Thompson of 'L' Division, Metropolitan Police, who happened by chance to have been drinking while off duty in the pub – waiting for an ambulance to arrive and take away the body. It was followed shortly afterwards by a police car, and Ruth Ellis was driven to Hampstead police station, PC Thompson still beside her.

At the police station Ruth Ellis was given a cup of tea. It was thought she might be in a state of shock. But she remained unmoved, drained of all emotion. She sipped the tea, like any hostess in any bar, and told the officers in a dull monotone: 'My name is Mrs Ruth Ellis. I am a model. I'm twenty-eight and I live at 44 Egerton Gardens – that's in Kensington.'

For the police it was a plain – if puzzling – case of murder. It was premeditated – taking the weapon along had been proof of intent – and if more proof of intent was needed, then she had fired all six shots into her victim, each time having to recock the revolver. But why? Under British law the prosecution do not have to prove motive, and to all intent and purposes is incurious as to motive, but they too are human and like everyone else

218

wanted to know *why*. What had driven this woman over the edge, to the ultimate extreme of action?

Ruth Ellis had been kindly treated by the police and felt obliged to try and explain her crime of passion as best she could – if she could. She told about her background, about meeting David Blakely for the first time. Of their affair, which had developed into a common-law marriage. Of how she had felt betrayed and abandoned . . .

The police tend not to be much interested in metaphysical abstractions, but far more keen on such mundane information as to where she had acquired the revolver. All she would say about it was: 'I was given it about three years ago in a pub by a man whose name I do not remember.' The police felt certain that she was protecting someone.

She was asked to account for the last few minutes of her lover's life, how and why she had shot him. She was vague about it all, explaining that as she walked towards the pub she felt herself to be 'somehow outside of myself, in a sort of daze'. Despite her efforts to cooperate, she remained detached from all that was happening around her, her inner calm as controlled as her platinum hair, which remained immaculately groomed.

Just after two in the morning Detective Superintendent Leonard Crawford went into the interview room and told Ruth Ellis: 'I have just seen the dead body of David Blakely in Hampstead mortuary. I understand you know something about it. You are not obliged to say anything at all about this unless you wish to do so, but whatever you say will be taken down in writing and may be given in evidence.'

Ruth Ellis looked at the officer intently. Then without hesitation she said: 'I understand what has been said. I am guilty. I am rather confused.' Then she began telling of her doomed affair with the victim and how rage drove her to kill. With a statement signed – a confession in legal terms – the police began putting together the elements of the case against the prisoner. The post-mortem revealed that four bullets had entered the body of David Blakely, the first of which must have been fired from just three inches away. In police eyes it was a straightforward case of murder, and the routine legal machinery was set inexorably in train. The prisoner was remanded in custody awaiting her trial, after appearing before the magistrates.

The trial took place in the famous No. 1 Court at the Old Bailey on Monday, 20 June 1955, before Mr Justice Havers. The jury were told the facts in the case, and then Ruth Ellis went into the witness box.

Telling the court of her affair with the other man, the bachelor businessman, Ruth said: 'David was getting rather jealous. He asked me what I had been doing and things like that, and, of course, I did not tell him . . . My association with David began again at his insistence. It was very difficult. I was running a business and he was there all the time. He was entitled to walk in: he was a customer and he was hanging around the bar all the time. He was spending money in my bar. I could not tell him to go.'

She recalled how, shortly after her divorce from George Ellis, Blakely had been desperate to see her. At the time her feelings for him were not so acute. She said: 'He phoned from the box just in the entrance to the club to my place upstairs and asked if he could please come up and I said "No". After half an hour he came upstairs and I was fooling around in the flat, doing one thing and another. He was very emotionally upset and he went down on his knees, crying and saying: "I'm sorry, darling. I do love you. I'll prove it." He asked me to marry him, but I declined.'

The jury heard all the details which were to be sensationally blazoned in the tabloid press. Of how, even when she and Blakely were living together as man and wife, she kept her other lover on the side.

Then she was cross-examined. Mr Christmas Humphreys, QC, asked her directly: 'Mrs Ellis, when you fired that revolver at close range into the body of David Blakely, what did you intend to do?'

Without pause and speaking tonelessly she replied: 'It is obvious that when I shot him I intended to kill him.' She signed her own death warrant with that single statement.

In his summing-up to the jury, Mr Justice Havers warned them that they could not return a verdict of manslaughter, given that statement of intent, and the jury of ten men and two women took less than fifteen minutes to return with a verdict of guilty of murder.

The black cap was placed on the judge's head and he pronounced the death sentence upon her. Ruth looked unmoved, and when he had finished speaking she murmured a brief 'thanks' and then turned and smiled at friends in the public gallery, before being led to the cells below, her high heels clicking and her blonde hair catching the last errant rays of sunlight as she disappeared.

She was held in Holloway Prison, and although her solicitor announced that there would be no appeal – his client did not wish one – organizations calling for the abolition of capital punishment collected fifty thousand signatures on a petition for a reprieve. In the death cell, she never showed any signs of remorse, apart from asking for a photograph of David Blakely's grave, which she kept on her bedside table. She wrote to Blakely's mother saying she was sorry to have caused her 'unpleasantness', but added: 'I shall die loving your son and you should feel content that his death has been repaid.'

After learning that she was not to be reprieved, she wrote a cheerful note to a friend saying she expected her execution to be no more painful than 'having a tooth out'. It has been suggested that a reprieve was refused because an innocent bystander had been wounded by one of the shots fired at Blakely. Certainly the bank offical's wife who had been wounded in the hand wrote in a London newspaper: 'If Ruth Ellis is reprieved we may

221

have other vindictive and jealous young women shooting their boy friends in public . . . '

The woman who had been called 'a vindictive and jealous young woman', a call girl and common prostitute, now achieved a dignity in the condemned cell which evoked the admiration of the women prison officers whose duty it was to watch over her.

When the final moment came, on the morning of 13 July, the grim procession of officials came to her cell: the governor, doctor, priest and hangman; but Ruth Ellis showed no fear. She drank the tot of brandy she was offered with a steady hand and then thanked the staff at Holloway Prison for all the kindness they had shown her. Then she almost hurried from her cell to the execution chamber, as if anxious to be done with life. She met death calmly and almost with gratitude, becoming the last woman ever to be hanged in Britain. Ten years later, in November 1965, capital punishment was finally abolished as a stain on a so-called civilized nation.

The man who hanged Ruth Ellis was Albert Pierrepoint, who was the most prolific hangman of this century. In his autobiography, published in 1974, Pierrepoint stated bluntly: 'I do not now believe that any of the hundreds of executions I carried out has in any way acted as a deterrent against future murder. Capital punishment, in my view, achieved nothing except revenge.' He went on to say: 'I don't really like talking about Ruth. I have met her family. They are a lovely family. She was a great woman. I have seen some brave men die, but nobody braver than her.' He also revealed that she had no famous 'last words' on the scaffold. 'She said nothing.'

In December 1973 details of a statement about the murder weapon, said to have been made by Ruth Ellis to her lawyers just prior to her execution, were published in Britain. It was claimed that Ruth Ellis stated that her jealous second lover both supplied her with the gun and drove her to her rendezvous with death. She had suppressed this evidence at her trial so as not to involve the man. This evidence, kept secret for so long, did not lead to any further police action. The police did interview the man named, but since he denied all knowledge of the affair the matter remained closed.

In 1985, *Dance with a Stranger*, a film based on the case of Ruth Ellis, was released. It portrayed her as a woman who had killed almost in a trance, under the influence of anti-depressant drugs following a miscarriage caused by her lover's ill-treatment. Legal experts believe that had the jury known Ruth Ellis had had a miscarriage shortly before the act of murder, she would have been regarded in the same light as a mother who commits infanticide – and deemed not responsible for her actions. It was certainly odd that her defence counsel did not seek to put forward an insanity plea.

But surely she knew what she was doing . . . In her case the act of murder was a form of suicide note. She wanted to die, to be rid of an unhappy life, but she was determined to take her lover with her. In death she was to achieve the status of a cult martyr-figure. That surely would have made her giggle.

15

RATTENBURY AND STONER, 1935:
THE IMPOSSIBLE DREAM

There exists no case in the annals of murder which arouses so much pity and terror as does the story of the fatal liaison between Alma Victoria Rattenbury and George Percy Stoner. It is the ultimate crime of passion, as real, modern and disturbing as the film *Fatal Attraction*.

But this was a real case with real people. We can recognize the passion which moved this couple, a passion which remains an almost tangible presence over the years and retains the power to touch us still – and terrify.

Murder, like every other human activity, takes many forms. At its lowest it is represented by people like the Moors Murderers. At its highest it illustrates human beings at their most extreme, desperately seeking to attain the impossible dream. Such is the Rattenbury and Stoner case, at once forbidding and incredibly romantic.

The general outlines of the case are well known. I do not wish to linger over them here, since ideally an examination of the trial should allow the events which preceded it to emerge in the transcript. The case has been made the subject of novels, films, plays and TV dramas. To those readers who missed all of them, the basic facts are these.

A mature married woman falls in love with a young boy she takes into her home as a chauffeur-handyman. They become lovers. The boy, having only just attained eighteen years of age, becomes insanely jealous of the elderly alcoholic husband and, unknown to the wife, attacks and kills him with a mallet. She, in an excess of devotion, at first attempts to take the blame for the murder to protect her young lover.

As a general rule, the more respectable the society in which a murder takes place, the more sensational the crime appears. In the hypocritical and prudish era of the 1930s the Rattenbury and Stoner affair was a drama of the highest calibre. Today it would seem a rather mundane murder, committed by a half-witted boy in love with a half-baked woman.

Widely written about as the case has been, it has been reported over the years with a mixture of prejudice and half-truths. Even F. Tennyson Jesse – easily the best writer on the case – accepts the conventional view that Alma Rattenbury was a nymphomaniac. This is sheer nonsense. She was in fact a modern woman born before her time, a woman with an artistic temperament who was in love with the *idea* of love – a born romantic.

But so prudish and ill-informed were people of the time that the learned counsel for the prosecution felt driven to ask a medical witness if regular sexual intercourse between a mature woman and a boy of eighteen would not inevitably ruin the boy's health. Mr Justice Humphreys told the jury that because Mrs Rattenbury had committed adultery they 'could not feel anything but disgust for her' – a view which prosecuting counsel stressed in his closing speech. It was as bad as the old canard that masturbation leads to blindness and stunts the growth.

There are a number of such prejudices surrounding the case which must be quashed. For example, it was generally assumed that in such a situation, the older woman must be the dominant partner. In fact the reverse is true. It is the young lover who calls the shots, whose love the older person is anxious to retain. The young lover tends to become demanding and wields the power.

There is another point to which F. Tennyson Jesse rightly adds emphasis. The real reason why the jury did not convict Alma Rattenbury was because the case had

225

too many echoes of the notorious Bywaters and Thompson case of 1922, in which a grotesque miscarriage of justice had taken place and an innocent woman had been hanged by a judge and jury who obviously regarded adultery as being on a par with murder. The jury were anxious not to make the same mistake, and the judge stressed that they should not convict a woman of murder simply because of her moral character. Truly the ghost of Edith Thompson haunted the courtroom.

The Rattenburys had come to England from Canada. Mr Francis Mawson Rattenbury had been a successful architect, married, with grown-up children. He had begun an affair with a married woman – Alma – who was cited in his divorce and whom he subsequently married. She was his second wife, he was her third husband. She had a small boy called Christopher, born in 1922, from a previous marriage.

The marriage of Francis Rattenbury and Alma Victoria Clark took place around 1927 in Canada, and a boy, John, was born a year later. After the birth of the child the husband and wife ceased to have a normal sexual relationship and slept in separate bedrooms. That same year – 1928 – the couple came to England, possibly to escape the scandal, and bought a house at 5 Manor Road, Bournemouth, named Villa Madeira.

They were an ill-matched pair from the start. Mr Rattenbury was an old sixty-seven who would sooner embrace the bottle than his wife. In fact, he drank himself unconscious most nights. He was a dull, melancholy man, unsociable, and given to bouts of irritation when he had imbibed too much whisky. She was thirty-eight, attractive and healthy, with the normal desires of a woman in her prime.

Mrs Rattenbury was a highly volatile woman, even to the point of being frivolous. She would wear pyjamas in the daytime and often stayed awake all night to play the gramophone. She was a good pianist and had once written song lyrics for a living. In fact, she was a music-hall type of person. She needed affection, both to give and receive. She liked to touch people, to laugh often, to drink cocktails until she began to talk and act wildly. She would have been at home in the theatre, where everyone calls everyone else 'darling'.

And yet the relationship was basically a happy one. They slept apart – he on the ground floor, she having the upper floor as her quarters – but she was genuinely fond of 'Ratz', as she affectionately called him, and was a caring wife. He was a little tight-fisted. True, he allowed her a thousand pounds a year, but this sum had to pay for everything: household bills, wages for domestics, school fees for the elder boy, clothing, and her husband's huge drinks bill. Mr Rattenbury was strange about money. He would sooner part with large sums than small ones, and it was easier for Alma to coax a hundred pounds out of him than five pounds. He was generous in big things, petty in small ones.

We know a lot about life at Villa Madeira, in the quiet tree-lined Bournemouth suburbs, because we have a witness who lived there. Miss Irene Riggs was the living-in maid and companion, and confidante to both husband and wife. She reported that Mrs Rattenbury always treated her kindly, and that she had never once heard Mr Rattenbury say a word against his wife. And so life at Villa Madeira might have continued . . .

In September 1934 Alma advertised in the *Bournemouth Daily Echo*: 'Willing Lad wanted, age 14-18, for house-work. Scout training preferred.' Cycling to the house to apply for the job came George Percy Stoner, seventeen, a semi-literate lad who lived with his grandmother and worked part-time in a garage. Unusually for the time, Stoner could drive a car. He was hired on the spot at a pound a week. Stoner – he was never called anything but 'Stoner', even by Alma Rattenbury – drove his mistress about, as well as helping in the house and garden. At first he lived out, but soon began to live in.

Stoner had his eighteenth birthday in November of

that same year, and by Christmas he and Alma had become lovers, spending nights in each other's arms, to the disapproval of the companion, Miss Riggs, who was a devout Catholic. At this time Mrs Rattenbury told the family doctor, Dr O'Donnell: 'There is something I want to tell you. I am afraid you will be shocked and never want to speak to me again.' She confessed the details of her affair with Stoner. Dr O'Donnell warned her that such a liaison was unwise, but she retorted: 'I am in love with Stoner.'

Was it really love or simply physical lust? After all, Alma wrote cheap, sentimental lyrics about love. There is one infallible test to decide whether it was love or lust. If it was merely lust, then when danger threatened and she found herself in the dock with him facing a capital charge, she would quickly have abandoned her lover. She did not. She stood by him until the end, and even died for him.

For weeks after the arrest she insisted to her solicitor that she wanted to take the blame for the murder of her husband, to clear Stoner. Her solicitor pleaded with her, telling her that her lie would be detected in the witness box and she would hang without saving Stoner. Still she persisted. Only when her son Christopher was sent to the prison to plead with her did she relent, but in court she said as little against Stoner as possible. For his part, Stoner refused to go into the witness box or say anything damaging about Alma. He was ready to confess to the murder alone.

Usually, when a couple are jointly charged with murder, the so-called 'cut-throat' defence is adopted, and each tries to place the blame on the other. It happened like this in the Milsom and Fowler case of 1896, in Field and Gray (1921), and, as we have seen, with Ruth Snyder and Judd Gray. The Rattenbury and Stoner case is unique in that each defendant tried to protect the other, and it is certain that Alma Rattenbury would happily have hanged if by so doing she could have saved the life of Stoner.

We come now to the background to the murder. Despite Irene Riggs' disapproval, she had managed to adapt to the situation. Stoner was a quiet, polite boy who gave no offence. On 19 March 1935, Alma asked Stoner to drive her to London, telling her husband that she was going to have an operation. She had had several minor operations before this. 'Ratz' generously gave her £250 for the trip.

Once in London the couple booked into the Royal Palace Hotel in Kensington, posing as brother and sister. They had opposite rooms. It was a four-day excursion for the couple, during which Stoner found himself being treated as Alma's social equal and called 'sir' by the servants. It must have quite turned his head.

Mrs Rattenbury took Stoner shopping, buying him silk pyjamas and made-to-measure suits. One has to make the mental effort to imagine what effect this had on a working-class lad in a class-conscious society. Suddenly he must have seen unimaginable vistas of becoming a gentleman opening up for him. Only the husband stood in the way, the classic 'eternal triangle'.

They returned from the trip to the Villa Madeira, and Mr Rattenbury did not even ask his wife about her operation or express any interest in her outing. He was in a mood of extreme depression because a business scheme for a block of flats had fallen through, leaving him worried about his finances. He talked of suicide, saying he admired anyone who had the courage to take their own life.

In an attempt to cheer him up, Alma took him for a drive before they had tea together. Then Alma suggested they should go and visit a family friend, Mr Jenks, at Bridport. She telephoned Mr Jenks and he invited them over for the Monday, suggesting that they should stay overnight.

Alma had been making the call in a separate room.

229

Mr Rattenbury could not hear the conversation, and was going deaf anyway. At that moment Stoner came into the room and overheard the arrangements Alma was making. Shaking with rage, he brandished an air-pistol he was holding and threatened to kill her if she made the trip to Bridport. It was not the trip he objected to, *but the fact that Alma would be sleeping with her husband.*

The jealous lover could not bear this. He had often in the past accused his mistress of having sexual relations with her husband. But what really lay behind his anger was the sense of betrayal. He had lived like a gentleman for four days, only to return to his position as a servant. Alma managed to pacify him, telling him that she and her husband would have separate rooms at Mr Jenks' house.

Stoner brooded. At eight o'clock that evening he went to his grandparents' house and borrowed a carpenter's mallet, and returned with it to Villa Madeira.

Alma had spent the evening playing cards with her husband. It was Irene Riggs' night out. Alma kissed her husband good-night and went up to bed. Miss Riggs arrived home at 10.15 p.m. and went to her room. Ten minutes later she went downstairs to find something to eat, and heard the noise of laboured breathing from the sitting room. She assumed that Mr Rattenbury had fallen asleep in his armchair again. She went upstairs to bed, coming out of her room a couple of minutes later to go to the toilet. She saw Stoner on the landing, looking down over the banister. She asked him what was wrong and he said he was looking to see that all the lights were out. In fact, Mr Rattenbury was slumped in his armchair breathing his last, his skull having been bashed in with blows from the mallet.

After visiting Irene's room to tell her about the trip to London, Alma went to her own room. Ten minutes later Stoner slipped into bed beside her. He seemed agitated, and she asked him: 'What is the matter, darling?'

He said he was in trouble but couldn't tell her about

it. He added: 'You won't be going to Bridport tomorrow.' Later he said he had hurt Ratz. He said he had hit him over the head with the mallet to injure him and prevent the trip from taking place.

Alma jumped out of bed and ran downstairs in her bare feet, only to find Ratz lying slumped in his chair with a black eye. In fact the injuries were to the back of his head and were concealed by his position. However, there was blood on the floor.

Alma immediately became excited and called for Irene, and told her to telephone for the doctor. She then went 'raving about the house' – to use Miss Riggs' phrase – drinking whisky furiously and crying out: 'Oh, poor Ratz! Poor Ratz! Can't somebody do something?' She screamed once when she trod on her husband's dental plate, which was lying on the floor.

Dr O'Donnell arrived at 11.45 p.m. and found Alma very drunk. He had sent for a surgeon, Mr Rooke, and together they decided that in view of Alma's hysterical condition it would be better to have Mr Rattenbury taken to a nursing home. There, after shaving his head, they found three wounds which had obviously been caused by extreme violence. Dr O'Donnell telephoned the central police station and asked for police officers to be sent to a possible case of murder. The wounds were, in his opinion, likely to prove fatal.

At about 3.15 a.m. Inspector Mills, who had already been to Villa Madeira, arrived at the nursing home. He collected Dr O'Donnell and Mr Rooke and took them back to Villa Madeira. Stoner, who had been sleeping in the Rattenburys' car outside the nursing home, drove Dr O'Donnell, following the police car.

At Villa Madeira every light in the house was on and the gramophone was playing loudly. Four police officers were in the house attempting to question an extremely drunken Mrs Rattenbury, who kept trying to kiss one of the officers. Dr O'Donnell turned off the gramophone and attempted to warn Mrs Rattenbury about the gravity of her husband's condition, but she was unable to comprehend what he was saying. She was simply too drunk to take it in.

Inspector Mills then said to her: 'Your husband has been seriously injured and is in a nursing home.'

Mrs Rattenbury replied: 'Will that be against me?' Inspector Mills then cautioned her and she made the following statement. 'I did it. He has lived too long. I will tell you in the morning where the mallet is.'

Dr O'Donnell remonstrated with the inspector, saying that Mrs Rattenbury was in no fit state to know what she was saying. He took her up to her bed and gave her a large injection of morphia – half a grain. But Alma managed to stagger back downstairs again and was once more being questioned by Inspector Mills. The doctor said to him: 'Look at her condition. She is full of whisky and I have just given her a large dose of morphia. She is in no condition to make any statement.'

Dr O'Donnell took Alma back to her bed and then went home – it was now well after 4 a.m. At 6 a.m. Inspector Carter arrived on the scene and awoke Mrs Rattenbury, getting Miss Riggs to make coffee to sober her up. He got a police matron to help the retching women bathe and dress. It will be recalled that Mrs Rattenbury had been drinking whisky from 11 p.m. the previous evening until 3.30 in the morning, and had also received a large dose of morphia, and was now prevented from sleeping it off.

At 8.15 Inspector Carter considered her to be competent to make a statement, which he wrote down in his notebook. It read:

About 9 p.m. on the 24th of March I was playing cards with my husband when he dared me to kill him, as he wanted to die. I picked up a mallet and he then said: 'You have not the guts to do it.' I then hit him with the mallet. I hid the mallet outside. I would have shot him if I'd had a gun.

232

Mrs Rattenbury signed the statement and was taken to Bournemouth police station, where she was charged with attempted murder. Before being led from Villa Madeira she had said to Miss Riggs: 'You must get Stoner to give me the mallet.' The fact was that despite her 'confession', she simply didn't know what Stoner had done with the mallet after he struck Ratz.

At the police station she was formally charged at 8.45 and replied: 'That is right. I did it deliberately and would do it again.' When she appeared before the magistrates later, the police did not mention that she had been drunk when answering police questions, and Mr Rooke, noticing this omission, made a point of telling Mrs Rattenbury's solicitor the true facts. Indeed, the medical officer at Holloway Prison found that Mrs Rattenbury was still under the influence of drugs three days later.

Stoner and Miss Riggs were left alone at Villa Madeira. Miss Riggs knew that Alma was innocent and suspected Stoner of being the assailant. Accordingly, she asked her mother and brother to move into the house with her, where they stayed until Stoner was arrested on Thursday, 28 March.

Stoner had a couple of days of freedom. He got drunk one night, going along the road shouting: 'Mrs Rattenbury's in jail and I put her there!' Miss Riggs was in a highly nervous state, determined to keep her mistress's secret about the liaison with Stoner, despite everything. Dr O'Donnell called on the morning of Thursday, 28 March, and found Miss Riggs alone. Stoner had gone to Holloway to visit Alma. Dr O'Donnell told Miss Riggs Mr Rattenbury had died, and pressed her to tell the police anything she knew which could help her mistress, pointing out that secrets meant nothing when a life was at stake. He himself knew of Mrs Rattenbury's affair with Stoner, he revealed.

He asked Miss Riggs if she thought her mistress had killed her husband. Miss Riggs replied: 'I know she did not do it.' Asked how she knew, she said that Stoner had confessed the crime to her, saying there would be no fingerprints on the mallet as he had worn gloves. Dr O'Donnell communicated this information to the police, and as a result, when Stoner returned home he was arrested and charged with murder. He told the police: 'Do you know Mrs Rattenbury had nothing to do with this? I did the job when he was asleep. I hit him and then came upstairs and told Mrs Rattenbury.'

Eventually Rattenbury and Stoner found themselves in the dock at the Old Bailey from 27 May to 31 May 1935. Both defendants made it difficult for their counsel: Stoner by inventing a fantastic story that he was a drug addict; Alma by her refusal to implicate Stoner.

Mr O'Connor, defending Mrs Rattenbury, told the jury that he would not seek to condone, much less commend, her conduct. His defence consisted of portraying Stoner as an insanely jealous youth. He went on: 'I am not here to cast one stone against that wretched boy, whose position there in the dock may be due to folly and self-indulgence on her part, to which he fell victim.'

He said of Stoner: 'Can you doubt, seduced, raised out of his sphere, taken away to London, given a very high time there; a lad who was melodramatic and went about with a dagger, violent sometimes, impulsive, jealous, his first love; a lad whose antecedents had been quiet, whose associations had been prosaic; never mixed with girls; flung into the vortex of this illicit love; unbalanced enough, and in addition to all these things, either endeavouring to sustain his passion with cocaine or already an addict of drugs. You may, as moral men and women, as citizens, condemn her in your souls for the part she has played in raising this position. She will bear to her grave the brand of reprobation, and men and women will know how she has acted. That will be her sorrow and disgrace so long as she lives. You may think of Mrs Rattenbury as a woman, self-indulgent and wilful, who by her own acts and folly has erected in this poor young man a Frankenstein of jealousy which she could not control.'

The trial began with Mr R. P. Croom-Johnson, prosecuting, telling the jury the background to the murder charge, to which both defendants had pleaded not guilty. He related how the wife and the boy had gone to London and booked into a hotel. How Alma Rattenbury had purchased a large number of articles for Stoner, including pyjamas, underclothing, suits and boots and a gold watch. She had also paid £15 10s for a diamond ring, which she then accepted from Stoner as a present.

The prosecutor said: 'It is our submission . . . that the relationship between Mrs Rattenbury and Stoner had ceased to be that of the wife of the employer and the man employed, but had become an adulterous intercourse . . . '

The prosecution submitted that the murder had been a joint enterprise between Mrs Rattenbury and Stoner: 'A common object and a common design.' Mr Croom-Johnson mentioned that when Mrs Rattenbury was being led from her house, under arrest, she had said to Stoner and Miss Riggs: 'Don't make fools of yourselves', to which Stoner had replied: 'You have got yourself into this mess by talking too much.'

Irene Riggs testified that she had been in Mrs Rattenbury's employ for some four years. On the night of the murder she said she had heard Alma calling out her name. She went downstairs and saw Mr Rattenbury slumped in his armchair. He appeared to have a black eye and was unconscious. There was some blood on the floor.

Stoner was called and helped carry Mr Rattenbury to his bed. Miss Riggs bathed the injured man's head, while Mrs Rattenbury tried to clean up the blood in the drawing room – 'because she did not want little John to see it in the morning'. (The prosecution claimed that the cleaning-up was done to cover up evidence of the crime.) Miss Riggs said that Mrs Rattenbury had been 'in a terrified state' and was drinking whisky 'continuously'.

She was asked about her experiences at Villa Madeira: 'Did you find it a very curious atmosphere there indeed?'

She replied: 'It was a little unusual.'

'She used to do strange things, did she not, sometimes walk about the garden late at night in her pyjamas?'

'I did not think it strange.'

'Did she sometimes stay up all night playing the gramophone?'

'Yes.'

'Did you think that was strange?'

'No, because I used to be with her.'

'All night long?'

'Yes.'

She admitted that she had been 'hurt' when her mistress started sleeping with Stoner, and agreed that Mrs Rattenbury used to drink too much and become 'excited'.

Dr O'Donnell testified on the second day of the trial. He told of being called late at night to attend to Mr Rattenbury. 'There was a bloodstained towel wrapped around his head. His head was bathed in blood, which was clotted and clinging to his hair, and I could not make any proper examination there. He was unconscious – laboured breathing. His left eye was very contused – purple and swollen. His pulse was slow and rather irregular.'

He said that Mrs Rattenbury had been very excited and was holding a glass of whisky and soda in her hand. He asked her what had happened and she said: 'Look at him, look at the blood. Somebody has finished him.' He said he was of the opinion that at four o'clock that morning Mrs Rattenbury was incapable of making a statement. She was too drunk and had received an injection of morphia. Yet the police persisted in questioning her.

In cross-examination Mr O'Connor, for Mrs Rattenbury, asked him: 'Did she tell you that Stoner was her lover?'

'She did.'

'What date was that?'

'12 February 1935.'

236

'Did she tell you of anything that Stoner had tried to do to her?'

'She told me he had tried to strangle her.'

He was taken back to the night of the murder. Mr O'Connor asked him: 'When you got back to Manor Road, at half-past three, describe what Mrs Rattenbury's condition was then.'

'She was very excited.'

'Was the gramophone playing?'

'Yes. She was running about the passage when I got there.'

'Running about?'

'Yes, staggering about . . . running from one room to the other.'

He told of giving Mrs Rattenbury an injection of half a grain of morphia.

'Half a grain is a very substantial dose?'

'Yes.'

'A dose which is likely to be effective and would persist for a considerable period of time?'

'It should do.'

'Would you be surprised in the case of Mrs Rattenbury to know that the effect persisted for as long as three or four days?'

'No, I would not.'

The doctor next saw Mrs Rattenbury in the police station the following day at 1 p.m. 'She could not walk – she had to be supported to the room where I was . . . She could not stand; she tottered when she tried to stand.'

'Was she trying to vomit?'

'She was trying to be sick.'

'Was she in a fit condition to make a statement?'

'I do not consider so.'

'What do you say as to her fitness to make a statement at six, seven, or eight o'clock that morning?'

'I should not place any credence on a statement given under such circumstances.'

In reply to Mr Casswell – appearing for Stoner – the

237

doctor said that Mrs Rattenbury had been suffering from tuberculosis. (A well-known side-effect of this condition is an increased sex-drive.)

Mr Casswell: 'With regard to Stoner, a boy of seventeen and a half, was that the sort of atmosphere you would put a boy in?'

'Well, it is very easy to be wise after the event. I should say no to that question.'

Mr Casswell tried hard to get the doctor to agree that Stoner was a cocaine addict. The doctor refused to confirm this from his own experience. He had been *told* so, but did not know it to be a fact.

Under re-examination, the prosecutor tried to get the doctor to agree that the police action in forcing Mrs Rattenbury to drink coffee and have a bath, after an excess of alcohol and a drug injection, would have helped her. He refused to agree with this. The judge asked him: 'Would you like to place any reliance at all on any statement made by a person under the influence of morphia?'

The doctor replied: 'No, my Lord.'

Mr Rooke, the surgeon, then testified. He had formed an opinion that 'three separate blows with a blunt instrument' had been inflicted upon Mr Rattenbury from behind. Cause of death was a fracture of the skull which injured the brain. Mr Casswell tried to get him to agree that the blows might have been struck from the front, but the surgeon refused this suggestion.

Constable Arthur Bagwell testified that he had been in the drawing room at Villa Madeira when Mrs Rattenbury – 'who was under the influence of drink to a mild extent' – said to him: 'I know who done it. I did it with a mallet. Ratz had lived too long. It is hidden. No, my lover did it. I would like to give you ten pounds. No, I won't bribe you.'

The constable said that he had looked for the 'hidden mallet' and found it outside the front door hidden behind the trellis-work. 'I examined the mallet and found a piece of flesh on it.' Constable Bagwell was the officer Mrs

238

Rattenbury had tried to kiss. He denied that she had ever been particularly excitable or drunk that night. 'She was not very drunk . . . '

Inspector William Mills said that he found Mrs Rattenbury 'very excited . . . and under the influence of drink.' He then recited the statement Mrs Rattenbury had made, in which she had admitted striking her husband with a mallet. He agreed that Dr O'Donnell had warned him that Mrs Rattenbury was not in a fit condition to make a statement.

Inspector William Carter followed him into the witness box. He had arrived at Villa Madeira at 6 a.m. and taken charge of the inquiry. He woke Mrs Rattenbury with coffee immediately. He then busied himself taking a statement from Stoner, who denied knowing anything of how Mr Rattenbury had come by his injuries.

'At 8.15 a.m. I went into Mrs Rattenbury's bedroom . . . She appeared to me to be definitely normal . . . I told her I was a police officer and then I arrested her. After I arrested her I charged her . . . I said to her: "I charge you that you did, by wounding, do grievous bodily harm to one Francis Mawson Rattenbury in an attempt to murder him on Sunday, 24 March 1935 . . ." She made a statement to me and I took it down.' It was the statement in which Mrs Rattenbury admitted striking her husband with the mallet. After it had been read back to her she had signed it.

Inspector Carter then told of arresting Stoner and searching him. He found a gold watch in Stoner's possession. 'Stoner said: "Be careful of that watch. It was given to me by Mrs Rattenbury and is worth twenty pounds." I also found on him letters from Mrs Rattenbury and two photographs of Mrs Rattenbury.'

Inspector Carter was cross-examined by Mr O'Connor, a very shrewd barrister. The following exchange is of great importance.

'You took a statement from her at 8.15?'

'Yes.'

'And you have told us she was quite normal?'

'I did.'

'How can you judge whether a person you have never seen before in your life was quite normal?'

'I saw Mrs Rattenbury when she woke up at 6 a.m. and she was not then in a normal condition; but it was at 8.15 that I decided she was in a normal condition, before I attempted to take a statement from her.'

'Do you know the medical officer at Holloway Prison has reported that she was still under the influence of drugs three days later?'

'He has never reported it to me.'

'Is your evidence to the jury that, from the time you began to take the statement until she left your charge, she did not appear to be under the influence of drugs?'

'She did not.'

'Not at any time?'

'Not at any time.'

Later in the trial Mr Justice Humphreys was turning over the pages of Inspector Carter's notebook when he came across an entry which had not been given in evidence. This was a statement Mrs Rattenbury made when she first woke up at 6 a.m. The judge drew the attention of defence counsel to this fact, and so made an important contribution to the defence.

Inspector Carter was recalled and Mr Justice Humphreys asked him: 'Did Mrs Rattenbury make any statement to you about the alleged crime before 8.15?'

'No statement to me, my Lord. Mrs Rattenbury said the words I have written into that book directly she woke up. I did not put them down in statement form. I did not refer to it in my evidence for this reason: when Mrs Rattenbury woke up I said in my evidence that, in my opinion, she was not in a normal condition.'

'Then in your opinion she was not in a condition to make a statement at 6.15?'

'No, my Lord.'

'Then what was said at that time was something said

by a woman who was not in a condition to make a statement that can be acted upon?'

'Not in my opinion, my Lord.'

The judge declared that the inspector had made a mistake. 'I think he was mistaken . . . in not informing the Director of Public Prosecutions that that statement had been made by the accused and that he had it in his notebook. It is not for the police officers . . . to decide what is admissible in evidence.'

The important point about that first entry in the inspector's notebook – the entry which he did not put in evidence – is that it is practically identical, word for word, with the statement he took at 8.15. In other words, she made the same statement when she was considered to be fit as she had made when unfit. Obviously she didn't know what she was saying at 8.15 any more than she had at 6.15 or even at 1 p.m. at the police station when she was still hopelessly unfit to make any statement.

In fact, she could not remember much of what had happened for days after her arrest. She did not remember signing a statement or even being driven away in a police car. Her self-incriminating statements were now badly tarnished.

Mr O'Connor got the inspector to admit that he had made up his mind to arrest Mrs Rattenbury *before* he had even questioned her. He did not arrest her at 6 a.m. out of a sense of decency. He wanted her in a sane condition before he charged her. But other police witnesses insisted that Mrs Rattenbury had not been drunk, Detective Constable Bright even asserted that he would have allowed Mrs Rattenbury to drive a motor vehicle that morning, so normal did she appear. Yet other witnesses had spoken of her being unable to stand, barely able to hold a coffee cup, incoherent and trembling . . .

On the third day of the trial Dr Roche Lynch, a Home Office pathologist, testified about the weight of the mallet and the human matter found on it. Under cross-examination by Mr Casswell he was asked numerous questions about cocaine addiction. That it makes a person do foolish things, can cause insane jealousy, and so on. It was all unnecessary – since Stoner had not been proved to be a cocaine addict – but all the medical terminology was designed to impress the jury into believing that perhaps the lad *had* snorted coke . . .

The senior medical officer at Brixton Prison testified that Stoner had put on eight pounds in weight since becoming an inmate. Once again Mr Casswell cross-examined about the nature and effect of cocaine addiction in great detail. The prosecution revealed that when asked to describe cocaine, Stoner had said it was 'a brownish powder with black specks in it'. It is, of course, a white crystalline powder.

That same third day of the trial came the highlight, when Alma Rattenbury went into the witness box. Asked 'Was your married life happy?' Alma replied: 'Like that,' tilting her hand from side to side. But she said that the marriage had been 'cordial'.

Turning to the hiring of Stoner, in September 1934, she was asked: 'When did you become Stoner's mistress?'

'In November.'

' . . . from that time until your husband's death did relations take place between you and Stoner regularly?'

'Yes.'

'In his room or yours or both?'

'Yes.'

'What attitude did your husband take toward this, if he knew it?'

'None whatsoever . . . He told me to lead my own life quite some years ago.'

It all came out in full shameful detail: the trip to London, the buying of expensive presents, the fact that she had sex with Stoner in her bedroom while her six-year-old son lay sleeping in the same room, until the night of the murder itself. 'He told me he had hurt Ratz. It did not penetrate my head what he did say to me at all until I heard Ratz groan, and then my brain became

242

alive and I jumped out of bed.' She denied murdering her husband or taking part in the planning of it, and said she had completely lost her memory of events from the night of the murder until about three days later.

In cross-examination Mr Croom-Johnson asked her: 'What was the last occasion on which you were intimate with Stoner?'

'Saturday.'

Questioned about her loss of memory, she said it was all 'an awful nightmare'. She did not remember Dr O'Donnell's arrival at the house, or being arrested and taken to the police station or appearing before the magistrates. Yet she had signed two cheques in the police station for the wages of Miss Riggs and Stoner.

She was asked: 'Did it not occur to you that if you went to Bridport, Mr Rattenbury might want to treat you as his wife? You know exactly what I mean by treat you as his wife?'

'Yes, exactly.'

'When had you last been intimate with your husband?'

'About six years ago.'

On re-examination Mr O'Connor read out a letter from the governor of Holloway Prison: 'She was received into my custody on the evening of March 25th, and I saw her early next morning. She was very depressed and seemed very confused, repeating the same sentence over and over again . . . ' Expert medical testimony was given to the effect that loss of memory could follow the administration of morphia.

The defence of Stoner seemed to rest solely on the fact that he was a cocaine addict and was therefore not responsible for his actions. That and the unhealthy influence of the older woman . . .

Dr Gillespie, noted psychologist and doctor, was asked by Mr Croom-Johnson: 'Is regular sexual intercourse between a boy of eighteen with a member of the opposite sex . . . a woman twice his age . . . likely to do him harm or good?' Counsel tried to get him to agree that it would make the boy pale and anaemic and fatigued. He asked him: 'Do you really find any difficulty in answering the question?'

Dr Gillespie replied: 'I find difficulty in answering the question as I believe you expect it to be answered.'

Mr Casswell, in his closing speech on behalf of Stoner, asked for a verdict of guilty but insane of murder, or guilty but insane of manslaughter, citing the cocaine habit as causing 'an uncontrollable impulse', and the harmful influence of Mrs Rattenbury.

The Crown then made its closing speech – Mrs Rattenbury's counsel having the right to speak last because it had called no witnesses. Mr Croom-Johnson referred to the case as 'a story of immorality and vice'. He too referred to Stoner as having been dominated by Mrs Rattenbury, saying: 'I suggest to you it is the key to the problem.' He dismissed talk of her loss of memory and said she was just as guilty as Stoner. It had been a joint venture, 'a common object'. As for Stoner, the proof against him was overwhelming, and the defence submission that he was somehow not responsible for his actions was 'extraordinary'. By fetching the mallet hours before he did the deed, Stoner had shown premeditation.

Mr O'Connor then got up to make a brilliant speech in defence of Alma Rattenbury. Stoner had sat in the dock looking unmoved during the trial, but Mrs Rattenbury seemed to have aged twenty years. The defence ridiculed the prosecution theory that Mr Rattenbury had somehow 'stood in the way', and that Mrs Rattenbury was willing to exchange the comforts of Villa Madeira to go and live with Stoner on a pound a week. There was a complete absence of motive. And her drink-sodden statements were absurd. On the evidence presented by the Crown 'no jury in the world could convict this woman'. He urged the jury to acquit, saying: 'She has been punished enough. Wherever she goes she will be a figure of shame.'

Then on the fifth day, Friday, 31 May, Mr Justice Humphreys summed up. He was scrupulously fair but his words must have cut Alma Rattenbury to the quick. She was, in the words of F. Tennyson Jesse: 'A woman at the extreme edge of what it was possible to bear and go on living.' She heard the judge describe her husband as 'that very unpleasant character for which, I think, they have no suitable English expression, but which the French call *un mari complaisant*, a man who knew his wife was committing adultery and had no objection to it – not a nice character'.

Of Alma Rattenbury he said: 'If indeed she is a person who has any moral understanding at all ... a woman lost to all sense of decency, so entirely without morals that she would stop at nothing to gain her ends, particularly her sexual gratification ... we have this orgy in London ... members of the jury ... it may be, having regard to the facts of this case, that you will say you cannot possibly feel any sympathy for that woman, you cannot have any feeling but disgust for her.' He might well have been speaking about a baby-killer ...

Nevertheless, when it came to the *facts* of the case the judge was very fair indeed – although he did try to suggest that Alma Rattenbury and Stoner *must* have been planning to live together. He said to the jury: 'Do you believe that while they were in London the future was not discussed? What they were going to do when they got back? Could life go on in the same way? Would not something have to be done with – or to – Mr Rattenbury?' However, he dismissed the statements made by Mrs Rattenbury when drunk and under the influence of morphia, saying: 'It seems to me it would be very unfair to form any conclusions against the woman on the grounds of a statement made in those circumstances.'

The jury retired at 2.48 p.m. and were out for forty-seven minutes. They found Alma Rattenbury not guilty. They found Stoner guilty of murder, but added a rider recommending mercy. The judge sentenced Stoner to hang.

Mrs Rattenbury was led from the court a broken

woman, looking closer to sixty than thirty-eight. Her relatives gave her refuge, but the flat was besieged by newspaper reporters and she had to flee into a nursing home. She had reached rock-bottom and was ill both physically and mentally. Life held nothing for her. The man she loved was to be hanged. The love they had shared had been cheapened into 'an adulterous intercourse'.

On 3 June she slipped out of the nursing home and took a train to a quiet meadow spot beside a river. There she spent hours writing on the backs of envelopes, declaring her love for Stoner, her hounding by the press, the impossibility of going on living. She had failed to grasp the impossible dream, to make love come true between May and September.

William Charles Mitchell, a Christchurch cowman, testified at the inquest held on Alma Rattenbury. He said that on 4 June at 8.30 p.m. he was walking across a meadow adjoining Stoney Lane, Christchurch. He saw Mrs Rattenbury sitting on the bank of a stream, smoking a cigarette. She was alone. He crossed the stream by the bridge and as he did so looked over and saw that she was standing by the water's edge. He saw a knife in her hand. She appeared to fall into the water. He ran to help, but found her lying face-down in the water, with blood in the water. She was too far out for him to reach, so he went for the police.

The inquest verdict was suicide. She had stabbed herself in the breast no less than six times, three of the wounds penetrating the heart. This raises interesting questions of pathology. For example, when the Baader-Meinhof terrorists committed suicide in Stammheim Prison on 18 October 1977, of the four prisoners, two were found dead in their cells, one was dying, and another injured. Irmgard Möller had four stab wounds in her left breast, all about one and a half inches deep. Professor Eberhard Hoffmeister operated on her at the University Hospital of Tübingen. He said afterwards: 'I have never come across a case of a woman trying to commit suicide by stabbing herself in the breast. There would be an inbuilt inhibition towards such an act.' This led to press accusations that the terrorists had been murdered in their cells by the authorities. The case of Alma Rattenbury was obviously unknown to the good doctor . . .

The coroner read out extracts from the notes Alma had left behind, including one which read: 'If only I thought it would help Stoner I would stay on, but it has been pointed out to me all too vividly that I cannot help him. That is my death sentence.' Another read: 'What a lovely world we are in! It must be easier to be hanged than to have to do the job oneself . . . God bless my children and look after them.'

The irony of it all was that Stoner was reprieved a few days later, after 300,000 people had signed a petition for leniency. He served seven years of a life sentence, and got married in the 1960s. Even if Alma *had* stayed on it would have made no difference. The impossible dream had been shattered by the cruel and scornful eyes of the world as much as by that mallet.

There is an epilogue to this case. Fifty-five years later, in September 1990, Stoner made the headlines again when he once more appeared in court. Now a frail pensioner aged seventy-four, he pleaded guilty to the sexual assault of an eleven-year-old boy in a public toilet in Bournemouth. He narrowly escaped a prison sentence, getting probation instead. The man who had arrested Stoner all those years ago and who rose to become deputy chief constable was still alive too, aged eighty-three. He commented: 'I couldn't believe it when I heard he had been arrested for assaulting a young boy. He never struck me as that kind of chap. He was reserved and introspective. I would not have thought he would have degraded himself in this way . . . He always had regrets about what he had done. He took one life and was indirectly responsible for another.'

247

It is a sad and sordid footnote which takes all the romance out of the tale. But then, real life is never a romance story.

16
KIM NEWELL: DEATH OF A KILLER LADY
1967

As we entered the new year of 1991, the death from cancer was reported of Kim Newell, the notorious woman in the 'Red Mini' murder case of 1967. Since her release from prison on completion of a life sentence, she had suffered an unhappy life and begun to express regrets about the past. It is worth recalling the case simply to remind ourselves of something which philosophers and dramatists have been trying to teach us for centuries: we are punished not for our sins, but *by* our sins. Kim Newell, like Lady Macbeth, found that the act of murder came back to haunt her . . .

And although there is no obvious parallel with the previous case of Rattenbury and Stoner, we have the same sense of a self-indulgent woman who was punished by her sins.

The case had its origins in what might have been a typical *crime passionel*, the adulterous relationship between Raymond Cook and Kim Newell, but in reality the motive for murder was sordid greed. A murder for profit which profited no one. It was intended to be the 'perfect murder', an elaborate plot to stage a car accident, but it fooled no one. The credit for quickly spotting the apparent accident as a deliberate murder goes to a village constable with the unlikely name of Sherlock . . .

It began as a routine accident report. Constable Sherlock, stationed at Nettlebed, near Henley-on-Thames, was on patrol in a police radio car on the evening of 2

March 1967 when he got a message to go to the scene of an accident on the road to Rumerhedge Wood, about three miles away. It was 10 p.m. and dark. Arriving at the scene, on a sharp bend in the road through the forest, he found two cars illuminating a third car with their headlights. The third car, a red Mini, apparently had its bonnet buried in the trunk of a beech tree. Three men at the scene had not been involved in the accident but had stopped to render assistance. They told the constable that an ambulance had already taken the two occupants of the Mini to hospital; the male passenger seemed dazed, but the female driver was unconscious. One of the men, a nearby garage owner, said he had arrived first on the scene to see a man bending over the body of the woman on the ground. The man had then gone to his car and driven off. Whoever the mystery man was, he appeared to be driving a Cortina.

PC Sherlock carried out the routine investigation. He noticed that there were no signs of tyre-marks on the road: no sign of any skid or any brakes having been applied. The Mini was only slightly damaged; even the windscreen remained intact. From his experience, the car could only have been travelling at 10 mph when it crashed.

Yet when he examined the interior of the car he found heavy bloodstaining on the driver's side, none on the passenger side. The constable had assumed, because of the slight damage to the car, that neither of the occupants could have been seriously injured. After straightening the wing away from the off-side front wheel, he reversed the car back to the road, then got the garage owner to drive it to his garage.

Sherlock drove home to his police house in Nettlebed, taking a woman's handbag from the car and a pair of woman's shoes found outside the car. He made a routine phone call to Battle Hospital in Reading to enquire about the condition of the driver, and was astonished to be told that the woman was dead. The male passenger appeared to be drunk, not dazed.

After alerting his headquarters to the fatality, Sherlock drove to the hospital to view the victim for himself. He found that the woman had extensive injuries to the face and head, and had been close to death on admission to hospital. Surgeons had performed an emergency tracheotomy to help the woman breathe, but in vain. Sherlock interviewed the male passenger, who smelt of alcohol and was incoherent in his speech. The constable put this down to shock. The man said he was Raymond Sidney Cook, a thirty-two-year-old draughtsman who worked in Reading. The dead woman was his wife, June Serina Cook, a schoolteacher of forty-one and the mother of two young sons.

The constable offered to drive Cook home to Spencers Wood, just outside Reading. He had to ask directions and was surprised that Mr Cook gave the directions precisely, yet replied with vague mumbles when questioned about the cause of the accident.

On arrival at Cook's home, Sherlock sent for the local doctor, then went to speak to Mrs Cook's parents, who lived next door. They were shattered by the news of their daughter's death. The constable gained the impression that the couple disapproved of their son-in-law, and they talked of rows their daughter and Cook had had recently. Sherlock made a mental note: another woman? He tried once more to get a statement from Cook, but had to give up when he met with incoherent nonsense.

Sherlock drove straight to police headquarters. He reported to a senior officer and told him that he was not satisfied with the accident story: he suspected foul play. Asked to substantiate his claims, Sherlock replied that the damage to the car was so slight that the accident could not have caused the serious injuries to Mrs Cook. And why had the husband received no injuries at all? He was also suspicious about the fact that the husband had refused to talk about the accident. As he talked to the detective, Sherlock grew more and more certain in his own mind that something was badly wrong with the 'accident' as it presented itself.

Indefatigable, he drove back to the accident scene for another look. The car was gone, but he noted bark knocked from the tree. He stood and ruminated. The windscreen had been unbroken . . . Then he remembered that when he had got into the car to back it up, he had not needed to adjust the rearview mirror – even though the woman was six inches shorter than himself. The ignition and lights had been off, but the handbrake had been on. Why? Who would pull on the handbrake after a head-on collision with a tree? And who was the mystery man seen bending over the body? The constable went back home and telephoned headquarters again, requesting that a Scene of Crime Officer be sent to the accident scene when it was light.

After a couple of hours of snatched sleep, Constable Sherlock was again on the case, even though it was his day off. He went first to the garage to examine the Mini in daylight. The driver's seat and steering wheel had been washed clean of blood, but he could see that the outside of the car was also covered in blood, and above the off-side rear wheel arch he found a human hair plastered in blood and stuck to the paintwork.

Sherlock then went to see Cook again, determined this time to get some answers. Cook said that he and his wife had been driving home from dinner at a hotel in Pangbourne. He had stopped the car, feeling sick, and allowed his wife to take the wheel. Soon afterwards a car coming in the opposite direction had dazzled them with its headlights. He remembered nothing after that. Presumably that was when the car had crashed. He signed his statement.

Sherlock went away, determined to trace that mystery man who had been at the scene before anyone else and might have vital information. Meanwhile, Sherlock took the Scene of Crime Officer, Sergeant McMiken, to the accident site.

The sergeant took photographs of the damaged tree, and then moved back to get a long shot of the bend in the road. It was then that he spotted a large patch of blood on the road, at least seven inches across. This was seventy-five yards from the crash site. The sergeant took a scraping of the blood. Both officers then went to inspect the Mini, and photographed that trapped human hair *in situ*. The most puzzling feature was the sheer amount of blood both inside and outside the vehicle. It suggested that the victim had suffered at least two injuries: one inside and one outside the car.

Detective Inspector Insell now took over what had become a potential murder inquiry. The Mini was transported to Henley police station for forensic tests. The inspector went to the hospital, where the pathologist told him that there was a high level of alcohol in the dead woman's blood, and the wound to her skull had been so severe that her brain was exposed. He suggested that the woman must have been thrown through the windscreen to hit her head on the tree – *but the windscreen was unbroken.* Told of the discovery of a large patch of blood seventy-five yards away, the pathologist said that the victim could not have walked that distance with such a serious injury. Insell requested a second post-mortem and had blood samples sent to the forensic lab. He also arranged for the BBC to broadcast a report of the accident and appeal for the Cortina driver to come forward.

Now came the classic confrontation of all crime fiction and fact. The inspector paid a visit to Raymond Cook, who had just come back from identifying his wife's body at the mortuary. The inspector had Sherlock with him, and both officers listened politely as Cook repeated his version of events. When asked what he had done with the clothing he had been wearing at the time of the accident, Cook said it was at the cleaner's, apart from a shirt he had asked his mother to wash. He had burned his leather driving gloves because they too were soaked with blood.

Cook went on to say that he and his wife had been married for eight years and had got into the habit of dining out every Thursday night. He repeated his original statement, but Sherlock noted that he spoke very slowly, as if weighing each word. It took him three hours to tell of dining at the George Hotel, and then the dazzling headlights.

More productive was an interview with the dead woman's parents. They had given the house to the couple as a wedding present, even though they disapproved of Raymond Cook. They disclosed that he had left his wife the previous autumn to live with another woman, a girl called Kim Mule who had been a nurse at the Borocourt Mental Hospital when Raymond Cook worked there.

The following day Insell set up a squad of six officers to investigate the background to the people involved, particularly the relationship between Cook and Kim Mule – who was now known to be Kim Newell, or Valerie Dorothy Newell. Insell also began to feed tantalizing scraps of information to the press, suggesting foul play. It would not hurt to apply a little psychological pressure to the suspect.

Information came in about the Cortina. One witness had seen it parked on the road at 9.20 p.m., but another man who used the road had not seen it at 9.30 p.m. On 6 March 1967, Home Office pathologist Dr Derek Barrowcliff first examined the Mini, then went with Insell to search the area of the crash site. After patient sifting, they found minute skull splinters. In the opinion of the pathologist, Mrs Cook had been hit on the head with a blunt instrument while being held. It was murder.

Scotland Yard detectives were now called in, and Detective Superintendent Ian Forbes and Detective Sergeant Peter Hill from the Murder Squad took rooms at the George Hotel in Reading. Forbes was a Scot with a strong accent who had solved all fourteen murders he had worked on. That night he spent reading the statements and examining the evidence. He arranged for the red Mini to be taken to the Yard's own forensic science lab in Holborn. A prudent decision, since the Mini was to divulge a wealth of evidence.

The sergeant held a press conference the following day and uttered the usual formula: 'Foul play cannot be ruled out.' It was more psychological pressure. It meant that reporters were hounding Cook, the obvious suspect, for interviews.

Cook told reporters that he remembered nothing of the crash, but did remember a man's voice telling him to sit still and someone pushing him back into his seat. That man was a fireman, who told police that Cook had been difficult, fighting and falling out of the car. The fireman remembered seeing the Cortina, and described it in detail. It was dark blue with a deluxe model grill and without wing mirrors.

All the newspaper publicity paid off when a house painter named Angus Macdonald told the police that he had seen a dark blue Cortina being driven into Reading from the Oxford direction on the night in question, and the driver was being directed by his woman passenger. Macdonald had been on his way to visit his mother, who lived next door to Kim Newell, and she had been the woman in the Cortina... He could even remember the registration number of the Cortina: it was 7711 FM. The pieces of the puzzle were falling into place.

Kim Newell, a good-looking blonde who wore tight ribbed sweaters, was put under observation. She was not working, but it was known that Cook was supporting her and phoned her regularly. Meanwhile, Detective Inspector Insell went to the dry cleaner's and collected Cook's clothes, along with a sample of the cleaning fluid used. These were sent to the Yard's lab. The Cortina was traced to a heavy plant hire company in Wrexham, and police watched the driver get into the car. His name was Eric Jones. He told officers that he had not been driving the car on the day of the murder anywhere near Reading, but had been in London all that day, having travelled via the M1 motorway.

Cook and Newell were revelling in the press attention, Newell striking poses for them like a model, and Cook using them to get information about the progress of the investigation. He was feeling frustrated because the police had not been to question him. In fact, Superintendent Forbes was deliberately ignoring Cook, playing a game of cat-and-mouse with him. He knew all he needed to know about the pair, having compiled a dossier on their backgrounds.

June Cook was a Reading girl who trained as a teacher, married, and emigrated to America with her husband in 1949. The marriage failed and she returned to England, getting a divorce in 1958. Less than a year later she married twenty-four-year-old Raymond Cook, then working as a draughtsman. She was twelve years his senior. They subsequently had two children, and Mrs Cook returned to teaching. She was worth more than ten thousand pounds in savings and the rent she received from properties she owned; even in the swinging sixties, ten grand was still a lot of money and a prime motive for murder.

But Mrs Cook controlled the purse strings, leaving Raymond Cook short of money to keep his mistress, Kim Newell. When Cook left his wife, she changed her will, leaving her money to her children. He returned only on the understanding that she would make a new will leaving him everything. And when he returned to her, in January 1967, he made sure they had an insurance policy which paid out a thousand pounds in the event of her death in a motoring accident. And there were rumours that Kim Newell was pregnant by Cook . . . It all made interesting reading, but as evidence it was purely circumstantial. What was needed was positive scientific proof.

The forensic people supplied that. All the blood in the red Mini was found to be Mrs Cook's, and it was heaviest around the driving seat. Blood on the passenger seat indicated that the seat had been empty when Mrs Cook bled, and blood had spurted in several directions, indicating that she had been moving her head when hit more than once. Crucially, the evidence revealed that she had been struck *before* the car hit the tree, as proved by bodywork which had been dislodged by the crash and had blood partially over it.

The pathologist was able to add to this, following a new postmortem examination. Mrs Jones had been killed by at least seven wounds to the front of the head, four of which had been inflicted at the same time. She must have been in a kneeling position outside the driver's door when hit, and had been struck repeatedly over the head from above. Her neck had been broken by someone standing over her and twisting her head by her hair.

The inquest on the dead woman opened on 17 March and then adjourned. Immediately afterwards Superintendent Forbes arrested Cook, telling him: 'I saw the dead body of your wife June Cook at the mortuary ... and as a result of inquiries we have made I am now going to take you to police headquarters where you will be charged with her murder.'

Jones was now brought in. Evidence had been uncovered linking him with Cook and Newell, and when interviewed again he admitted having been in Reading on 2 March. He had gone to see Kim Newell, who wanted an abortion. He said he had known Newell for six or seven years, and had seen her in December 1966, when she introduced him to her boyfriend, a tall man she called 'Ray'. But he denied any knowledge of a murder plot.

Superintendent Forbes now interviewed Kim Newell at the police station. She had been a student nurse and nanny, and on her first job away from home had become pregnant by Eric Jones. Later, Jones aborted her. When she began working at the mental hospital, she began an affair with Raymond Cook. Questioned about her movements on 2 March, she said she had cashed a cheque for ten pounds for Cook that day. He had told her, to spend five pounds on a dress and called in the afternoon to collect the change. Cook made sexual overtures to her but she rejected them. Cook told her that he could no longer afford to pay her rent – and Newell admitted having received hundreds of pounds from Cook in previous months. She said she felt that Cook owed her the money as she had become pregnant by him and lost her job as a result of their affair. She stated that she never had any intention of marrying Cook, although he did not realize this.

Jones had called that evening to ask her if she was still pregnant and wanted anything doing about it. She went with him in the car to show him his direction home, and he dropped her off at her flat at about 7.40 p.m. She had stayed in the rest of the night. She admitted having visited Raymond Cook every day save for Wednesday, 22 March, the day before her statement was taken.

Newell was interviewed again a few days later. This time she mentioned that Raymond Cook had met Eric Jones at Wrexham, but made no further admissions.

Superintendent Forbes learned that Newell had told her sister Janett that Eric Jones killed Mrs Cook by hitting her over the head with a car jack. There had been a previous conspiracy to drown June Cook by running her car into a river, but Cook had vetoed that. The murder plot had been arranged so that when Cook took his wife to dinner, Jones would flag him down for a lift on the pretext that his car had broken down.

Cook was to have pointed out the proposed murder spot to Jones on the early evening of 2 March but he was late home. Kim Newell had to show Jones the spot. That put her in the frame as an accessory before the fact.

Telling her sister of the actual murder, Newell related that Jones had hit Mrs Cook but failed to stun her. He then said: 'I'll bloody well have to kill her now,' and proceeded to do just that. Afterwards Jones threatened

Cook and his children with death to protect himself from ever being incriminated in the deed.

Superintendent Forbes now had enough of the pieces. On Sunday, 16 April, he arrested Kim Newell. She finally broke and told the full story in a statement which took her almost three hours. Soon afterwards Jones made a statement admitting his part in the plot.

Cook, Jones and Newell were tried for the murder at the Oxford Assizes. Later the charge against Newell was altered to one of being an accessory before the fact. All three were found guilty and jailed for life, after the prosecution had described twenty-three-year-old Newell as being 'at the heart of the plot'. Jones had become a prosecution witness and testified against his former partners in murder.

After the case Superintendent Forbes said Kim Newell was 'the most evil woman I have ever met'. Two months afterwards Newell gave birth to a son, Paul, in prison, and gave him away.

Later, a court ruled that the will of Mrs Cook, leaving £10,651 to her husband, could not stand because under the law a murderer cannot benefit from his victim's estate. The money went to the bereaved children.

The men were released before Kim Newell, even the husband who had watched as his wife was beaten to death. She was deemed to be the worst of the three because she had been an avaricious temptress, scheming and pitiless. In prison she was intractable, and served thirteen years before being released. While inside, she met someone even more evil than herself, Myra Hindley, and admitted to liking her. 'I was surprised by her . . . I had read so much about her and she still came across as a normal woman. In a way I liked her. I have asked myself how she could have helped kill those children.'

Kim Newell walked free from prison in 1980 and joined her parents in a bungalow on a Welsh hillside. She married a decorator she had met in prison. The marriage did not last; it was bleak and without children. Then she began having pains in her back, and soon cancer was diagnosed. She spent her last few years in pain, her good looks ravaged.

Towards the end she began talking about the past – a sort of death-bed confession. But she never fully admitted her guilt. She said: 'I never used men, they used me. If they saw me they would stop in the street. Chat me up perhaps, or offer me a lift . . . I had a sort of power, I suppose, because of the effect I had on men. But I didn't know that Cook was going to do it. When I read in the paper she had died I was fearful. Fearful for me. Fearful for what would happen to my dog. I loved my dog . . . Jones and Cook? Oh, I never loved them.'

Then, talking about the only person she ever felt anything for, the weary, gaunt woman said: 'Paul, where is he? When will he come?' The baby she gave up at the age of ten months.

The blonde beauty is gone. Cancer is a terrible way to die, but perhaps at least one can say about Kim Newell – unlike the thousands of innocent people who die each year from it – that she deserved it. She wasn't upset by the brutal murder of her rival in love, but was more concerned about the fate of her dog. Murder brought her pain but no gain. The grim story of so many killers.

17
THE CASSERLEY AFFAIR, 1938

Sheer physical lust is all too often the driving motive for murder. A man in the grip of sex is like a man possessed: cabinet ministers have thrown their careers away for it, top businessmen have been ruined, clever men made to look like idiots, and desperate men to kill. When the murder involves some sordid adulterous affair, it is hard to feel pity for the protagonists, and when they protest: 'But I was in the grip of passion!' it is like the familiar excuse of every rapist, mugger and opportunist thief: 'I had too much to drink, your honour . . . '

In short, sex may dress in silk and wear a pretty painted face, but underneath the façade lies a dangerous and even ugly emotion.

However, now and again – rarely, in fact – there comes along a case which is not mere sex but true love; a shining and inspiring affection which transcends time, the courts of law, the confines of prison, and has the traditional happy ending. Such was the Casserley affair, a half-century ago. It is a story of passion, tragedy and faith which still has the power to thrill the heart of anyone who is not a hopeless cynic. It is proof that love can and does exist in a bleak and hostile world.

Percy Arthur Casserley, the husband in the case, was a miserable creature who gave his wife a life of hell – perhaps because he was twenty years older than his wife Georgina when they married in 1927. He was then forty-seven and she twenty-seven. Perhaps it was not exactly the marriage of spring and autumn, but it was a considerable age gap which did not presage well for the future.

Percy Casserley had made his way in the world and was the managing director of John Watney & Co., the London brewers. His salary was £1,500 a year – a small fortune for the time – and by 1937 he and his wife Georgina lived in some comfort at a villa in Wimbledon: 35 Lindisfarne Road. Casserley was a tall, athletic-looking man – he had once been a runner with the South London Harriers – but his appearance belied the true man. In fact he was a chronic alcoholic who abused his wife.

His losing battle with the bottle forced his early retirement that September. With no work to occupy him and at a loss to spend his time, he began drinking even more – his daily consumption was a bottle and a half of whisky. Although he did not abuse his wife physically, his conduct amounted to mental cruelty. He was moody and irritable, never once took his wife out, and regularly stayed up until past midnight drinking. More importantly, perhaps, following an operation he had become impotent. His wife remained a healthy and vigorous woman with repressed desires building up inside her until she was like a ripe fruit, waiting to fall into a convenient hand.

That hand belonged to Edward Royal Chaplin, a brawny, handsome man of thirty-five, who was divorced. He was a building foreman, and in the spring of 1937 work had begun on the construction of houses close to the Casserley home, near Wimbledon Common. Edward Chaplin was the site foreman, and one imagines that Mrs Casserley must have often secretly watched the powerfully built man as he worked, stripped to the waist, on the house near by. Certainly she invited him into her house for a cup of tea one day, and from there romance blossomed.

By January 1938 Mr Casserley was in such a poor state of health that he had to become an in-patient at a nursing home for alcoholics, and he stayed there between

16 January and 17 February. While the husband was away, Chaplin was staying overnight at 35 Lindisfarne Road, occupying the master's bed and his wife. And Mrs Casserley was known to have visited Chaplin at his lodgings in Abbotsbury Road, Morden.

When Percy Casserley returned to his home his wife gave him some traumatic news: she was pregnant. The news absolutely shattered him, and the humiliation caused another breakdown. His pride and manhood destroyed, he told his brother-in-law: 'One way out would be for me to shoot myself.' He was evidently under the impression that his wife's lover was a tea-planter on six months' leave from Ceylon – proof that when 'lovely woman stoops to folly' she displays an extraordinary ability to deceive. Mr Casserley returned to the nursing home suffering from a nervous breakdown. He was there from 8 to 22 March, and while he was away Georgina and Edward continued their dalliance.

The coming baby was a problem. Abortion was out of the question then, and both parents were anxious to make the child legitimate. Divorce was the only solution. At thirty-eight, Georgina was desperate to become a mother, and Edward Chaplin wanted both mother and child to bear his name. Georgina plucked up her courage and wrote to Percy in the nursing home, begging him to grant her a divorce. His reply was a curt note. 'Do you think I am such a fool as to give you up for someone else?'

The conclusion to this marital discord was dramatic. Mr Casserley returned home on 22 March 1938, and the following evening he was dead – murdered by the lover, the police were to claim. A vital witness in the case was the living-in maid, Lydia Scott, who had become Mrs Casserley's confidante and carried messages to the lover.

Lydia Scott later testified at the murder trial of Edward Chaplin about the events of Wednesday, 23 March 1938. She said she had suggested to Mrs Casserley that they should both go out to the cinema that night, and Mrs Casserley had agreed. Later, however, Mrs Casserley complained bitterly that her husband had forbidden her to go out and threatened to shoot her if she so much as set foot outside the house. 'She was in a state of fear and distress,' claimed the housekeeper. When Lydia Scott left the house alone at 6.45 p.m., Mrs Casserley asked her: 'If you happen to see Ted, tell him I shall only be able to see him for a minute or two. I won't be able to get out. If he comes to the back door I'll be able to see him . . . Do try and see him.'

Chaplin had arranged to meet Mrs Casserley at 7.30 p.m. at Coombe Lane, and was surprised when Lydia Scott appeared instead. She told him: 'Madam can't get out tonight. Will you go up to the house to see her, if only for a few minutes?' She explained that her mistress was in great distress and mentioned Mr Casserley's threat of violence.

A grim-faced Ted Chaplin walked to the Casserleys' house, arriving just as Mrs Casserley left in tears. She had made a pretext of going to the local off-licence to get her husband a bottle of whisky: it was the only way she could leave the house. Together, she and her lover walked to the off-licence at Copse Hill, arriving there at about 7.45 p.m. She purchased the bottle of whisky, but then told Chaplin that she was afraid to go home, fearing violence from her husband. Chaplin assured her that he would personally see to it that she came to no harm.

Chaplin walked her back to the villa in Lindisfarne Road and followed her into the kitchen, where they held a whispered conversation. Chaplin was dressed in clothing suitable for a blustery and cold March day. He wore a raincoat over his jacket and trousers, with a hat on his head and gloves on his hands. His clothing was later to be brought into question as being proof of premeditation. Chaplin told Mrs Casserley to go up to her bedroom and stay there, saying: 'Ena, you had better leave this to me. I'll have it out with him.'

From her bedroom Mrs Casserley heard the sound of men's voices raised in anger, then a scuffle followed by two gunshots. Then someone came up the stairs and opened the door to her bedroom. It was Ted Chaplin. It could just as easily have been her husband, come to finish her off, she told the police.

Chaplin's own account of that fatal evening was told in court. He had entered the lounge intending to have a 'man-to-man talk' with Percy Casserley. He found the husband sitting in an armchair by the fire. He announced himself by saying: 'Good evening', and removed his gloves to shake hands. Percy Casserley stood up abruptly, his spectacles falling to the floor, his face mottled with rage. He had not expected the mystery lover to have the effrontery to beard him in his own den.

Chaplin then said: 'I've called to see what the trouble is between you and Mrs Casserley. I've just left her and she's terribly upset. You know about her condition. I'm responsible for it. I want to suggest to you that she either comes away with me tonight or I'll phone and get her police protection, as I understand you have threatened her.'

Percy Casserley stared dumbfounded at the other man. At last, recovering his wits, he shouted: 'Oh, so it's you, you swine!' Chaplin pulled his gloves back on, preparing to leave the room. Percy Casserley went to a bureau, where he sat with his head in his hands for a moment or two. Then he opened a drawer and took out a pistol. Chaplin said that he had anticipated such a move and immediately dived at the husband, seizing his right arm with both hands and twisting it until Percy Casserley was forced to drop the weapon. At this point, said Chaplin, he released the husband 'because he looked ill'. He was having to half-support the husband, who had obviously taken too much to drink and was distraught with anger and despair.

But Percy Casserley took advantage of the temporary truce to pick up the pistol with his *left* hand. Chaplin countered by grabbing the gun with his right hand. With his left hand he grabbed the husband's right wrist and they had a stand-up face-to-face struggle, with Chaplin desperately trying to keep the muzzle of the pistol pointing upwards and away from himself. In the course of the struggle the gun went off, causing a superficial wound to the back of Casserley's neck. Chaplin changed his grip, intending to seize the other man around the waist and wrestle him to the floor, but as he did so Casserley's right hand gripped his testicles – Casserley's left hand was still gripping the pistol.

In agony from what he termed in court 'a portion of my anatomy', Chaplin grabbed a large torch which was lying on top of the bureau, and with his left hand struck the husband three times over the head. The torch became broken, but the blows had the effect of making Casserley release his ferocious and painful grip.

By now both men were in the position of wrestlers executing a difficult hold. Casserley was stooping, his head on a level with Chaplin's waist, and his left arm – the pistol clutched in the fist – was twisted up high in Chaplin's right-handed grip. Then Casserley fell backwards, pulling Chaplin on top of him so that their faces touched. Chaplin banged his head heavily on a bookcase as he fell, and was dazed.

The husband, fifty-eight and in poor health, was still intent on murder, Chaplin claimed. He continued to struggle in his attempt to point the pistol at Chaplin, and the gun clicked a couple of times as it misfired.

'He was like a maddened bull,' Chaplin said – an unfortunate choice of simile, given that the husband was impotent and that he, the lover, had impregnated his wife. Chaplin went on to say that he used both hands to seize Casserley's left hand, twisting the gun away from himself, and in the process twisting his body so that he now lay across Percy Casserley.

The husband, unable to move because of the weight of the younger man, then said: 'All right. I give in.'

Chaplin relaxed his hold and began to get up. As he did so he heard another click and saw that Casserley was again pointing the gun at him and attempting to pull the trigger. He fell back on Casserley and forced his left hand upwards to the side of his head. The gun fired, and Casserley went limp. He had been shot in the head, just in front of his left ear.

Chaplin was now in a perilous position. There were no witnesses to the desperate struggle which had taken place, and on the face of it the evidence seemed to point to his having murdered the husband of his mistress. Unwisely, he removed the pistol from Casserley's left hand, wrapped it in a handkerchief and placed it in his raincoat pocket. He closed the open drawer of the bureau, after removing a box of cartridges he saw there, putting the bullets too into his pocket. He wiped his bloodstained gloves on his raincoat and then went upstairs to Mrs Casserley. His first words to her were: 'My God!'

Mrs Casserley followed Chaplin downstairs. He made her wait in the kitchen while he went back into the lounge where Casserley lay in a pool of blood. He was still alive and groaning. Chaplin touched the wounded man's head and thought briefly of sending for an ambulance, but it was obvious to him that Casserley was dying.

It was at this point that he panicked, setting the scene to look like a burglary gone wrong. 'I thought of staging a burglary to save the publicity and keep Mrs Casserley's name out of it as far as possible,' he said in court. He then told Mrs Casserley to phone for the police.

A hysterical Mrs Casserley ran to a neighbour's house at 9.10 p.m., sobbing that something terrible had happened: a burglar had broken into the house and murdered her husband. The neighbour, a Mr Churchill, went next door and saw Mr Casserley lying on the lounge floor, stretched out diagonally in front of a small bookcase, his head lying in a pool of congealed blood. Furniture had

267

been scattered about and it certainly looked as if the Casserleys had been burgled.

The police arrived on the scene at 9.30 p.m. and examined the injured man, who died a few minutes later. They noted the disorder in the room, and then questioned Mrs Casserley. She told them that she had gone out for a walk lasting about forty minutes, and on her return had found her husband dying in the lounge.

The house was in a mess. A coat-stand had been knocked over in the hall, silverware was stacked on the dining-table and other valuable items lay scattered about, as if the burglar had intended to take them with him but had been disturbed by the husband. The police noticed that one of the dead man's slippers was on the settee in the lounge, an empty cartridge case lay near his hand, and there was a bullet hole in the wall about a foot above the skirting board. A broken and bloodstained torch lay on the floor, and there was plenty of blood in evidence.

Chaplin, in the meantime, had returned to his flat in Morden, where he put the gun and cartridges in a bedside cabinet in which also reposed a cosh – then called a 'life preserver' – which Chaplin claimed he had bought for his father in October of the previous year.

Blood from the gun got on to that cosh . . . Chaplin washed the blood from his raincoat and burned his handkerchief. The following morning he went to Epsom, where he was working, and hid the gun and cartridges in the cavity-wall of a half-completed villa. He then carried on with his work, hoping to continue a normal routine which would divert any suspicion from him.

But he could not hope to fool the police, and from very early on in the investigation detectives realized that burglary had played no part in the death of Percy Casserley. Sir Bernard Spilsbury carried out an autopsy on the victim on 25 March, and by 29 March detectives called on Edward Chaplin at the site he was working on in Northey Road, Epsom.

'Are you Mr Chaplin – known as Ted?' inquired Detective Inspector Henry. Chaplin admitted his identity, and the detective went on: 'I wish to speak to you concerning the death of Percy Arthur Casserley.'

Chaplin replied: 'Yes, it's terrible. I read about it in the papers.' Told he was being taken to a police station for questioning, he fetched his raincoat from a shed and put it on. It was still damp and was missing a button. Police had found that button in the lounge in 35 Lindisfarne Road, close to the body of Percy Casserley . . .

Once at the police station, detectives confronted Chaplin about his relationship with the wife of the murdered man. The illicit romance had not escaped the attention of neighbours – the lovers had scarcely attempted to keep their affair secret – and Lydia Scott had been compelled to tell what she knew. While admitting that he had been having an affair with Georgina Casserley, Chaplin at first denied having been to the house in Lindisfarne Road on the night in question, but almost immediately changed his mind and confessed everything. He even led the police to the villa where the gun was hidden, saying: 'I'll show you where the gun is. You'll never find it on your own.'

The aftermath was predictable: on the same day that the victim was buried at Gap Road Cemetery, Wimbledon, with a wreath from the widow reading: 'Sorrowing Ena', Edward Chaplin was charged at Wimbledon police station with the murder of Percy Casserley.

Three days after that, Mrs Casserley was arrested at a nursing home, charged with being an accessory after the fact to murder and remanded in custody to Holloway Prison. There she was treated particularly harshly, being forbidden to have a bath and forced to scrub floors. Her solicitor made an energetic protest, saying that his client was a lady of good social standing and was pregnant. Her position did not justify such humiliating treatment. He was successful in getting Mrs Casserley released on bail.

In retrospect, it is surprising that the case did not

attract the press attention afforded the very similar case of Rattenbury and Stoner, but perhaps 35 Lindisfarne Road did not have the same ring to it as Villa Madeira.

The trial of Edward Chaplin began at the Old Bailey on Tuesday, 24 May 1938, in the famous No. 1 Court, before Mr Justice Humphreys. Chaplin was lucky to have the services of Norman Birkett, KC, a brilliant barrister who had won many 'lost causes'. The trial of Mrs Casserley as an accessory followed Chaplin's. She was defended by Mr St John Hutchinson. The prosecution was led by Mr G. B. McClure, KC, assisted by Mr Christmas Humphreys, later to become a famous judge in his turn.

The dilemma of Edward Chaplin was a very real one. He had certainly caused the death of a man, and the circumstances could be made to look black against him. Even the fact that he wore gloves during the death struggle could be construed as a deliberate attempt to avoid leaving fingerprints on the murder weapon. His attempt to fake a burglary scene, his deliberate hiding of the death weapon – all must seem as proof of guilt. And juries then did not have much time or respect for men who 'carried on' with married women. Adultery then was still very much frowned upon. Indeed, Mrs Thompson had been *hanged* for adultery . . .

Sir Bernard Spilsbury, the eminent pathologist, appeared as an expert witness for the Crown and testified that marks and injuries on the back of the deceased man could have been caused by the cosh found in Chaplin's possession. He pointed out that while the body of the victim bore no less than seventeen bruises, not a single mark or injury was found on Chaplin when he was examined by a police surgeon shortly after his arrest.

The prosecution case was that Chaplin went to 35 Lindisfarne Road with the intention to murder his rival-in-love. Knowing that Percy Casserley had a gun, Chaplin took his 'life preserver' with him, used it to batter the older man to the floor, and then shot him twice with his own gun.

It was alleged that Chaplin had intended to make the death look like suicide, but the brave struggle of Mr Casserley prevented that scenario from being carried out. The bullet wound on his neck must have been caused from a shot fired from at least a foot away, as there were no powder marks around the injury; and since both men were right-handed, the description of Casserley firing with his *left* hand, of Chaplin using his *left* hand to batter the victim with the torch, must be pure invention. If there had been a struggle in that lounge, it was because Mr Casserley was fighting to prevent himself from being killed – not attempting to kill Chaplin.

And there was the fact that a desperate struggle had been described in detail by the accused man, a fit man in his thirties with strong hands, against an ailing man of fifty-eight. Could Mr Casserley have really put up such a determined struggle as that described by Chaplin? A struggle witnessed by no one but Chaplin himself . . . And was it not strange that Chaplin had remained unmarked in his struggle against a man who was like 'a maddened bull'?

The prosecution pointed out that Chaplin had also made no attempt to get medical aid for the injured man, despite the fact that there was a telephone in the house. Under cross-examination by Mr McClure, Chaplin was asked why he had used such a large torch to batter Mr Casserley, when he could just as easily have used his large strong hands. 'Why didn't you hit him in the face with that large hand of yours?' Mr McClure asked. Chaplin replied: 'I had no intention of harming Mr Casserley.' It must have seemed a weak response.

In his closing speech, Mr McClure made more damaging points. Blood was found on the life preserver: how had it got there? Why was a diamond ring worn by Mr Casserley found in Chaplin's flat? He could not have been in the state of panic he had described to the police if he had taken the time to remove and steal the ring.

Chaplin had never mentioned seeing Mr Casserley cock

271

the pistol. Was he asking the jury to believe that the weapon had already been cocked when it lay in the bureau drawer? Why did he need a weapon to bludgeon a much weaker man? Would not the victim have been dazed after three blows from the torch, and thus incapable of further resistance? Why had Chaplin had so much difficulty in disarming a man holding a pistol in his left hand?

'Chaplin was holding the hand that was holding the pistol,' Mr McClure said. 'Whose was the force that was pressing that pistol against the skin? The man was flat on his back . . . I suggest that the accused made up his story of a struggle later, to fit the facts.'

The defence called firearms expert Robert Churchill to testify that the pistol, a .25 Webley & Scott automatic, had a defective mechanism and could more easily have been used by a man accustomed to its foibles. Casserley would have known how to clear a cartridge when the pistol became jammed. Against that was the fact that the pistol was not oiled, was in poor condition, and one had to conclude that its owner knew or cared little about guns.

The judge, in his summing-up, told the jury: 'What you have to decide is: did Chaplin unlawfully cause the death of Mr Casserley, and if he did, did he do it with the intention of causing his death or causing him grievous injury?' He reminded the jury that if they found that Mr Casserley had been shot 'in the heat of passion in the course of a quarrel so serious that the accused lost complete control of himself' they might convict him of manslaughter but not of murder.

On Friday, 27 May, the jury returned a verdict of not guilty of murder but guilty of manslaughter. Mrs Casserley, waiting outside the court, fainted when she was told the verdict. Within minutes the six-months pregnant widow was herself placed in the dock on the accessory charge.

Her counsel began by saying that for years his client

had been an excellent wife. The judge intervened to ask sarcastically: 'You are not putting her forward as an excellent wife *now?*' Counsel asked the judge to take into account Mrs Casserley's pregnancy. The judge retorted: 'We know she is pregnant, as hundreds of women are pregnant. But there's nothing the matter with her, no disease or anything like that. She can pull herself together if she wants to.' Sentencing her to eleven days in prison – which meant her immediate release – the judge castigated her: 'The less said about you and your part in this case the better. I am not going to treat you with leniency because I think there is nothing particular about your condition that calls for it. Your case has aroused the most ridiculous nonsense. A great many people have treated you as if you were some sort of heroine. You were a participant in a vulgar and sordid intrigue. Now please go!'

Edward Chaplin was sentenced to twelve years in jail. Released from Parkhurst Prison on the Isle of Wight after the end of the war, having served eight years and earned full remission for good conduct, he found Georgina Casserley waiting for him outside the prison gates.

The couple went straight to a registry office and were married on 17 May 1946. It is to be hoped that as man and wife they lived happily ever after. But Chaplin was a very lucky man to escape the rope, and possibly owed his life as much to Norman Birkett as to the innate good sense of a British jury.

18
BLIND FURY: THE WOMAN WHO MURDERED HER RIVAL IN LOVE 1988

Again, there is no exact parallel with the preceding case. Edward Chaplin killed Percy Casserley in defence of the woman he loved. But Yvonne Sleightholme killed for plain revenge, the product of a thwarted love.

As students of murder will have long since realized, women rarely resort to murder to solve their emotional problems and tend to be the victims rather than the perpetrators of violence. Official figures published in 1982 revealed that two per cent of all murder victims in this country were husbands killed by their wives, while eighteen per cent were wives killed by their husbands.

The statistics tell the story – or part of it. That two per cent of wives who killed their husbands can be further subdivided. More often than not the wife will incite another person – her lover, or, as is becoming common, a hit man – to commit the deed. The fictional murderess to be found in the pages of Ruth Rendell or P. D. James, plotting an involved and cold-blooded murder for revenge, is rare in life.

Which seems to contradict the old saying about the female of the species being deadlier than the male. But there is no contradiction. What it means is that in the rare cases where a woman turns to murder she becomes even more remorseless than any male killer. With a rage fuelled by jealousy, the woman can kill coldly and deliberately, regardless of the possible consequences – witness Ruth Ellis.

The case of Yvonne Sleightholme is destined to become a classic in the annals of murder and will earn itself a notch in the canon of the *crime passionel*. A saga of jealousy and hate festering in a small rural area of North Yorkshire and exploding into a terrible act of revenge which left her rival dead, the man who jilted her ruined, and the killer herself struck blind by the hysterical reaction to her own deed. It has all the elements of classical Greek tragedy.

If the starting point of any murder can be traced – which is often impossible, since an incident in childhood can predispose an individual to become a killer – then the seeds of this particular tragedy were sown in 1980 at a New Year's Eve party to celebrate the new decade. It was at this party, held at Malton Rugby Club, that farmer William Smith first met Yvonne Sleightholme.

Malton is a small town in the heart of North Yorkshire, an area of farms and rolling green pastures. Yvonne Sleightholme was a thirty-one-year-old doctor's receptionist, a pretty but shy woman, quiet and gentle, religious by inclination, whose hobbies included lace making and tapestry work. She came from a well-respected farming family. William Smith was a good-looking bearded man who farmed at Broats Farm, Salton, near Malton, and who was quickly entranced by this young woman who represented a clean and feminine world far removed from the muck of the farmyard. The couple danced together and chatted, discovering a mutual attraction. For six years they courted, finally becoming officially engaged in June 1986. For the woman it was like a fairytale come true. William was to become her man, to rescue her from spinsterhood and take care of her.

But the fairytale romance was soon over. Mr Smith began having doubts about the relationship and called it off. Yvonne was heart-broken. She tried to win back her errant lover by threatening to commit suicide, even telling him that she had leukaemia and would die if he left her.

275

It was emotional blackmail of the sort which only an obsessive and inadequate woman could have brought herself to use.

At this point a childhood sweetheart of Mr Smith's entered the picture. Jayne Wilford, a nurse, had known William since school days and confessed she had always loved him and cherished a secret dream that one day they might marry. She was an attractive woman of twenty-nine, some eight years younger than Yvonne Sleightholme.

This time romance came true. In May 1988 William Smith married Jayne Wilford at a ceremony at Old Malton Priory; it was a white wedding with all the trimmings. The couple went to live at Broats Farm and were blissfully happy.

But what of the rejected rival, Yvonne Sleightholme? For many months she harboured hatred and resentment in her heart and for many months she plotted the death of the woman who had supplanted her in her lover's affections. To men it would seem absurd. Why didn't she plot to kill William, the man who had jilted her? Why pick on the innocent Jayne, a woman she hardly knew and who could not be blamed for what William did? At least Ruth Ellis did the logical thing and killed the man who cheated on her . . .

This is to ignore the nature of the female psyche. Very often women do not blame the man, but the 'other woman'. And they rarely blame themselves. The American author Robin Norwood, in her book *Women Who Love Too Much*, explains: 'We who love obsessively are full of fear . . . fear of being ignored, abandoned or destroyed. We give our love in the desperate hope that the man with whom we are obsessed will take care of our fears. Instead, the fears – and our obsessions – deepen until giving love in order to get it back becomes a driving force in our lives.'

Yvonne Sleightholme felt full of fear, drained of any self-confidence by being jilted, and was convinced that only William Smith offered salvation. But he had been 'stolen' from her by another woman, and she was determined that the other woman would pay. The price was to be terrible . . .

On the evening of 13 December 1988, just seven months after her marriage, Jayne Smith arrived home from her job at the Rosewood Nursing Home in Malton. Her husband was not at home: he was enjoying his usual Tuesday night game of indoor football. In the darkened farmyard of Broats Farm, Jayne Smith was confronted by a figure wielding a .22 Winchester rifle. There was a deafening explosion which rent the night sky with a vivid yellow flash, and Jayne Smith fell dead, shot through the back of the head with ruthless efficiency. Nor did it end there: the body was defiled after death.

William Smith arrived home a couple of hours later to be greeted by the gruesome sight, illuminated by the lights of his vehicle, of a near-naked body lying sprawled in the muck of the farmyard. Walking closer to the body, William Smith suddenly recognized it as his wife's. Her underwear was torn off as though she had been the victim of a sex attack. Fighting down hysteria, Mr Smith phoned for the police.

By the dawn light detectives began the opening moves in their murder inquiry. The pathologist confirmed that there had been no sexual interference with the body, which ruled out the possibility of a random rapist. The question detectives asked themselves was: who had motive and opportunity? The husband had an alibi and would hardly kill a bride of just seven months – although he was investigated in depth as a possible suspect, as is normal in such cases. The rejected rival was mentioned and detectives made a note to check her out. Meanwhile, the murder itself had to be re-enacted, the sequence of events established. Who could have known when Jayne Smith would return home from work? Who knew the farm so well that they hid in the ideal spot for an ambush?

Yvonne Sleightholme was interviewed at her home at

Carr House Farm, Seamer, near Scarborough. She claimed to have an alibi of sorts. On the night of the murder she had been staying in a rented holiday cottage near Kelso in Scotland, all of two hundred miles away, with her new boyfriend. From there she had even sent the mother-in-law of the victim a Christmas card and a prayer book. She answered questions calmly and politely and was almost too good to be true.

But there was a significant clue at the murder scene which, although meaningless by itself, pointed straight at her. The murder victim's wedding ring was missing. That symbol of marriage which should have been Sleightholme's had been ripped from the finger of the dead woman. It was a classic psychological giveaway.

Police searched Sleightholme's house, and in a barn found the murder weapon, still covered in blood. Also in the barn was her Ford Fiesta car, the boot of which was covered in blood. How could she explain these things? She did not. Throughout hours of questioning she denied any involvement in the murder and was impossible to crack. She may have appeared soft and gentle, but inside were steel shutters. She maintained all along that she had been in a cottage in Scotland at the time of the murder, with her boyfriend, Mr Anthony Berry, a Filey ambulance driver. They had had sex that night for the first time . . .

Yvonne Sleightholme was to prove impossible to break. She resisted all questioning, and when cornered in an outright lie, came out with other lies to account for the discrepancy. It was always going to be a case for a jury of twelve good people and true to solve.

But before she could have her trial, and three months after being charged with the murder of her rival, Yvonne Sleightholme went blind. It was no trick: the blindness was certified as genuine by Professor Alexander Crombie, a leading eye expert. It was a hysterical reaction to her situation, described by psychologists as a symptom of her mind shutting out the truth, a truth too terrible to be faced. She had convinced herself of her own innocence and was now to set out to try and convince a jury.

The trial began at Leeds Crown Court before Mr Justice Waite on Monday, 22 April 1991, and was to last an astonishing fourteen days. The Listings Office had allocated just a week for it.

On the first day of the trial, Sleightholme arrived outside the court on the arm of one of her solicitors, carrying a white stick and apparently oblivious to the flashing camera lights of newsmen and TV crews. She was a slight-looking figure, quite touching in appearance, with a quiet dignity.

Mr Stephen Williamson, QC, prosecuting, told the jury in his opening speech that Elizabeth Yvonne Sleightholme, who had pleaded not guilty to the charge of murder, had been driven by hatred to shoot Mrs Jayne Smith through the back of the head. She had been a jilted bride-to-be who had bought her wedding dress and booked her reception – only to have her rival take her place.

Sleightholme, he said, had lain in wait at the secluded Broats Farm and had shot her victim through the back of the head with a single shot, killing her instantly. She had then dragged the body to another part of the farmyard and ripped off Mrs Smith's clothes to make it look like a rape-murder.

Mr Williamson explained that Mr Smith had ended his relationship with Sleightholme in 1987. She had been destroyed by his decision. She later told police: 'I was devastated – my world fell apart. There were no arguments. We were both very emotionally upset and crying. He told me he wanted to be free to find out how he felt about Jayne and he could not do that while he was attached to me. He was doing the honourable thing and I could do nothing other than agree.'

'Those might seem generous words,' Mr Williamson told the jury, 'but in reality she felt a deep-seated resentment and hatred that would result in the killing of Jayne

Smith.' He said Sleightholme's life had been geared to marrying Mr Smith, but a month after severing his connection with her, Mr Smith had asked Jayne to move into his home.

The prosecution then told of Sleightholme's cunning murder plot, which involved renting a holiday cottage in Scotland to set up an alibi. But she knew that Jayne did not leave work until 9.30 p.m., and that the husband would not be at home on the night of the murder. That Tuesday she drove two hundred miles from Scotland to Broats Farm, armed with a .22 rifle taken from her father's gun cabinet. She waited in the darkness for her victim to arrive, then ordered her at gunpoint to walk towards farm outbuildings. Then she killed her victim with a single shot through the back of the head fired at point-blank range.

Mr Williamson said simply: 'One bullet, one death.'

Sleightholme had made an attempt to put the body into the boot of her car, obviously with the intention of taking it away, but she could not manage this and left bloodstains in the boot. She then dragged Jayne Smith's body through the muddy farmyard.

Mr Williamson went on: 'In a final grotesque indignity her clothes were removed and her body was exposed. She was left there as if raped or sexually assaulted. Mr Smith found his wife's body was cold. There was no pulse and she was dead.'

After the killing Sleightholme returned the rifle to her parents' home at Carr House Farm and drove on to Scotland to meet her boyfriend. But on the way she made a mistake. She booked into a hotel in order to shower, to remove any traces of blood. After being told that she could not have a room until midday she had left, but staff there remembered her. In addition, evidence would be given that the bullet recovered from the victim had been fired from the rifle found at Sleightholme's house, and neighbours would be produced who had seen Sleightholme in the vicinity of Broats Farm on the evening of the murder. Despite all the planning, it had not been a perfect murder after all . . .

For the defence, Mr Paul Worsley, QC, accused the bereaved husband of having hired a team of hit men to murder his wife after his marriage began to fail. He said that Mr Smith had to have his wife murdered, because he knew that if she got a divorce she would get half of his 130-acre farm, worth £250,000.

Mr Smith denied the charges angrily. Telling of how he found his wife dead, he said: 'I touched the side of her neck to feel her pulse. Her body was cold and I knew she was dead. When I looked around I saw a pool of blood further down the yard. I knew I needed help. I did not touch anything else. I went in to phone the police. I thought my wife had been murdered and raped. I did not know how or by whom. There was no sign of anyone in the yard when I found her. It was something I could not cope with and I needed someone to help me.'

Mr Worsley put it to him that he had been involved with a group of drug dealers and it was through these connections that three men arrived at his farm to murder his wife. He also alleged that Mr Smith had been having an affair with Sleightholme while married to his wife.

More than that, the defence claimed, Mr Smith had arranged for Sleightholme to meet him in Pickering that night, and when he failed to turn up, she went to the farm. That was part of the plan; Mr Smith wanted the finger of suspicion to be pointed at her – she was a scapegoat. The defence also claimed that Mr Smith had shown virtually no emotion over his wife's brutal killing during hours of police questioning.

Angrily, Mr Smith said: 'It is total rubbish, lies, complete lies. I cannot believe it was a sensible suggestion.' He added that his seven months with his wife had been the happiest period in his life, and if he appeared to be emotionless when the police questioned him, it was because he was unable to show his emotions in public.

The defence questioned Mr Smith about his relationship with two of his friends, suggesting that one of them was of a homosexual nature. Mr Smith replied through gritted teeth: 'It was Yvonne who raised the matter. She said her parents did not like him going to their house with us. They thought he was homosexual.' Asked if he had ever had a homosexual relationship with any man, Mr Smith replied: 'I never did. I never have and I never will have.'

The prosecution then brought up the matter of Sleightholme's holiday in Scotland, claiming that the holiday had been a cover for murder. The woman who rented Sleightholme the cottage said that she noticed Sleightholme's blue car was missing on the night of the thirteenth. When she returned the next morning she seemed 'edgy and nervous', the witness said. Then the news came through about the murder and Sleightholme told her: 'I will have to leave because of a tragedy at home.' She was crying . . .

A neighbour testified to seeing Sleightholme near Broats Farm on the night of the killing, and Sleightholme's brother told of how a .22 rifle which had gone missing weeks before from a locked cabinet at their home suddenly reappeared on the morning of the fourteenth.

On the fourth day of the trial, Home Office pathologist Dr Siva Siva testified about the wound which had killed Jayne Smith. Defence counsel suggested to the doctor that it had all the hallmarks of a professional killing.

'It was certainly a very accurate shot,' Dr Siva said. 'It was someone who knew exactly what they were doing.' Dr Siva agreed that the killer had taken up the position of an executioner and had chosen exactly the right spot to kill instantly. The doctor had testified that bloodied handprints on the legs of Mrs Smith indicated that she had been dragged to another part of the farmyard to be stripped, but there was no evidence of any sexual assault.

A tape-recording of the emergency call Mr Smith made to the police after discovering his wife's body was played in court, for the jury to decide if he had showed emotion or not. On the tape Mr Smith was heard to say: 'My wife has been sexually assaulted and murdered. She is lain in the yard. There is blood all over the yard. Her clothes have been removed. She has been raped and murdered.'

An officer asked Mr Smith if he was feeling all right. He replied: 'I am not feeling very good but I am coping. I am well enough to cope. Things like this don't hit for a day or two. I will be all right.'

PC Jeremy Smith, one of the first officers to arrive on the scene, was assigned to sit with Mr Smith. He told the court: 'He was very quiet, more or less just staring at the ground. A couple of times he involuntarily wept quietly to himself for a short time. He was sat down with his hands on his forehead and wept quietly to himself. I asked him if he was okay and he said: "Yes, I'm sorry." '

The following day the jury of six men and six women were taken to the parking area below the court to examine Sleightholme's car and see for themselves the blood-stained boot. Dr Raymond Petrie, a Home Office forensic scientist, had told the court that the blood in the boot was of the same rare group as the murdered woman's. He also testified that he had found the outline of a palm print from a small hand on the stocking from Mrs Smith's right leg. He had compared a photograph of that mark with palm prints taken from Sleightholme and found she had the right size and shape of print to have caused the mark.

He told prosecuting counsel that blood had been found in the boot of the car, as well as in the driver's compartment. But the amount of blood in the boot suggested that someone had tried to get a body inside.

He went on: 'Bodies in my experience are not that easy to handle in confined spaces. My feeling is that there may well have been an attempt to get a heavily bloodstained body into the back of the car, failing, and taking it out again.'

Forensic scientist Dr Graham Renshaw had examined

a spent cartridge case recovered from the mud in the yard at Broats Farm and found it had been fired from the rifle recovered from Sleightholme's house.

The case against the slightly built blind woman in the dock was building slowly, point by point. There was the scientific evidence, the blood and ballistics, and now the evidence of witnesses. A receptionist at the Hotspur Hotel, Alnwick, told the court that a woman calling herself Yvonne Sleightholme had arrived at the hotel on 14 December 1988 at 7.45 a.m. and asked for a room. When told she could not have a room until midday, she asked if it was possible to take a bath or shower, but was told this was not possible. She paid for the room in advance, using a cheque and asking for a receipt. She had been friendly and chatty, but had never returned to take the room she had paid for.

The prosecution said that Sleightholme had made love to her boyfriend in their holiday cottage less then twenty-four hours after killing her arch-rival. They called the boyfriend, Mr Berry, described as a pillar of his local Methodist church.

He said he had spent a cosy evening with Sleightholme at the cottage, having arrived late on the fourteenth, drinking tea and holding hands. 'I was sat in a chair. She sat down beside me by the fire and held my hand. It was a very pleasant and cosy situation. She said: 'I would like you to spend the night with me.' We did. We made love and then went to sleep.'

Mr Berry said it was the first time they had made love since the start of their relationship six months earlier. Before that night they had never even hugged one another. The following morning, he said, he drew the curtains and found police officers outside. He and Sleightholme were taken to Malton police station to help police with their inquiries. He said that Sleightholme was crying and said she was sorry he had become involved.

Mr Berry added: 'She was saying that someone's

daughter had been killed and she was concerned for the parents of the woman who had been killed.'

Asked by the prosecution if she had ever mentioned her former fiancé, William Smith, Mr Berry said: 'As far as I can remember she said it was all in the past, and when people mentioned things about him she didn't want to know.'

Earlier, a close friend of Sleightholme's had described her as being a friendly, kind, helpful and truthful person. There were to be many other similar tributes to her virtues. The real Yvonne Sleightholme had been a very secret person, hiding her true nature under a façade of sweetness.

On the eighth day of the trial Yvonne Sleightholme went into the witness box to try and sway the jury with her blend of sweetness. She began by accusing her former fiancé of being involved in a drugs ring supplying people in York and Ryedale. Smith's role, she claimed, was to 'launder' drugs money by depositing it in a bank in Lithuania. She said that although she had been hurt when Smith jilted her, she had no hatred for Jayne Smith and had misgivings of her own about marrying Smith after he told her of his involvement with a drugs ring.

She said she had questioned Smith about his relationship with one of his friends, suspecting a homosexual liaison. She said: 'I confronted him as to what he had been doing. I thought he was messing about with men.' But Smith had laughed at her suggestion and explained his role in the drugs ring.

Sleightholme claimed she had once found a 'complicated-looking' gun wrapped in a fertilizer bag and hidden in a grain store at Smith's farm. Two weeks later she told Smith about her find, and he said he was looking after it for a friend.

She claimed she had become pregnant by Smith but miscarried six weeks into the pregnancy. She had told no one other than her doctor about it. She also claimed that Smith continued to have sexual relations with her after his marriage to Jayne. Often they would meet at a local beauty spot and make love in a grassy valley, she said.

Turning to the actual murder itself, she claimed that Smith had ordered the deed done and had framed her for it. He had told her that he had made a dreadful mistake in marrying Jayne, but had no intention of letting her have half of all he owned. Although it was her father's gun which had been used to shoot Jayne, she had taken it to give to Mr Smith after he said he needed it to shoot crows.

Mr Smith had lured her down to Broats Farm from her holiday cottage in Scotland on the night of the murder. She arrived at the farmhouse to find two men with Smith. When she asked him what was going on, he told her that their affair was over.

'He turned round and looked at me. He said, "This is the end, I am never going to see you again." He just stared at me. It was just cold, the most cruel stare I have ever been given in my life. He just looked straight through me with so much hate and coldness. I felt sick.'

She said that Smith walked out, leaving her with the two men. They took her outside into the farmyard where there was a third man holding a gun. She heard a car pull into the yard, then a female voice saying: 'This is ridiculous.' Then seconds later: 'Oh my God, you are not going to do it here.'

Sleightholme, who had spent a year in custody composing this lurid thriller scenario, went on: 'I thought it was Jayne's voice. I got hysterical. I started to scream. I was told to shut up but I couldn't. There was a very loud bang at the side of my head. I thought I had been shot. I fainted. I passed out.'

She said that when she recovered consciousness the men banged her head against a wall and threatened to kill her sister and her two nieces if ever she told anyone what had happened. She was shoved into her car and told to go back to Scotland and to keep her mouth shut.

Sleightholme said she drove to Alnwick, where she

286

spent the night in her car in a lorry park. Next day she booked a room in a hotel but did not stay there.

Under cross-examination, she admitted that she had lied and deceived the police and her family, but said she had done so to protect her sister and two nieces. Mr Williamson suggested that her story was a cover-up to hide her own guilt. She had constructed an alibi by sending the Christmas card from Scotland on the day of the murder, and she had taken the rifle from her father's gun cabinet and replaced it in the garage after the murder. Sleightholme denied all this, and denied a suggestion that she had killed her rival and left her near-naked body in the farm yard knowing that it would be discovered by the husband, who would be left with the cruellest memory he could possibly have of his wife.

Mr Williamson put it to her: 'You sent that Christmas card, hours before the killing, to convince the world that you had put all thought of William out of your mind after he jilted you and married Jayne instead.' A note enclosed with the card to Smith's mother-in-law read *I have a lovely boyfriend. He has been with me for quite some time now ... through all the worrying times.*

In his closing speech the prosecutor told the jury that Yvonne Sleightholme was a bitter woman who had murdered her love rival and then told a fantastic story to hide her own guilt. He said that Sleightholme was 'an accomplished liar who has come up with this sadly fantastic story' of her former fiancé hiring a team of hit men to execute his wife because she had been faced with the weight of evidence pointing to her guilt.

Mr Williamson asked the jury: 'What was the purpose of leaving Jayne Smith's body as it was left? She has ruined his life, hasn't she? Whatever else you make of this, wasn't it to hurt him? ... William Smith was all he said he was, a hard-working, rather dour farmer, perhaps fortunate to have the choice of two women and not know which to choose, and happy in the choice he made eventually.'

Saying there was not a scrap of evidence that Smith had carried on with an affair with Sleightholme after his marriage, Mr Williamson went on: 'You may shrink from the thought that someone, perhaps especially a woman, could do the evil that is alleged in this case, but someone did, of that there is no doubt.' He said that Sleightholme had admitted taking her father's rifle and added: 'She is not sufficiently ignorant not to know how to load a rifle and how to fire it into the back of someone's neck. It is not asking for a marksman, it may be asking for a rather cold and deliberate killer.'

Now came the defence closing speech. Mr Paul Worsley told the jury that the police had found such an obvious suspect in Yvonne Sleightholme that they had 'blindly ignored other theories about the killing'. Had she been the real killer, surely she would have got rid of the rifle and washed the blood from her car.

'Is she not too obvious a suspect? Someone has taken care for all the clues to be there for even the most flat-footed policeman to find, and I say that with no disrespect – the police have investigated very thoroughly. The police have pursued one theory, blindly ignoring the pointers that point somewhere else.'

He ended by saying that the jury were being asked to believe that Sleightholme, described by various witnesses as being kindly and caring, had turned into a cold-blooded killer lying in wait for the other woman. He said the jury would be aware from watching such programmes as *Rough Justice* that sometimes dreadful mistakes could be made and innocent people jailed. He suggested that Sleightholme's account was so incredible that it just might be true.

On the twelfth day of the trial the judge summed up the case to the jury. He said: 'The members of the jury are not investigators but judges. The question for the jury is not who committed this dreadful crime, but was it committed by the defendant?' He told the jury that they might have no difficulty in deciding that Jayne Smith

288

had been unlawfully killed at Broats Farm. She was a healthy young woman who had been shot through the back of the head and left with her clothing disarranged to give a superficial appearance of a sexual assault.

The judge went on: 'It is a scene evocative at first sight of the start of a thousand detective stories. You might have been struck by the contrast between an account of an episode of that sort which you will read peacefully by your fireside or watch in relaxation on a television screen, and the terrible reality of the sight which confronted the police when they were first called to the farm.'

The judge emphasized that the task of the jury was not like solving a fictional whodunnit. There was an essential difference between a storybook murder and reality. The essence of the fictional murder was that the reader or viewer joined the inquiry, pitting their wits against those of the amateur or professional detective, looking at the clues and motives to decide who had done the murder.

'That does not, of course, happen in real life. Certainly it does not happen in a criminal trial,' he said. Mr Justice Waite stressed that it was for the prosecution to prove Yvonne Sleightholme's guilt 'beyond reasonable doubt'.

She had been at the farm that evening, yet had lied to the police about her movements on the night of the murder. The jury were entitled to ask themselves why she had told those lies – 'but you must not allow your minds to slip into any automatic assumption of guilt simply because of admitted untruths. The mere fact that a defendant tells a lie is not in itself evidence of guilt.'

On Friday, 10 May 1991, the fourteenth day of the trial, the jury retired, returning with a majority verdict of guilty. Sleightholme broke down in tears in the dock as the verdict was announced.

The judge listened to defence counsel's speech in mitigation. Mr Worsley said that Sleightholme, with her blindness, and even without it, was not a danger to the public at all. He said there was very much another side to her character, spoken of by those who had appeared in court. Finally, because of her father's illness, she was unlikely to see him alive again. At this point Sleightholme began sobbing loudly.

Passing a sentence of life imprisonment on her, the judge told her: 'You planned in cold fury and you executed with ruthless precision the killing of your rival.'

He went on to say that Sleightholme had tried to escape justice with a wicked story. 'When the falsehood of your attempted alibi was exposed, you tried to escape justice by telling a wickedly untruthful story. Wicked is not too strong a word because it was a story which sought to cast upon the bereaved husband of your victim the further burden of public calumny which branded him a sexual deviant, a drug trafficker, and a man who would hire the services of a contract killer.' The judge added that the jury's verdict had removed any slur on Mr Smith's character and he could resume his place in society as a man entitled to both sympathy and respect. 'In his unhappiness he has one consolation today. By their verdict the jury has rejected this slur on his character.'

Sleightholme is expected to serve her sentence in a special unit in prison where blind people are catered for.

After the case, Mr Smith told of how he had bought another wedding ring and slipped it on to his wife's finger just before her burial. 'I was determined that she would be buried as my wife and nothing else.' Speaking of his wife's killer, he said: 'I still cannot believe that Yvonne was capable either of the killing or what she said about me. It was not the person I knew and loved all those years. At least I think I loved her. That was a sweet gentle person. Perhaps I loved an illusion.

'I am a simple farmer. The world I love and am happiest with starts at my farm gate. It is the world I know. Nature's cycle of life and death . . . The other world beyond the farm is something I find it difficult to come to terms with and what has happened to Jayne and what happened to me in court is part of the world I cannot grasp . . . I want to remember the Yvonne I thought I knew. The person who did this to us all is a stranger, someone I will never be able to recognize.'

This writer, present in court to see her sentenced, recognizes her. I cannot forgive her but I can understand her. Understanding is the key to the solving of any crime or human aberration. One simply has to delve deeply into the mysteries of the human heart.

We have examined in depth eighteen cases of crimes of passion, and one obvious conclusion cannot be ignored. Although methods of murder might change, murderers do not. They remain creatures of impulse, at the mercy of their passions.

Eugene Ionesco once wrote: 'People like killers, and if one feels sympathy for the victims, it's only by way of thanking them for letting themselves be killed.' That is far too cynical for me, but it does contain an element of truth. In a sense we are all voyeurs, leading artificial lives and never once experiencing the wind against our naked skin. It is natural that we should be fascinated by people whose passions are so strong and primitive that they lead to murder.

But let not their passion blind us to reality. Most of the leading characters in this book are, after all, killers who paid the price for their violent crimes. And their victims' deaths are tragedies that should not be forgotten.

INDEX

CANNIBALISM: THE LAST TABOO

Brian Marriner

In this gruesome yet compelling study, Brian Marriner charts a journey through the dark depths of the human psyche, tracing cannibalism from its prehistoric roots to the present day: from the Aztecs who ritually sacrificed and devoured their enemies to shipwreck survivors who ate the cabinboy; from the Japanese student who shot his girlfriend and sliced her thinly to eat raw, to the horrific murders committed by Jeffrey Dahmer and Andrei Chikatilo.

Drawing on historical evidence and recent criminal cases, Marriner's chilling catalogue of human flesh-eaters takes us to the frontiers of real-life horror . . .

STRANGE DEATHS
A chilling collection of terrifying true murders

John Dunning

Fifteen true stories of the most shocking and unusual murders of this century, each one retold in frighteningly accurate detail by an outstanding historian of crime. Stories that are guaranteed to send shivers of terror down your spine.

MURDEROUS WOMEN
Where the female is deadlier than the male.

John Dunning

A chilling collection of horrific crimes where women play a deadly role.

The gruesome details of these eighteen true stories – dramatically reconstructed by an outstanding crime historian from the newspaper files of three continents – prove that the female can sometimes be as deadly, if not deadlier, than the male.

MINDLESS MURDERS
Twenty chilling trues stories

John Dunning

A murder without a motive is the most chilling of all. And the twenty seemingly pointless murders described here are all the more horrifying because every one is true.

The dissected body found still partly deep-frozen in the park, the corpse cooked through in the sauna, the murder of an elderly woman from Black Mamba venom– these are just some of the extraordinary cases described in *Mindless Murders*.

CRYPTIC CRIMES
A horrifying catalogue of mysterious murders.

John Dunning

Behind the closed doors and the net curtains in perfctly ordinary cities, towns and villages something goes on . . . MURDER.

Reconstructed in graphic detail, here are the true stories of twenty horrific killings – baffling murder cases with strangely obscure motives. The victims were wives, grandparents, children . . . the murderers were the sort of people that you meet every day . . .

THE KILLER NEXT DOOR

Joel Norris

Inside the minds of seven serial killers

Serial killers – the curse of the modern age, the symptoms of a sick society, but a sickness that will never come near you, or touch your life.

Or will it?

Joel Norris (bestselling author of *Serial Killers*) examines the cases of seven well-known serial killers, each of whom gave off warning signs to their family and neighbours, but were still left to kill, and kill again. For those nearest to them failed to interpret the danger signals – the long periods of sullenness and the explosive violence.

Arthur Shawcross, the Cannibal of Genesee, Henry Lee Lucas who claims more than three hundred victims, Daniel Rakowitz who cooked a topless dancer and served her to the homeless. Norris meticulously examines their cases and four others, and shows how all of them suffered brain damage, chemical imbalances, addiction and childhood traumas that built up a powder keg of violence in them.

By reading this book, you too may be able to understand the mind of a killer, the killer who may be close to you now, *The Killer Next Door*.

SERIAL KILLERS:
The Growing Menace

Joel Norris

A controversial look at a terrifying trend

The rise in the number of multiple murderers is one of the most horrifying trends of recent times.

This carefully researched study examines the backgrounds and personal testimonies of a variety of serial killers and asks – and chillingly answers – the question: what is it about these people that drives them to commit these wanton and senseless killings? People like:

Charles Manson whose masterminding of the Tate/LeBianca murders with his 'family' was a manifestation of his helter-skelter vision of Armageddon.

Leonard Lake who financed his survivalist lifestyle by making gruesome snuff movies, and boiling his victims down for soup.

Carlton Gary the black avenger, who waits on Death Row while the doctors and lawyers argue whether his slayings of white matriarchs were mad or just bad.

'A brilliant and useful book about an epidemic that is threatening lives and destroying peace of mind on a scale unparalleled in history' JACK OLSEN, author of *SON*

THE EXECUTION PROTOCOL

Stephen Trombley

This is the first book to examine with absolute candour what it is like to live and die on America's death row and how America's executioners take a life.

Over a year of intense research, author Stephen Trombley immersed himself in the shadowy world of the capital punishment industry, embarking on an extraordinary personal odyssey that allowed him to hear of things, and witness scenes, that most people can't even bring themselves to think about.

The result is a shocking insight into the history and present practice of state-sanctioned killing.

In Cold Blood looked at the crime. *The Executioner's Song* looked at the criminal. *The Execution Protocol* looks at the executioners preparing their deadly machinery. It is a modern classic which will change the way we think of capital punishment.

'A grim, if compelling, journey into the world of America's legal death industry' ECONOMIST

'This is not a book to read on underground trains. Half-way through the first chapter, disgust and horror closed so tightly round me that I had to shut the book and leave the train at the next station. Trombley . . . writes . . . in a clear, neutral manner . . . the facts seem to burst through the prose' ANDREW BROWN, INDEPENDENT

'Utterly shocking' THE TIMES

TRULY, MADLY, DEADLY
Where truth is more deadly than fiction

John Dunning

This omnibus brings together the volumes *Truly Murderous . . . Madly Murderous . . . Deadly Deviates* previously published by Arrow Books.

A chilling collection of more than fifty extraordinary murders. Retold in horrifying detail by one of the century's foremost crime historians, *Truly, Madly, Deadly* chronicles some of the most bizarre killings of the lethally insane. John Dunning reconstructs these sordid, brutal and painful atrocities with painstaking accuracy and terrifying detail.

TRUE CRIME
TITLES AVAILABLE FROM ARROW

☐	Helter Skelter	Vincent Bugliosi	£6.99
☐	Stone Cold	Martin Dillon	£4.99
☐	Carnal Crimes	John Dunning	£4.50
☐	Cryptic Crimes	John Dunning	£3.99
☐	Mindless Murders	John Dunning	£3.99
☐	Murderous Women	John Dunning	£3.99
☐	Strange Deaths	John Dunning	£4.50
☐	Truly, Madly, Deadly	John Dunning	£5.99
☐	The Insider	Donald Goddard	£5.99
☐	The Murders of the Black Museum	Gordon Honeycombe	£5.99
☐	Born Fighter	Reg Kray	£4.99
☐	The Execution Protocol	Stephen Trombley	£5.99
☐	Cannibalism: The Last Taboo	Brian Marriner	£4.99
☐	The Killer Next Door	Joel Norris	£4.99
☐	Serial Killers	Joel Norris	£4.99

ARROW BOOKS, BOOKSERVICE BY POST, PO BOX 29,
DOUGLAS, ISLE OF MAN, BRITISH ISLES

NAME _____

ADDRESS _____

_____

_____

Please enclose a cheque or postal order made out to Arrow
Books Ltd. for the amount due and allow the following for
postage and packing.

U.K. CUSTOMERS: Please allow 75p per book to a maximum
of £7.50

B.F.P.O. & EIRE: Please allow 75p per book to a maximum
of £7.50

OVERSEAS CUSTOMERS: Please allow £1.00 per book.

Whilst every effort is made to keep prices low it is sometimes
necessary to increase cover prices at short notice. Arrow Books
reserve the right to show new retail prices on covers which may
differ from those previously advertised in the text or elsewhere.